THE GREAT WESTERN NORTH OF WOLVERHAMPTON

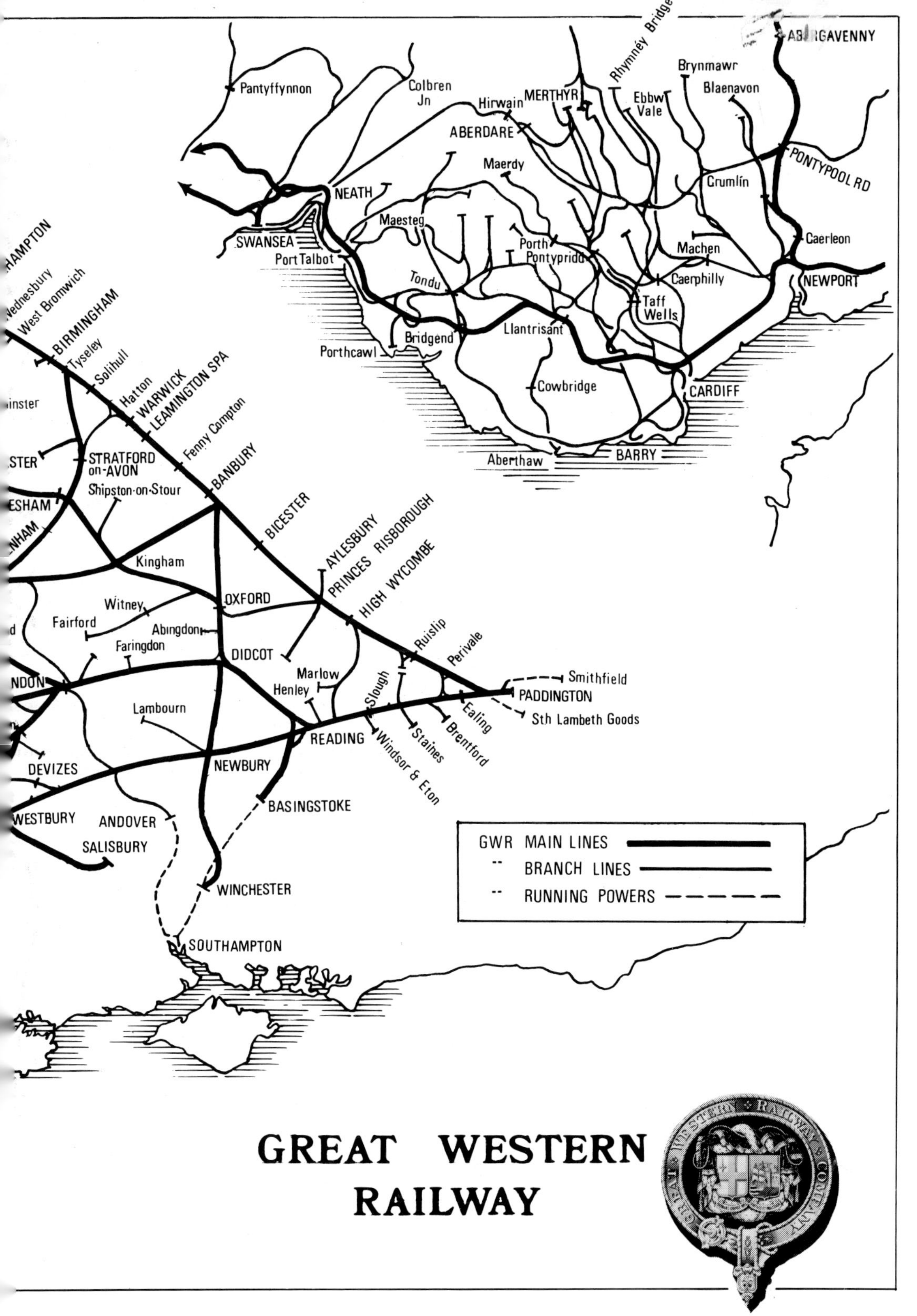

GREAT WESTERN RAILWAY

THE GREAT WESTERN NORTH OF WOLVERHAMPTON

KEITH M. BECK

LONDON

IAN ALLAN LTD

First published 1986

ISBN 0 7110 1615 1

Published by Ian Allan Ltd, Shepperton, Surrey;
and printed by Ian Allan Printing Ltd at its works
at Coombelands in Runnymede, England

Dedication

To the memory of my late uncle,
Harry Maylott, some time Chief Fitter
at Stafford Road Works,
Wolverhampton.

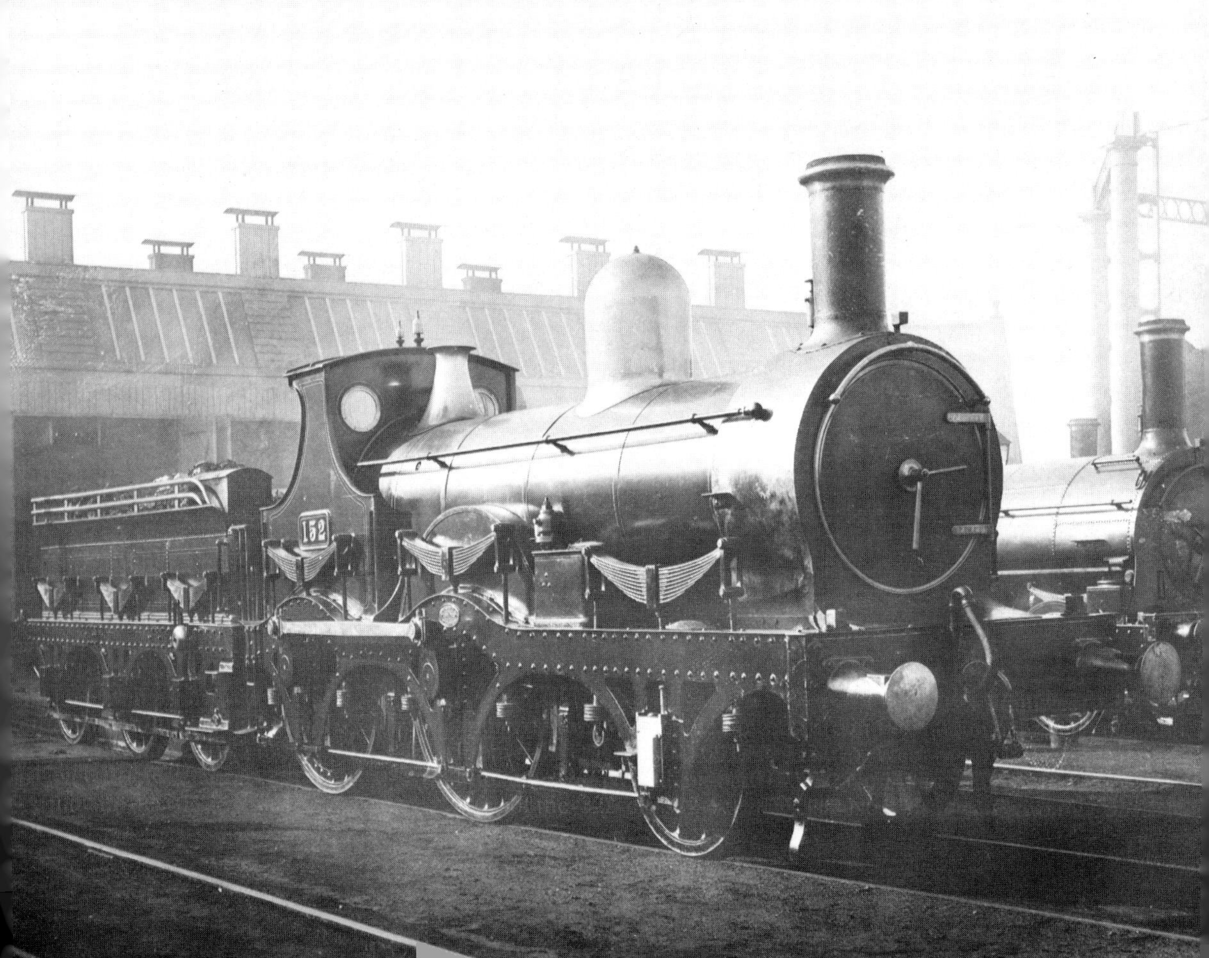

Contents

Above:
Stafford Road Works, the Lower Yard in 1883.
From right to left — 0-6-0ST No 1527; ex-West
Midland 2-2-2 No 214; ex-S&CR 2-2-2 No 14; an
0-6-0 of the '322' class: 2-4-0 '806' class No 806:
domeless 2-2-2 of the 'Queen' class (either No 999
or 1121): unidentified 0-6-0 (probably of the '322'
class); three 0-6-0STs of the '645' class. Note the
covered vans constructed on old tender frames!
Bucknall Collection

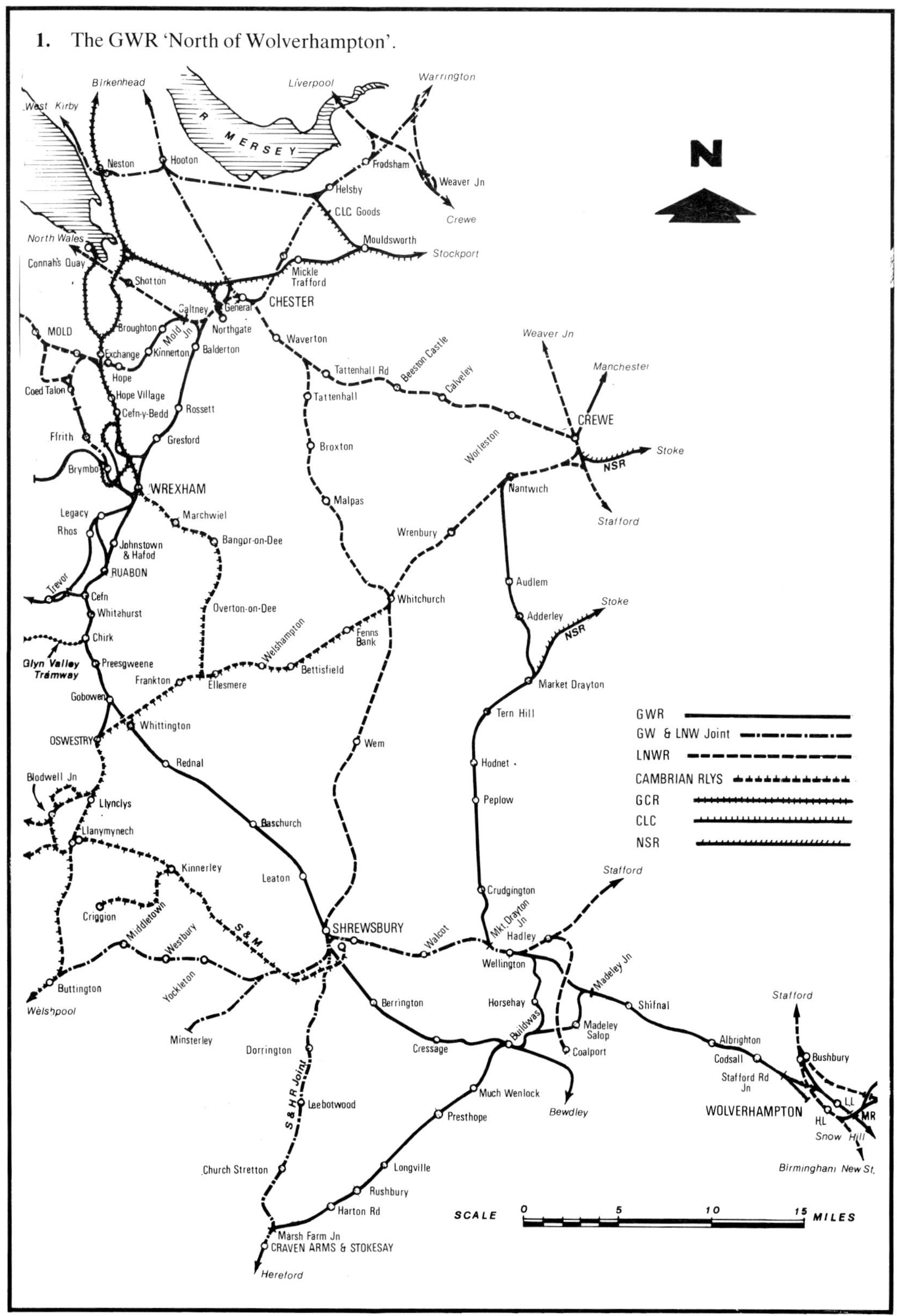
Birkenhead
Warrington
Liverpool
West Kirby
R MERSEY
Neston
Hooton
Frodsham
Helsby
Weaver Jn
CLC Goods
Crewe
North Wales
Mouldsworth
Stockport
Connah's Quay
Mickle Trafford
Shotton
Saltney
General
CHESTER
Broughton
Mold Jn
Northgate
Waverton
MOLD
Exchange
Kinnerton
Balderton
Hope
Tattenhall Rd
Beeston Castle
Calveley
Weaver Jn
Coed Talon
Hope Village
Rossett
Tattenhall
Manchester
Cefn-y-Bedd
Ffrith
Gresford
Broxton
Worleston
CREWE
Stoke
Brymbo
NSR
WREXHAM
Malpas
Nantwich
Legacy
Marchwiel
Rhos
Bangor-on-Dee
Wrenbury
Stafford
Johnstown & Hafod
RUABON
Trevor
Cefn
Audlem
Whitehurst
Overton-on-Dee
Whitchurch
Adderley
Stoke
Chirk
NSR
Glyn Valley Tramway
Preesgweene
Welshampton
Fenns Bank
Frankton
Ellesmere
Bettisfield
Market Drayton
Gobowen
Tern Hill
Whittington
Wem
OSWESTRY
Hodnet
Rednal
Peplow
Blodwell Jn
Llynclys
Llanymynech
Stafford
Kinnerley
Leaton
Crudgington
Criggion
Middletown
Westbury
S & M
SHREWSBURY
Walcot
Mkt. Drayton Jn
Hadley
Buttington
Yockleton
Wellington
Welshpool
Berrington
Horsehay
Madeley Jn
Shifnal
Stafford
Minsterley
Dorrington
Cressage
Buildwas
Madeley Salop
Albrighton
Codsall
Bushbury
S.H.R. Joint
Coalport
Stafford Rd Jn
Leebotwood
Much Wenlock
Bewdley
WOLVERHAMPTON
Presthope
LL
HL
MR
Church Stretton
Longville
Snow Hill
Rushbury
Birmingham New St.
Harton Rd
Marsh Farm Jn
CRAVEN ARMS & STOKESAY
Hereford
GWR
GW & LNW Joint
LNWR
CAMBRIAN RLYS
GCR
CLC
NSR
SCALE
0   5   10   15 MILES
N

Introduction and Acknowledgements

Although the Paddington to Birmingham and Wolverhampton section of the Great Western Railway received considerable publicity, both from the company itself and from those writing on locomotive matters, as the company's second main line, it was a different matter where the line north of Wolverhampton was concerned.

The change-over at Wolverhampton (Low Level) from the mighty 'King' class engine, which had brought the train for Birkenhead thus far from Paddington, to a 'Hall' or aged 'Saint' which would take it forward to Chester, seemed to symbolise the attitude of the GWR to all that beyond — as being of secondary importance. Yet it had one unique claim to fame; alone among all the company's main lines it had never been part of the broad gauge, being from the first laid on what Paddington insisted was the narrow gauge.

Wolverhampton became a natural frontier at which both passengers and goods traffic had to be trans-shipped until the narrow gauge rails reached Paddington and through services became possible. Thus the practice of changing engines at Wolverhampton was established; at first as an absolute necessity, and later as an operating convenience. It was also marked for many years by the use north of Wolverhampton of types and classes of engines which differed in many respects from those to be found further south.

The existence of the locomotive works at Stafford Road, Wolverhampton inherited from the former Shrewsbury & Birmingham Railway — and which continued as an almost autonomous establishment until the end of the 19th century — was largely responsible for the many differences to be found in the Northern Division of the GWR.

This volume is an attempt to trace the history and development of those lines from their earliest days up to the lamentable day when the GWR ceased to exist. Little now remains of what was once the Northern Division: at Wolverhampton both the Low Level station and the once great locomotive works and running sheds have disappeared; north of that place no branches remain — apart from three short freight lines — and the service on the remaining section of the main line is but a shadow of what it was in former days.

Though the differences in locomotive practice ended at the beginning of this century, it was not until many years later that all traces of the former individuality disappeared. Indeed, it might be claimed that it was only with the transfer of those lines to the London Midland Region and the demise of steam that the Northern Division died and was buried.

Acknowledgements

My thanks are due to a number of friends who have loaned material in the shape of timetables etc; without which this book would not have been written, especially the Rev Kenneth Tibbetts, Michael D. Rumsey, Steve Buck and Geoffrey Bannister. My thanks are also due to all who have kindly provided me with photographs, and especially Hubert Wheeller, Geoffrey Bannister, Gordon Coltas, William Potter and R. C. 'Dick' Riley.

Keith M. Beck

1 The 'Fighting Shrewsburys' and the Battle for Birkenhead

The Shrewsbury & Chester Railway

A railway from Chester to the Wrexham and Ruabon coalfields was projected as early as 1839, when George Stephenson was engaged as the Engineer but the scheme was abandoned owing to the commercial depression of that time. Revived again in 1842, it was again abortive, due to the opposition of the landowners and apathy on the part of local industry. However, the promoters were successful in obtaining a Bill in 1844 to incorporate the North Wales Mineral Railway (NWMR). The line was to commence at the River Dee at Saltney and terminate close to the old mansion of Bryn-y-fynnon at Wrexham, the Engineer being Henry Robertson. The Chester & Holyhead Railway (C&HR), which was authorised in the same session, was to be used to reach the already existing terminus of the Birkenhead Railway in Chester, two miles from Saltney.

Despite the title, the NWMR had no connection with any of the collieries or iron works in the Wrexham area! The proposed branch intended to provide such access had to be abandoned owing to the disputes between the rival mine owners — all of whom were in favour of such a branch, providing it gave only their colliery a rail outlet for coal! However, in the following year an extension of the line from Wrexham to Ruabon was authorised, with a branch to Brymbo and Minera, the latter giving access to collieries and works in the area.

Among the proposals during the 'railway mania' year of 1845 was that for a rival line from Chester to Shrewsbury, promoted by the Chester &

Below:
The northern approaches to the Joint station (later known as Low Level) at Wolverhampton, in 1854, with mixed gauge trackwork. Wednesfield Road Bridge is in the foreground. Note the 'side-stepping' of the narrow gauge track on the right, also the unusual disc signal under the bridge, and the broad gauge carriages in the station.
LGRP courtesy David & Charles (17793)

Holyhead company and the Birkenhead Railway. The NWMR's answer was to promote a continuation of their own line under the title of the Shrewsbury, Oswestry & Chester Junction Railway (SO&CJR): this was eventually passed unopposed, and in the following year the two companies were amalgamated to form the Shrewsbury & Chester Railway (S&CR).

The line to Ruabon was opened on 2 November 1846, at the same time as the C&HR's line from the Birkenhead's station in Chester to Saltney. The first section as far as Rossett was over level country, after which its progress up the side of the Gresford Vale required deep cuttings and embankments to Wrexham. At Saltney there was a short branch to a wharf on the River Dee, with an engine shed and workshops; while another branch, six miles long, passed through the centre of the collieries and iron works to Minera. The NWMR's line terminated near Rhosymedre, a mile beyond Ruabon, at which point the SO&CJR section began.

Between Ruabon and Shrewsbury there were two great viaducts over the valleys of the Dee at Cefn and the Ceiriog at Chirk. The former, 510yd long and 148ft high, having 19 stone arches with a span of 60ft each, was the largest in the country at that time. It was built by Thomas Brassey, the ceremony of keying the last arch being performed on 25 August 1848 by W. Ormsby Gore, MP, the first Chairman of the S&CR. A great gathering of people from Chester and the surrounding countryside witnessed the event, and at a luncheon held in the goods shed at Ruabon, 300 people were present. No less than 23 separate toasts 'were enthusiastically responded to in eloquent and glowing terms' — one imagines that both the eloquence and the glow increased as the toasts were drunk!

The Chirk Viaduct was a smaller work, 283yd long and 100ft high, with 12 arches; these were 10 stone arches of 45ft span, with the extreme arch at each end being of laminated timber and having a span of 120ft. (The timber arches were replaced by stone arches in 1858.) There is no record of the number of toasts drunk on the occasion of the completion of this work!

The line was opened between Ruabon and a temporary station at Shrewsbury on 16 October 1848, this being the first railway to enter Shrewsbury. On 12 October a special train left Shrewsbury at 9.30am, conveying the Mayor, Town Clerk and Magistrates, with other officials and local gentry. Chester was reached at 12 noon and the party returned at 12.30pm, and on arrival back in Shrewsbury attended a public dinner (tickets 3s 6d [17½p]) in the Music Hall — the day being declared a local public holiday.

A large joint passenger station was built at a cost of £100,000, as Shrewsbury was faced with the prospect of being the meeting place of no less than four lines; the Shrewsbury & Chester, the

Shrewsbury & Birmingham, the Shrewsbury & Hereford, and the Shropshire Union — though the latter was to share a line from Wellington with the Shrewsbury & Birmingham. The station was finished in time for the opening of the joint line from Wellington on 1 June 1849.

In Chester, the General station, opened on 1 August 1848, was also the joint property of four companies; these were the C&HR, the S&CR, the LNWR and the Birkenhead, Lancashire & Cheshire Junction (commonly known as the Birkenhead Railway). A most unusual feature of the Chester General station was the oversight by a body of Commissioners, who even owned a small locomotive (later taken into GWR stock).

Despite Oswestry being included in the title of the SO&CJR, that town was left more than two miles from the railway as constructed. In 1846 the company obtained powers to construct two branches; one being from Gobowen through Oswestry to join the already-authorised Crewe and Newton line of the Shropshire Union Railway & Canal Co at Crickheath, near Llanymynech, while the other was to be from Leaton to the little town of Wem. The former was opened as far as Oswestry on 23 December 1848, but the remainder of the line, as well as the whole of the Wem branch, was later abandoned.

For the first year or so, the S&CR led a peaceful life as a local line whose affairs were of little interest further afield. Relations with the neighbouring LNWR and the Birkenhead Railway were friendly and might have continued to be so, but for the opening of the Shrewsbury & Birmingham's line which created a through line from Wolverhampton to Chester. Bitter warfare then ensued; which was to last until both the Shrewsbury railways became part of the GWR.

The Shrewsbury & Birmingham Railway

The proposal to link Birmingham with Shrewsbury by a railway running through Dudley and Wolverhampton was first made in 1844. The project was warmly supported by the London & Birmingham Railway (L&BR) who entered into a provisional agreement to lease the line as part of their strategy to combat the ambitions of the Grand Junction Railway (GJR). Then came the surprising agreement of the L&BR and the GJR to amalgamate as the LNWR, and this was followed by the repudiation of the provisional agreement to lease the S&BR. At the same time, the LNWR withdrew its support from a rival proposal for a line between Birmingham and Shrewsbury, though they continued with the promotion of the Shropshire Union's (SUR) line from Stafford.

The S&BR promoters readily agreed to a suggestion that they should leave the construction of the expensive Birmingham to Wolverhampton section to a separate company to be promoted jointly by themselves, the LNWR and the Birmingham Canal Co, each of whom was to subscribe a quarter of the capital, the remainder to be raised by public subscription. Entitled the Birmingham, Wolverhampton & Stour Valley Railway (BW&SVR), it was more commonly known as the Stour Valley. The S&BR was left with responsibility only for the line from Wolverhampton to Shrewsbury, of which the section from Wellington to Shrewsbury was to be jointly owned with the SUR.

Bills for the S&BR, the BW&SVR and the SUR line from Stafford were all passed in 1846. The S&BR Act authorised a railway from Shrewsbury to Wolverhampton, a distance of 19½ miles, with a branch from Shifnal through Madeley to the iron works at Dawley. The 10 miles between Welling-

Above left:
Madeley station was closed to passengers in 1915, though it was re-opened for two months in the summer of 1925. The down line was always used as a siding. Note the inside-keyed track on the line nearest to the platform. 1932.
LGRP courtesy David & Charles (11920)

Top:
Oakengates Tunnel was constructed to dimensions large enough to allow the laying of broad gauge track — much to the alarm of the LNWR. The south portal. *Real Photos (59031)*

Above:
As was often the case, different decor was given to the portals at each entrance. Oakengates, north portal. *Real Photos (59030)*

ton and Shrewsbury were to be jointly constructed and owned by S&BR and the SUR.

The company's Engineer was William Baker, a disciple of Robert Stephenson, who was also Engineer for the SUR. As early as September 1846 the Directors considered making the bridges and tunnels wide enough to take the broad gauge. Six months later, they ordered the only tunnel on the line, near Oakengates and 471yd long, to be made 28ft wide instead of the normal width of 24ft.

However, in the autumn of 1846 the LNWR took two steps destined to have far-reaching effects upon the fortunes of the S&BR: these were the leasing of both the SUR and the Stour Valley from the owning companies. Opposition to these leases on the part of the S&BR was eventually ended by an agreement that all traffic between Shrewsbury and other stations on the joint line to Wellington and stations south of Rugby should be pooled and divided into certain proportions; and that the LNWR should not use the Stafford line to compete for traffic which properly belonged to the S&BR.

In the meantime, the LNWR had acquired the Birmingham Canal Co, so that they held half the capital in the Stour Valley company, whose line they proposed to lease. A clause in the Act gave full running rights over the line to the S&BR, but provided that these running powers should cease if that company should be leased to, purchased by, or amalgamated with the GWR, the Oxford, Worcester & Wolverhampton Railway (OW&WR) or the Birmingham, Wolverhampton & Dudley Railway (BW&DR). It was obvious that the LNWR already envisaged the possibility that the broad gauge would eventually invade the north via Shrewsbury, because of the Directors making provision for broad gauge track. At the same time, in July 1847, agreement was reached that the station at Wolverhampton, and the line between it and the point where the Stour Valley line to Bushbury diverged from the Shrewsbury line, should be the joint property of the two companies. This was confirmed by a clause in the S&BR Act of 1847.

11

Left:
What was possibly once a broad gauge carriage, in use as a store behind the engine shed at Wellington. If so, this was the furthest north ever reached by a broad gauge vehicle! *H. Wheeller*

Below:
Wellington shed c1930 with 'Stella' class 2-4-0 No 3201. This shed is believed to have been converted from a goods shed c1876, the building being of S&BR origin. *W. Potter*

The SUR line from Stafford being ready before that of the S&BR from Wolverhampton, the opening of the joint section to Shrewsbury took place on 1 June 1849. Oakengates Tunnel not being finished, the only portion of the S&BR to be opened at that time was that from Wellington to Oakengates station. However, the rest of the line was opened to a temporary station at Wolverhampton (High Level) on Monday 12 November 1849.

From the moment of its opening until it amalgamated with the GWR five years later, the S&BR was involved in a long and bitter fight with the LNWR. In this conflict, the S&CR was its close ally, so that the two companies were well described by MacDermott as the 'Fighting Shrewsburys'.

The 'Fighting Shrewsburys'
The L&BR had supported the proposed S&BR line in the hope that some of the traffic between Birmingham, Chester and Birkenhead, previously the monopoly of the GJR, would be diverted to the new line. Quite naturally the S&BR and the S&CR also hoped that this would be so; they therefore arranged to work such traffic through and to divide the proceeds according to their mileage. However, they also rather rashly attempted to attract passengers to their route by charging lower fares. This was something which the LNWR could not tolerate, and action was forthcoming. The LNWR's General Manager being the redoubtable — and notorious — Capt Huish, it was to be expected that both threats and underhand manoeuvres would be employed.

The opening shot was a politely worded — though menacing — letter from Huish to the Secretary of the S&CR, Mr Roy, in which the latter was asked if the reported low rates were a fact and which warned that if this was so, a general fight would result! The reply did nothing to assuage the wrath of Capt Huish or of the LNWR. It stated that 'it is intended to carry through passengers only, first, second and third class, at reduced rates, with each of our regular trains . . . as an addition of a few through carriages to our local trains occasions scarcely any expense'. It concluded, 'If a "general fight" as you express it, arise, it is not of our seeking nor from any unreasonable views on the part of this Company'.

In the eyes of Huish, anything which did not accord with the dictates of Euston *was* unreasonable, so that this letter meant nothing less than a declaration of war! While the Shrewsbury companies were quite within their rights in joining to compete for the through traffic, their method of doing so was a suicidal policy. It left them wide open to wholesale retribution on the part of the LNWR.

The first battle took place at Chester. The Commissioners of the General station refused to allow passengers to be booked to Wolverhampton or beyond via Shrewsbury: when the S&CR persisted in this matter, their booking clerk was dragged out of the office and his tickets thrown after him! The Birkenhead company having declined to convey third class passengers by more than two trains, one very early in the morning and the other late at night, the S&CR introduced a service of horse-drawn buses to and from Birkenhead. They were excluded from the station approach by barricades of wood and chains, while the company's time bills and notices were torn down. All this taking place in a station of which the S&CR were part owners! They quickly obtained an injunction to stop such behaviour.

On the whole, relations with the Birkenhead Railway remained fairly peaceful, though that company refused to join in any competition against the LNWR of whom they were frankly terrified! Considerable quantities of goods traffic continued to be exchanged between the two companies at Chester. However, in April 1850, their Chairman, Alderman Charles Bancroft, was frightened into making an agreement with Capt Huish by which all facilities were withdrawn from the Shrewsbury companies except those which they could demand by law.

Passengers had to change trains and re-book at Chester, while all cattle from Birkenhead were loaded into LNWR trucks and sent by that line. The S&CR lost about 40 trucks of cattle which they had been carrying every Monday. The company countered by chartering a steamer to work flat-bottomed boats on the Dee to and from Saltney, and sent their goods traffic that way. The answer was a concerted plan by the LNWR and the Birkenhead Railway to attack all the S&CR's traffic by canal and road competition. All goods traffic from Birkenhead was sent to Shrewsbury and Wellington via Stafford, to Wrexham by wagons, and to Ruabon and Oswestry by canal! The LNWR undertook to bear the loss involved in such measures.

This continued for nearly six months, until Bancroft had considerable difficulty in defending it to his shareholders. The tonnage of goods which had been received from the S&CR during the half year to June 1850 was 38,795, whereas that received from the mighty LNWR had been a mere trickle of 2,245! What frightened the Chairman even more was a proposal of the S&CR to apply for running rights over his railway! A truce was hastily arranged and the worst obstructions were removed, at the same time the S&CR gave up the use of boats on the Dee and buses to Birkenhead. However, they pressed ahead with their Bill to obtain running powers.

The LNWR, by no means averse to fighting on two fronts at once, also commenced hostilities further south at Wolverhampton. Disregarding the Agreement of 1847, by which the S&BR's opposition to the lease of the SUR had been ended, they started a fierce competition at low fares and rates between Wolverhampton and Shrewsbury via Stafford; a distance of 46 miles compared with that of 29½ miles by the S&BR line.

As at Chester, physical violence was part of the warfare. Unable to deal with goods traffic for places south of Wolverhampton, owing to lack of communication with the Birmingham Canal adjoining the last half mile of their line, which was joint property with the Stour Valley, the S&BR attempted to lay a siding for this purpose in April 1850. Their men were forcibly prevented from doing this by their late Engineer, William Baker, who had been replaced by Henry Robertson, late of the S&CR, immediately after the opening of the line. A large force of navvies, under Baker's command — he was afterwards known locally as 'General Baker' (!) — accompanied well in the rear by the LNWR lawyer, were marched on to the ground to stop the work, and only prompt action by the police and military prevented a pitched battle being fought! The reason for this behaviour was stated to be that the plan had not been approved by the Joint Committee.

An injunction soon put a stop to this illegal action, and under its protection the S&BR made the siding, which was later followed by the construction on their adjoining land of the Victoria Basin with its wharves and sidings.

Meanwhile, very slow progress was being made with the construction of the Stour Valley line, leased by the LNWR, which was to provide the S&BR with their access to Birmingham. As the LNWR had the old GJR station at Bushbury — which they called Wolverhampton, though situ-

ated a mile from that town — they had no need to hurry. The Stour Valley's representatives helped by staying away from the Joint Committee from May 1850 until August 1851, thus ensuring that no progress could be made with the new station at Wolverhampton.

However, Huish had been 'too clever by half', as his activities forced the two Shrewsbury companies to look elsewhere for support; and this was forthcoming from Paddington and the GWR. That company was already poised to reach Wolverhampton by means of the BW&DR, with whom — and the OW&WR — the S&BR were to be partners in a proposed Low Level station. An agreement over traffic between the two Shrewsbury companies and the GWR was sealed on 10 January 1851. This provided for the mutual interchange of traffic, the division of the net receipts according to mileage, and the appointment of a joint committee to manage the through traffic. As the GWR was opened only as far as Banbury, goods were to be forwarded over the intervening country by canal.

Huish was, quite naturally, 'not amused' by this alliance with the LNWR's greatest rival, and the strife became even more bitter. The S&BR was attacked through the buying of shares which were divided among residents of Euston Square and Camden Town who happened to be employed by the LNWR! Much money was spent in strengthen-

ing an existing opposition to the Directors, so that the half-yearly meeting agreed to a Committee of Investigation and adjoined for a month to await its report.

The Committee stated that they had re-opened negotiations with the LNWR and had made a 'preliminary arrangement' with that company by which the S&BR were to cease being carriers and hand over their line, together with their rolling stock, to the LNWR who would work it for 21 years; and pay them, *out of the traffic receipts of the S&BR*, dividends beginning at 3% and rising to 4% after four years!

The meeting was again adjourned for a month to allow time for this 'arrangement' to be considered, during which time the opposition demanded a special meeting to consider the LNWR proposals. This lasted four days, during which time the uproar and confusion was tremendous. The Chairman, Directors and Officers were all abused in turn, without mercy — especially the Secretary, Knox, who was the objective of particular hatred by the pro-LNWR party, as he had taken a leaf out of their book by arranging the splitting of stock among the company's staff, his own children, and friends!

The Chairman, Ormsby Gore, was forced to remain in the chair while a poll was taken in an adjoining room, while most of the shareholders went away for refreshment — though protesting loudly against any adjournment of the meeting — and spent his time reading a volume of 'Household Words'. At 9pm he brought from his pocket a white night-cap, which he drew over his head, and appeared to go into a peaceful slumber! The meeting eventually agreed to adjourn, and the next day the resolution accepting the LNWR's terms and handing over the railway to them, 'lock, stock and barrel', was carried with immense applause — despite a warning by the chairman that without an Act of Parliament it would be totally illegal and void. The meeting then rejected the Directors' Report, and illegally appointed new Directors who were members of the opposition.

The next move lay with the GWR, who in April made an offer to both the Shrewsbury companies which 'floored' the opposition; this was for a future amalgamation of all three companies in 1856 or 1857, at the choice of the small companies, on the basis of their net revenues in the preceding year. There was also a guarantee out of the whole revenue from the through traffic between London and places beyond Birmingham of a dividend beginning from January 1852 at 3% and rising to 4% in 1855. The offer was accepted by the legal S&BR Directors and a special meeting of the company was called for 8 May to consider it.

The opposition held their meeting on 7 May, when Ormsby Gore made a brief appearance to inform them that it was not a legal meeting, but this did not deter them. A forgery of the company's seal was produced — Huish had employed such tactics on several previous occasions — and the agreement with the LNWR was solemnly sealed 'amidst boisterous cheers'. Next day the special meeting called by the Directors was held, and the Agreement for Amalgamation with the GWR and the S&CR was approved and sealed with the genuine seal of the company. Huish and the LNWR were forced to accept the situation: they now concentrated their efforts on the S&CR, in an attempt to ensure that trains from Paddington should never reach the banks of the Mersey.

In readiness for the special meeting of the S&CR a lively and noisy opposition was procured by the usual methods. A special train brought the famous Euston troupe, 140 strong, to Chester. However, once again one of the Directors played the LNWR at their own game and 'spiked the enemies' guns' by distributing a share or two apiece to a crowd of S&CR employees who made as much noise as the opposition! The meeting was adjourned for a month, the interval being devoted to a war of circulars and canvassing. Eventually, at the adjourned meeting the GWR Agreement was accepted. Thus the GWR extended its influence as far north as Chester, though there were to be another three years of strenuous fighting before the amalgamation was made effective. Ironically, the author of this undreamed-of extension to the original GWR was none other than its inveterate enemy, the General Manager of the LNWR!

In 1851 the Associated Companies, as the GWR and the two Shrewsbury companies came to be called, made overtures to the Birkenhead company to join the alliance. Birkenhead with its docks, and with Liverpool just across the Mersey, was an obvious prize and would make a more fitting northern terminus than Chester. The Birkenhead, whose full title was the Birkenhead, Lancashire & Cheshire Junction Railway, had just opened a line from Chester to a junction with the LNWR near Warrington, from which point it worked its own traffic into Manchester over the latter's line — by agreement with the LNWR.

Meanwhile, the S&CR introduced a Bill asking for running powers over the C&HR's line between Saltney and Chester — enjoyed only by agreement with that company — and also over the entire Birkenhead system, and authorising the S&CR to make a station on the South Reserve at Birkenhead. Though the LNWR backed both the small companies in their strenuous attempts to resist these powers, they were granted. The Birkenhead's Chairman, Bancroft, concluded from such a portent that it was time to make terms with the Associated Companies!

An agreement between the four companies was made in October 1851, this being confirmed by the Birkenhead proprietors the following month, for a perpetual lease of that railway *and the benefits of its agreements with other companies*, to the Associated Companies in return for a guarantee of dividends beginning at 3% and rising after three years to 4%. There was also an option for the Birkenhead to amalgamate with them before January 1856. In the meantime the Associated Companies were given powers to convey traffic over the Birkenhead's lines, paying the latter 60% of the receipts. Hence, at the end of 1851 a line from Paddington to Birkenhead, as well as access to Manchester, seemed assured for the GWR.

Back in the south, at Wolverhampton, the LNWR still had 'some shots left in its locker' in connection with the still unopened Stour Valley line. The line was practically finished early in 1851, but no attempt was made to open it — much to the very vocal annoyance of the local population! In November the S&BR gave notice of an application to Parliament to open the line themselves, which

forced the LNWR into declaring that they intended opening it on 1 December.

On hearing of the intended opening, the S&BR directors notified the LNWR that they would forthwith exercise their running rights over the line. That company replied, regretfully, that as the S&BR had now amalgamated with the GWR their running powers had ceased — as provided in the Act. The response from the S&BR was that they had *not* amalgamated with the GWR, but had only agreed to do so at a future date; therefore their running powers were in full force and they intended exercising them! The LNWR decided to postpone the opening of the line on account of 'imminent risk to the public from such a hostile attempt and the danger to be anticipated of a collision': the S&BR responded with a counter notice that their trains would arrive at the new station at Wolverhampton at specified hours, 'and proceed over the Stour Valley Railway to Birmingham, as specially authorised by the Stour Valley Act of Parliament in 1847'.

An exciting account of the ensuing conflict appeared in the *Wolverhampton Herald*.

'The first Shrewsbury & Birmingham train was to leave about 9.15, and on arriving at the Wolverhampton station from Shrewsbury several persons were desirous of going through, and others who had booked from the new station were waiting to be conveyed to Birmingham. The London & North Western had caused their powerful engine

Above:
The Chirk Viaduct, carrying the Shrewsbury & Chester Railway across the River Ceiriog. The end sections were originally spans of laminated timber. *H. G. W. Household*

Right:
The Chirk Viaduct. Detail on the pillar which originally united the stone arches (right) with the laminated wooden arches (left).
H. G. W. Household.

Swift to be placed on the up line a little beyond the signal post upon the bridge leading to Mr Bayley's chemical works, thus causing an obstruction to the progress of the Shrewsbury & Birmingham train. Several officials, policemen and other persons connected with the London & North Western, surrounded the engine, quietly waiting for any further proceedings on the part of the Shrewsbury & Birmingham people. A little further up the line an engine and tender were placed across the up and down rails. Hundreds of people congregated upon the line, and shortly after 10 o'clock a strong party of borough police were marched, under the command of Colonel Hogg, to the bridge on which the LNWR engine rested. As a breach of the peace and serious disturbance was expected when the train from Shrewsbury proceeded towards Birmingham, the military under the command of Capt Bellairs, stationed in the town, were ordered to be in readiness. The Mayor was also in attendance,

16

and an army of police waited in the hall of the station.

'About quarter past 10 o'clock, the passengers having previously alighted, the engine of the Shrewsbury & Birmingham with guards and a 3rd class carriage filled with men, who appeared to be servants of the Company and with G. Knox Esq and several other Directors and gentlemen standing on the engine carriage, proceeded towards Birmingham, the whistle of the engine emitting the shrillest sound to signify their advance to the obstructing engine before them, two fog alarm signals, which had been placed on the rails, exploded. No notice, however, was taken by the parties belonging to the London & North Western engine, save the continuous waving of red danger flags, which a number of policemen held in their hands, and one of which was tied to the signal post.

'The engine of the Shrewsbury & Birmingham slowly advanced in spite of the red flags hoisted, and amid cheers and shouts of the assembled multitude, bunted against that of the London & North Western, which being a very powerful engine, and the brakes being screwed tightly on,

received but a slight shock from the concussion. The parties in charge of the LNWR engine were then requested to move on, but declined, and Mr Baker, the engineer of the Stour Valley, who was on that engine, in reply to several questions knowingly shook his head. The two engines standing opposite each other in the closest proximity with the steam power of their gigantic bodies issuing from various safety valves in voluminous quantities with a hissing noise presented an exciting spectacle, representing the antagonism of their respective proprietors.

'As no satisfactory answer could be got from the LNWR officials, the Directors and other gentlemen on the opposing Company's engine got down and immediately obtained a summons from the Borough Magistrates against Mr Baker, the engineer, who was in charge of the engine, and Thomas Newbold, the engine driver, for obstructing the free traffic of the line.'

Unlike most other battles for access, no physical violence ensued. A meeting was held at the Town Hall, and this produced an agreement that the LNWR's Directors should meet at once to consider suggestions made by the Magistrates and that the S&BR should refrain from further action for a month.

The LNWR appealed to the Board of Trade, maintaining that there was extreme danger to the public in opening the line. The Board took refuge in requiring a second inspection of the line — which they had already approved for opening — and the inspecting officer found that certain signals were missing! The Board then ordered the LNWR to postpone the opening: that company protested that they were anxious to open it, but were now prevented by the Board; and that all this was the fault of the S&BR!

Eventually the LNWR agreed to open the line on condition that the S&BR refrained from attempting to enforce their running powers until a judgement had been obtained. So the Stour Valley was, at last, opened on 1 July 1852. However, the LNWR were not defeated; they ensured that no trains connected with any from Shrewsbury and no through bookings were allowed, while goods traffic from the S&BR continued to be transferred to and from the canal at Victoria Basin.

Although the Bill for the amalgamation of the three Associated Companies was passed in 1852, it required the approval of four-fifths of the shareholders of each company. Once again, the Euston troupe set forth on their journeys to attend the meetings of the two Shrewsbury companies; needless to say there was little chance of a peaceful acceptance at either meeting!

The GWR then took the bold step of applying for powers, irrespective of amalgamation, to run over both the Shrewsbury Railways and the Shrewsbury & Hereford line; while the entire system of the Birkenhead company, as well as the two intervening miles of the C&HR and the Birkenhead Docks were included. They proposed to lay broad gauge rails over all these lines, at their own expense, creating through broad gauge routes from both Hereford and Wolverhampton to Birkenhead! Only the S&BR accepted this, even the S&CR opposed it, and the Bill was rejected. Thus perished the first — and, as it turned out, the only — attempt to obtain powers to extend the broad gauge north of Wolverhampton and to the banks of the Mersey.

Although both companies stood by the agreements with the GWR, it was in the face of constant opposition. However, this collapsed dramatically in 1853 when the GWR made a guarantee of a fixed 3½% dividend and half surplus profits. This offer was accepted by enormous majorities, and a Bill effecting the amalgamation was introduced in the 1854 Session. Despite concerted opposition by the LNWR and its satellites, the Bill passed unanimously — the amalgamation being described 'as being of a special character and of great importance to the public interest'. The 'special character' was probably the amalgamation of two gauges!

However, the GWR had to pay a price, being forced to agree that no application to extend the broad gauge north of Wolverhampton would be made until the Board of Trade should have reported that this was desirable in the public interest. Alas, the Board never did this! Thus the GWR was destined to remain a company with two gauges and two Divisions, whose divergences of practice gave it such interest during the 19th century. On 1 September 1854, the stormy and troubled existence of the two Shrewsbury companies came to an end and the GWR extended its territory to Chester, with running powers to Birkenhead and the prospect of access into Manchester.

Apart from the two viaducts on the S&CR there were few works of note on either line, whose permanent way was of the usual standard gauge type. The signals were of the normal semaphore pattern, with double-armed signals for both lines situated on the platform of each station. The telegraph had been installed throughout both lines in 1852. The train service was worked by time intervals, though by 1863 the section from Hollinswood to Oakengates and the Gresford incline were both worked on the block system by single-needle and bell. Well into the 1870s much of the line north of Wolverhampton was still being worked by the old time interval system, but by 1883 the only remaining section was the line from Wellington to Nantwich.

A joint committee to manage the working of through traffic had been set up prior to the opening of the S&BR, and this was merged into a larger one, on which the GWR was represented, in 1851. James Grierson — destined for high office on the GWR — was Secretary of this committee and early in 1854 he became Traffic Manager of both lines.

William Ormsby Gore MP, of Parkington, near Oswestry, was the first Chairman of both companies (as well as of the Shrewsbury & Hereford), and has a right to be regarded as 'the father of railways in Shropshire'. Neither company was allowed by the LNWR's persecution to become in any way at all prosperous; the S&BR did not manage to pay even its preference shareholders in full! It was small wonder that the shareholders of both companies were so eager to accept the GWR's final offer — and enter into 'the Promised Land'.

A peculiar consequence of the amalgamation was that the GWR found themselves in the curious position of having joint ownership of both stations at Wolverhampton — and in both cases the premises were shared with a company with whom relationships were, to say the least, strained if not always in a state of warfare! Low Level was shared with the OW&WR — the 'Old Worse and Worse'. The GWR used both stations for northbound traffic from November 1854; the carriages from High Level being joined to those from Low Level at Stafford Road Junction. There was, however, no corresponding division of trains in the reverse direction, all passengers being carried into Low Level. In 1858 this practice ceased, all passenger traffic being dealt with at Low Level and all goods traffic at Victoria Basin. The GWR then sold their interest in High Level to the LNWR.

The Battle for Birkenhead
At the end of 1851 the Birkenhead Railway was on friendly terms with the Associated Companies, having agreed to lease its line to them with a view to eventual amalgamation, and a Bill to authorise this was deposited for the 1852 Session. Huish forthwith frightened the company by the promotion of *two* rival lines between Chester and Birkenhead — one by the LNWR, the other by the C&HR. The Birkenhead decided that 'discretion was the better part of valour' and promptly withdrew the Bill for the lease of its line — much to the consternation of the Associated Companies. Bancroft, who was always pro-LNWR, arranged for the immediate handing over of the line and its rolling stock to the LNWR on a lease: the reward for such subservience being the withdrawal of the Bills for the competing lines — neither of which had a remote chance of being passed! A Bill to permit this lease was then introduced, but was promptly rejected.

War had already been declared on the S&CR by raising the charges for trains running over the Birkenhead's line. The S&CR at first took no notice, continuing to pay the original 60%. When bailiffs invaded the goods shed and siezed property to pay for the extra tolls, they simply ceased to run over the Birkenhead's line and handed over their traffic at Chester. Unprepared for this, the Birkenhead could not handle the increased traffic. Bancroft complained bitterly that owing to the wickedness of the S&CR his company had been forced to buy six new engines to work the traffic! The result was that Parliament granted further powers to the S&CR in respect of the Birkenhead's lines.

When the Birkenhead shareholders discovered that the amount of traffic received from the S&CR was *over three times as much* as that from the LNWR there was a rebellion, four Directors being replaced. The new board attempted to conclude a working agreement with the GWR with an option for the lease of the line; but the LNWR managed to get this defeated at the half-yearly meeting. The Birkenhead then once again took up a hostile position, refusing any facilities for through traffic.

The GWR took steps to obtain their own premises in Birkenhead, and also in Liverpool and at Timperley near Manchester. Premises and wharves were leased in Birkenhead Docks, and the GWR commenced running their own goods trains from Chester on terms settled by arbitration: no attempt appears to have been made to run to Manchester via Timperley. Early in 1856 through mineral traffic began to be worked between South Wales and Birkenhead, and on 1 May 1857 GWR passenger trains commenced running to and from Birkenhead by agreement with the Birkenhead company — the latter having decided that welcoming profitable traffic was more sensible than refusing it to please the LNWR!

Access to Manchester via Walton Junction was gained by the GWR, together with the LNWR's Liverpool Road goods station and sundry other benefits, following the retirement of Huish — who appeared to have an almost pathological hatred of the GWR. Finally, in 1860, the Birkenhead Railway came into joint ownership, with the rolling stock and engines divided between the two companies. The Birkenhead, desirous of being rid of its responsibilities, obtained powers from Parliament by which it could make an arrangement jointly, but not separately, with the GWR and LNWR. Thus neither Euston nor Paddington could complain! At last, the GWR extended to the banks of the Mersey, and Paddington also had the satisfaction that it had also penetrated into Manchester, previously a Euston preserve.

Below:
Prior to the opening of the Vale of Llangollen Railway in 1861, Llangollen was served by a station on the main line several miles distant. Closed in 1862, the station buildings at Llangollen Road still survived in 1949. *LGRP courtesy David & Charles (19582)*

Bottom:
An 0-6-0PT of the '6400' class creeps across the 510yd length of the Cefn Viaduct, 148ft above the River Dee, with the morning auto-train from Gobowen to Ruabon. 8 September 1956. *Norman Jones*

2 The Great Western's Second Main Line

In 1854 the GWR found itself in possession of a second main line, no less than 230 miles long, from Paddington to Birkenhead. However, no trains could run from Paddington to the banks of the Mersey, owing to the change of gauge at Wolverhampton. The extension of the broad gauge northwards being out of the question, the only alternative was to extend the standard gauge southwards to Paddington.

As early as 1852 the line from Oxford to Birmingham had the third rail added, and in 1854 the section northwards to Priestfield Junction — where it joined the OW&WR — was opened on the mixed gauge. By the end of 1856 the mixed gauge had been extended to Reading, and on 1 October 1861 Paddington saw its first standard gauge trains. The first train for Birkenhead left at 9.35am that morning, in the charge of one of the Beyer, Peacock 2-2-2s which had hitherto worked the express trains north of Wolverhampton. Broad gauge trains between Paddington and Wolverhampton ceased to run at the end of March 1869. The GWR had gained a second main line and access to Liverpool — albeit by means of a ferry — but the price was the hastening of the end of the broad gauge.

The withdrawal of the broad gauge from Wolverhampton enabled the station at Low Level to be altered and improved; formerly the joint station, it had been in the sole ownership of the GWR since the amalgamation with the West Midland Railway in 1863. There was also an opportunity to make improvements to the complex and inconvenient premises of the Locomotive Department at Stafford Road, which had become the largest running centre on the GWR — a distinction it was to retain for many years.

In its final form, Low Level was quite a spacious station. The up and down platforms, (the former having been lengthened in 1911), were long enough for the maximum loadings on the main line, and there were bays on both sides at the up end and on the down side at the north end. An island platform, sharing a line with the down platform, had been removed soon after the withdrawal of the broad gauge, thus allowing four lines to be situated between the up and down platforms. Until the early 1930s a large overall roof covered the platforms and running lines.

Below:
Wolverhampton Low Level station after the removal of the original overall roof. No 4944 *Middleton Hall* enters on the Birkenhead to Bournemouth through train formed of Southern stock. 23 August 1936.
S. W. Baker, courtesy R. C. Riley

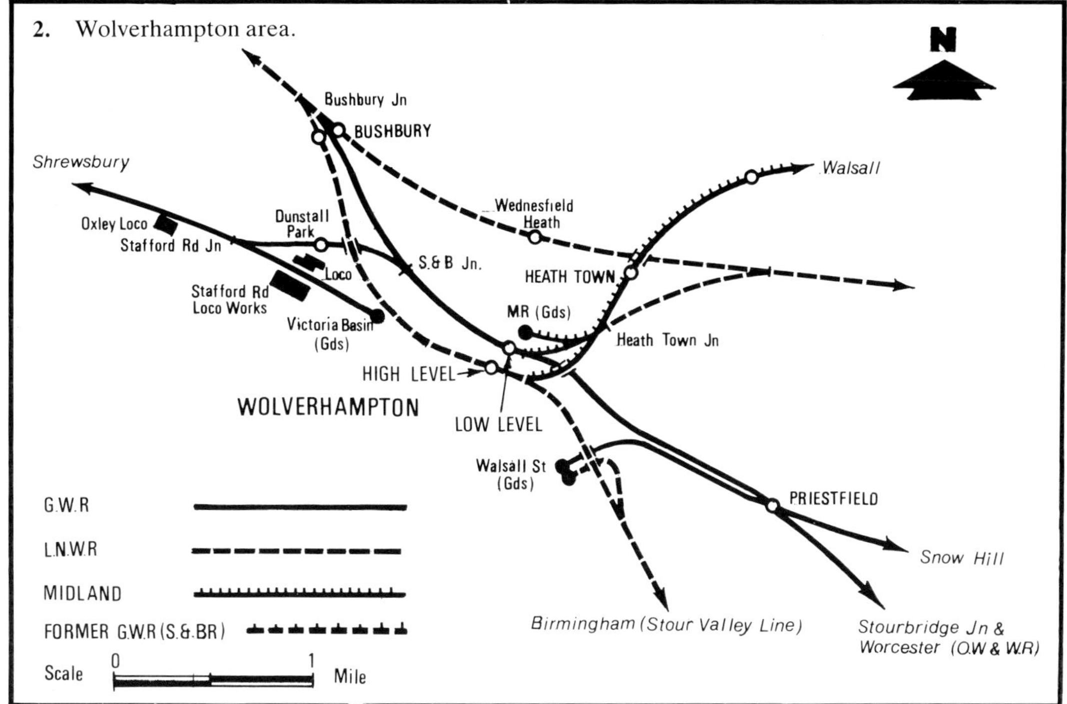

From the earliest days of a through train service between Paddington and Birkenhead it was the practice to change engines at Wolverhampton; though at one period in the 19th century some engine changing took place at Birmingham. In later years there were some through workings to and from Shrewsbury; while Chester engines, 'Saints', 'Halls' and (later) 'Counties', worked as far south as Oxford on through trains between Birkenhead and the South Coast resorts.

Between Low Level and the Stafford Road complex the main line made use of a short section of the former 'Old Worse & Worse' line to Bushbury Junction where it joined the LNWR. Apart from a very short-lived service between Wolverhampton (Low Level) and Manchester during the period 1864-67, the final section to Bushbury Junction was used almost exclusively for goods traffic. However, there was an annual and notable exception during the latter years of the 19th century; this being its use by the Royal Train on the occasions of visits by Queen Victoria to Balmoral, when the GWR conveyed the train to or from Windsor — the Single No 55 *Queen* being the engine normally used. The line was also used for special Ambulance Train workings during both World Wars.

Leaving Wolverhampton for the North, the extensive premises at Stafford Road were on the left of the short section of line — originally broad gauge — between Cannock Road Junction and Stafford Road Junction (where the GWR and the S&BR joined each other). Opened in November 1849, the first shed had a brief existence as it had to be demolished only five years later when the connecting line was built from Cannock Junction to create a through route northwards from Low Level. Replaced by another building on the opposite side of the ex-S&BR line to High Level, this was closed when extensions were made to the works in about 1881.

The first GWR shed, opened in 1854 for broad gauge engines, was sited at a lower level and on the opposite side of the Stafford Road to the S&BR premises. Additional accommodation being require ˙ for standard gauge engines, a second shed was opened in 1860. Although adjacent to the broad gauge building, access was from the ex-S&BR line near the Works. When the broad gauge shed became redundant, it was converted to a tender shop, an erecting shop having been built alongside.

Two additional turntable sheds (Nos 2 and 3) were built adjacent to the original standard gauge building (known as No 1 shed), all being linked internally. An additional terminal building, with access from No 3 shed, was added in the 1890s; at a later date this became a road motor repair shop. Following the opening in 1932 of the new repair shop on the far side of the ex-S&BR line, the former broad gauge premises reverted to being used as engine sheds. Two straight, terminal sheds

(Nos 4 and 5) took the place of the old tender shop.

Beyond the junction with the ex-S&BR line, and shortly after crossing Oxley Viaduct, the main line passed through the Oxley marshalling yards. Originating as a few up and down sidings opened by the S&BR in the 1850s, they had been extended in 1897 to provide up and down yards, each having about a dozen sidings. The down yard was divided into the Crewe and Birkenhead yards, while at a later date the up yard was divided into the Old and New yards.

To the north of the down yard was Oxley engine shed, opened in July 1907 to provide some relief for the over-crowded premises at Stafford Road. A standard Churchward two turntable unit, it was unique in the siting of the units behind one another rather than side by side.

Well over 100 engines were shedded at Oxley in the last days of the GWR, compared with just over 70 at Stafford Road (though prior to Oxley being opened there had been well over twice that number). Oxley was the Wolverhampton freight shed, Stafford Road being mainly concerned with passenger engines. However, Oxley had no less than 31 4-6-0s, most of these being 'Halls'.

Immediately beyond Oxley shed was Oxley Middle Junction, followed by Oxley North Junction, from both of which lines led to Oxley Branch Junction from whence a single track branch line ran to make an end-on junction with a branch of the former OW&WR from Kingswinford Junction to Baggeridge. The Oxley to Baggeridge Junction section was not opened until May 1925 and during its early years was provided with a passenger service on which steam railmotors were used (from Stourbridge Junction shed), but this was withdrawn in October 1932 and the line was then used only for freight traffic.

The line had several unusual features. At Oxley Branch Junction the double tracks from the Middle and North junctions became two tracks, and only three chains later merged into a single track! This was probably unique on the GWR. However, it had originally been intended that the new line should be double track throughout, and two platforms were built at Tettenhall and Himley, though only one was ever used! Despite its single track as far as Baggeridge (the old ex-OW&WR branch being double track) the line carried a considerable volume of goods traffic.

From Oxley to Cosford the line was on a down gradient of 1 in 100, followed by a similar rise from Shifnal to beyond Madeley Junction. A spur for

banking engines was provided at Shifnal, the majority of down goods trains being banked as far as Hollinswood which was the junction for the Stirchley branch. The latter line, just over a mile long and for goods traffic only, was opened in 1908 to serve chemical and iron works; it was an extension of an older and much shorter line, the Dark Lane branch!

Shortly after passing through Oakengates tunnel and Oakengates station the line from Buildwas, via

Above:
Stafford Road Works: the new Erecting Shop in 1932. The majority of locomotives under repair appear to be of the 'Bulldog' or 'Duke' classes, though there are also two small 2-6-2Ts, a pannier and a 'Barnum' class 2-4-0. The 'Bulldog' in the foreground is No 3388 *Ian Allan Library*

Left:
Oxley Sidings in 1935. 'Aberdare' class 2-6-0 No 2633, with a '2800' class 2-8-0 to the rear. August 1935. *H. Wheeller*

Above right:
The coal stage at Stafford Road in 1948, with a very begrimed No 6877 *Llanfair Grange* (of Worcester). *G. Bannister*

Right:
Outside Stafford Road Works in 1935. 0-6-0PT No 1712 and other panniers wait for admission. August 1935. *H. Wheeller*

Above:
Many goods trains were routed over the line between Oxley Junction and Kingswinsford Junction, thus avoiding Wolverhampton. No 3860 heads a Crewe to Stoke Gifford train passing Tettenhall in 1954. *G. Bannister*

Left:
Oakengates station, looking towards Wellington, with a superb example of a brick-built goods shed on the right — note how the two centre bays are wider than the others. 1932.
LGRP courtesy David & Charles (11940)

Below left:
Wellington station, the junction for the LMS (ex-LNWR and Shropshire Union) line to Stafford and for the GWR's branches to Crewe and to Buildwas and Craven Arms. 0-6-0PT No 2713 of the '655' class passes through on a down goods in August 1935. *H. Wheeller*

Above right:
The bay platform at Wellington, with 2-6-2T No 4406 on the 4.30pm to Much Wenlock and LMS (ex-LNWR) 'Coal Tank' No 58904 on the 3.53pm to Coalport. *J. Edgington*

Right:
Although still often to be seen on express passenger workings, 'Star' class No 4061 *Glastonbury Abbey* is in charge of a down stopping train leaving Shrewsbury in 1950. No 4061 was shedded at Shrewsbury for many years.
Real Photos (K946)

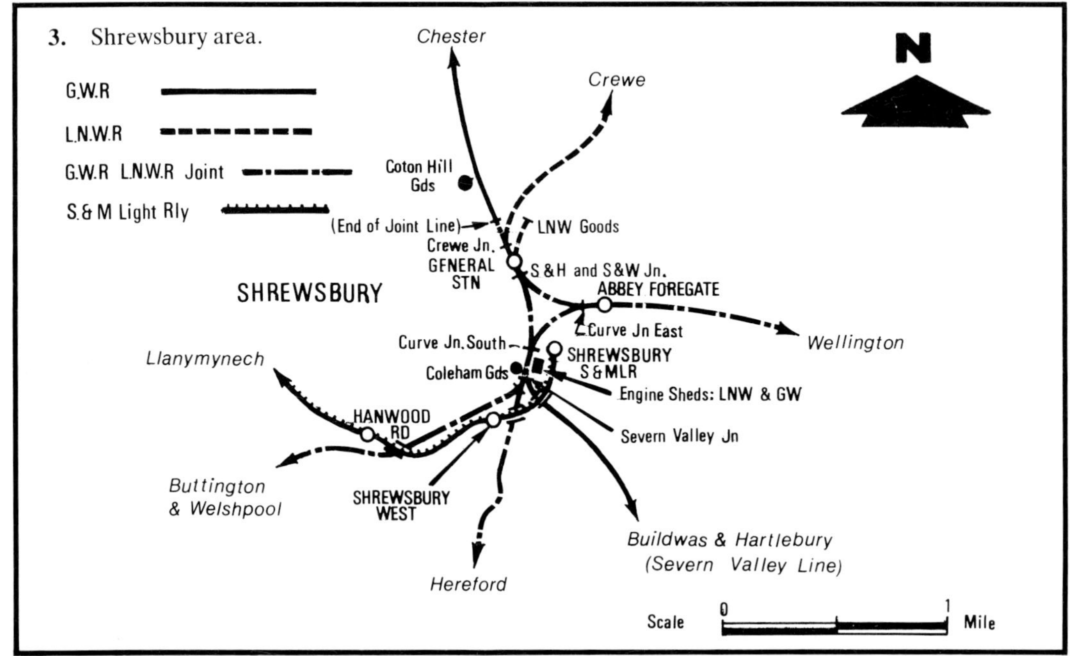

Lightmoor, joined the main line at Ketley Junction. Half a mile further along the line, the LNWR's line from Stafford made a junction on the up side. From this point the line was owned jointly as far as Shrewsbury, and it was also 'downhill' for most of the way.

Wellington was the largest and most important station between Wolverhampton and Shrewsbury, being the junction for two GWR branch lines to Buildwas, Much Wenlock and Craven Arms, and to Market Drayton, Nantwich and Crewe. It also served as the junction for the LNWR's branch to

Below:
Gobowen station's importance was due solely to being the junction for the branch to Oswestry and the former Cambrian Railways' system. The branch can be seen curving away to the right beyond the site of the engine shed (which was closed in 1922). The building behind the water tank is the pumphouse which formed part of the shed. *LGRP courtesy David & Charles (13549)*

Coalport, which diverged from the line to Stafford. The Much Wenlock and Craven Arms trains used a bay at the east end of the down platform, which was also used by the LNWR's Coalport trains.

A three road engine shed was situated on the up side beyond the loop line, the building being of considerable antiquity and dating from the early days of the S&BR. A lithograph of 1850 reveals that it was then in use as a goods shed: in 1876 it was recorded that a goods shed was to be converted for the purpose of stabling GWR and LNWR engines. Wellington shed was responsible for the services over the Crewe branch and the line to Much Wenlock and Craven Arms. For the former, a succession of some of the GWRs locomotive antiquities — all of them 2-4-0s — were employed until the mid-1930s, despite the service running into the citadel of the LNWR. (One wonders if the practice had originated as a gesture of contempt towards Crewe and all its works!) The shed was also provided with a succession of 'Dukes' and 'Bulldogs' for that line; while for the Craven Arms line, five of the small-wheeled 2-6-2Ts of the '4400' class were shedded at Wellington from 1935 onwards. Until the mid-1930s there had been a turntable; but this was removed after the demise of the last 2-4-0s — being too small to turn anything larger. The normal allocation was about 20 engines.

From the early days of the railway, Shrewsbury was a large and important junction and eventually there were no less than nine signalboxes! The LNWR's presence was much in evidence by reason of its joint ownership of the lines from Wellington, Hereford and Welshpool, in addition to its own line from Crewe. The jointly-owned line to Welshpool was opened from Sutton Bridge Junction to Minsterley in June 1861, and on to Buttington Junction, to join the Oswestry & Newtown Railway, in the following January. In 1867 the Abbey Foregate curve was opened from Abbey Foregate Junction to English Bridge Junction, thus ending the need for reversal on through services between London and Mid Wales. In later years it was used by the 'Cambrian Coast Express' to and from Paddington.

Situated partly on two bridges crossing the River Severn, Shrewsbury station was somewhat restricted in layout. The main 'Baronial Mock Tudor' building, somewhat reminiscent of Bristol Temple Meads, was crowned with a 70ft tower. Originally of two stories only, excavations at the end of the 19th century produced the present three storey facade. The original timber roof disappeared during the 1899 rebuilding and enlargement of the station, after which the southern ends of the platforms were covered by a great overall roof of peculiar appearance, having a flat top and sloping sides (the northern portion of this roof was replaced by platform awnings in 1924). The only other railway building resembling this, which comes to mind, was the Great North of Scotland's engine shed at Elgin!

At the south end were bays for the Hereford, Stafford and Severn Valley line trains, the latter's little 0-4-2Ts or antiquated 2-4-0s being a familiar sight at the turn of the century. Although there was an up through line, none was provided in the down direction. For many years up and down trains used the same platform — a common practice on the LNWR. A short tunnel, passing under the station wall at the south end, gave access to the Shropshire Yard where there was an old, but extensive, goods warehouse and which connected with canal wharves. For many years an LNWR

Above:
Gobowen station, with unusual motive power for the Oswestry auto-train on 28 August 1952. The delightful Italianate station building can be seen beyond the goods shed. *B. E. Morrison*

Below:
Looking south from Ruabon station, showing the engine turntable on the right. The junction for Llangollen and Barmouth is beyond the bridge.
LGRP courtesy David & Charles (19277)

'Special Tank' was used for shunting in this yard. The most impressive feature of the south end of the station was the huge signalbox.

From 1862 a Joint Superintendent was in charge and each company had its own offices. Joint control ceased in February 1932, after which the station came under the GWR's District Superintendent at Chester. During the period of joint superintendency, all parcels and miscellaneous traffic, other than that for local stations, handed in without any route being specified, was dealt with on alternate 'red' and 'black' days. The former were GWR, the latter LNWR (LMS) — eg: on a 'red' day parcels for Swansea were sent via Hereford and Cardiff, while on a 'black' day they travelled via the Central Wales Line! Had this been at Chester, one might have suspected that the cathedral authorities were responsible for suggesting the idea: after all, it was 'God's Wonderful Railway' which had the 'red' days, and 'Red Letter Day' rank above 'Black Letter Days' in the Prayer Book Calendar!

The Shrewsbury engine sheds of both the GWR and LNWR were situated at Coleham, on the S&H Joint line. The GWR sheds were considerably enlarged in 1932, when the old wagon repair shop was demolished and an additional straight shed built in its place. The allocation in 1947 was 53 engines.

The GWR goods depot was situated to the north of the station, on the up side and just beyond Crewe Junction. It was distinguished by an extra-large advertisement — carefully placed so as to be visible to all who travelled by the LNWR line — which extrolled the merits of the GWR's fast goods trains, the latter being something in which the company led the field and of which it was justly proud.

Northwards from Shrewsbury, past Coton goods marshalling yard, the line climbed for over four miles, the first mile and a half being at 1 in 80. At Whittington, one and a half miles south of Gobowen, it passed under the Cambrian Railways' line from Whitchurch to Oswestry. The latter town was connected to the main line by a branch from Gobowen, where the branch lines used a bay at the rear of the south end of the down platform whose station name board proclaimed to main line passengers that this was indeed Gobowen, where they should change for Oswestry, but simply informed passengers on the branch train 'All Change'!

From Gobowen the line ascended again towards Preesgweene (later Weston Rhyn), after which it crossed the first of the two great viaducts, this being the Chirk Viaduct over the River Ceiriog. Though only serving a small village (though this

did include Chirk Castle), the station at Chirk was important in former days as the interchange point with the Glyn Valley Tramway. The latter's narrow gauge trains, with their tramway-type engines, ran up the valley to Glynceiriog until the little line closed in 1935.

Shortly before reaching Cefn station the line was carried over the River Dee by the magnificent Cefn Viaduct; while to the north of the station, on the down side, was the junction for the important

Above left:
Ruabon station from the south, 1949. The extra-large station name board was a notable feature of the station for many years.
LGRP courtesy David & Charles (19276)

Left:
An Edwardian view of the fine station canopy on the up platform at Ruabon. Winston Churchill's name appears on one of the newspaper advertisements. *Lens of Sutton*

Above:
The approach to Chester, with the evening Chester to Barmouth train hauled by Mogul No 5330 crossing the Dee bridge near Saltney Junction on 10 August 1962. *Derek Cross*

Right:
The immense length of the GWR's original engine shed at Chester (inherited from the Birkenhead Railway) can be judged from this photograph taken during the 1920s, showing large 2-6-2T No 3120. Engines of this type were at that time used on mineral train workings from the North Wales coalfield to Birkenhead. *Lens of Sutton*

cross-country line to Dolgelley and Barmouth. The original Ruabon station was fairly small, with only up and down platforms and a goods yard on the up side, but was later enlarged to have four running lines and an additional island platform. Ruabon was situated at the centre of an industrial area from which bricks and chemicals were the main products, as well as a considerable amount of coal.

Between Ruabon and Wrexham the line ran through an extensive coalfield served by a number of mineral branches, that to Brymbo and Minera making a triangular junction with the main line at Croes Newydd, just south of Wrexham. The southern chord of the triangle was used by the heavy trains of iron ore from Banbury and bound for Brymbo steel works. Croes Newydd engine shed was situated within the triangle, having been opened in 1902 when it replaced two small and ancient sheds dating from the days of the NWMR. Primarily concerned with coal traffic from the local

collieries and with working iron ore and steel to and from Brymbo, it was also responsible for some of the passenger workings to Barmouth and for a number of local trains to Chester, Oswestry and Shrewsbury.

Croes Newydd was one of the first sheds to be opened in this century, and was the last to be constructed on the old northlight roundhouse pattern. A small repair bay was attached to the shed building, the only access being across the turntable and through the rear wall of the shed! The coal stage was an early example of the ramped type with water tank forming the roof. About 45 engines were shedded there in the latter days of the GWR, half the allocation being tender engines, including 2-8-0s, Moguls, and 4-6-0 No 7817 *Garsington Manor*.

Above left:
The hoist was a familiar item of equipment at many larger sheds. 'Saint' class No 2950 *Taplow Court* has had its bogie removed at Chester shed in August 1933. *W. Potter*

Left:
More drastic measures have been adopted for No 4984 *Albrighton Hall* seen suspended from the hoist at Chester c1939. *W. Potter*

Below:
Halton Tunnel on the Birkenhead Joint Line, the east end — with Edwardian train spotters?
Real Photos (59022)

Wrexham station, which had been rebuilt and enlarged betwen 1910 and 1912 (and not before time!), was the largest between Shrewsbury and Chester. In addition to the main line platforms and those for the Barmouth trains there was an extensive goods yard and interchange sidings with the Great Central Railway (later the LNER). The latter's unlikely presence in North Wales was due to acquiring a ramshackle and impecunious local line, which had spent much of its existence in the hands of the Receiver, the Wrexham, Mold & Connah's Quay Railway. LNER trains had their own platforms adjacent to those of the GWR, but that company also had its own station, Wrexham Central, which was also used by the GWR for its Wrexham and Ellesmere service (inherited from the Cambrian Railways).

To the north of Wrexham, Wheatsheaf Junction gave access to a mineral branch leading to Wheatsheaf Yard and Gwersylt Colliery (but which had originally served Brymbo). Beyond the junction there was the descent of Gresford Bank, graded at 1 in 80 and subject to a speed restriction of 40mph due to colliery subsidence. One further branch left the main line before the junction with the LNWR (LMS) at Saltney; this was on the down side and ran to wharves and workshops on the bank of the River Dee. Originally the engine shed and works of the S&CR had been situated on this branch; however, the latter had been turned into a carriage and wagon works after 1854.

Access into Chester and its General station was over the LNWR's Holyhead line, consequently all GWR trains were controlled north of Saltney Junction by LNWR (LMS) signalboxes and signals.

Direct running to Birkenhead was possible by means of a loop line which formed a triangle with the Holyhead and Birkenhead lines, Chester station being to the southeast of the triangle. The direct line was mostly used by goods trains; though the GWR also used it to run express trains such as the 'Zulu' which did not stop at Chester, while in later years Grand National Specials and the Isle of Man Boat Trains also took that route. The inside of the triangle, which had four running lines on each side, was almost empty, there being only a turntable from which radiated four spurs. The scene was dominated by a typical LNWR signalbox built on 'stilts'.

Chester Joint (or General) station's original platforms were covered by an overall roof. Considerable extension took place in 1890, when a new island platform was provided. The GWR's interest in the station was largely confined to two long bays on the 'down' side (the orientation being from Euston), adjacent to which were the company's divisional offices. As Chester's Station Master was one of the select company on the

Above:
Halton Tunnel, the west end portal was quite different from that at the east end, its design suggesting some influence by the local landed gentry. *Real Photos (59023)*

'Premier Line' who wore top hats — as befitted such an ancient cathedral city — there was the unique situation of a Divisional Superintendent having his office at a station under the direction of a 'foreign' Station Master!

The GWR's engine sheds consisted of two separate and quite distinct buildings. Immediately to the east of the Chester to Birkenhead line was a three-road 'through' shed, originally belonging to the LNWR. A much larger three-road shed was situated nearer to the station, this being the former Chester & Birkenhead Railway's premises. Over 300ft long, the building, with its arched windows set within the bays of its brick walls, was the background for the photographs of numerous GWR engines — mostly of venerable appearance — which were taken there during the latter years of the 19th century.

In those days, Chester had a varied assortment of aged engines which inspired the late E. L. Ahrons to write, 'It has always seemed that there must have been some arrangement between the Great Western Railway locomotive department and the local and ecclesiastical authorities of that ancient city, whereby it was stipulated that the architecture of the engines should harmonise with the Roman appearance of that beautiful place. American visitors who spent some time at the cathedral should not have missed the Great Western engine shed. For during the 1880s and the early part of the 1890s there was hardly a locomotive shed in the kingdom — always excepting those of the North Eastern at that other cathedral city York — that had collected together a more miscellaneous and assorted lot of old stagers than were to be seen at Chester . . . Any old paleozoic specimens that the Great Western possessed were promptly sent down to Chester and a visit to this engine shed on a Sunday afternoon, when they were all at home, was an education in the history of the locomotive engine'.

Chester being the furthest point to which GWR express engines normally worked, the shed usually had several express passenger engines allocated for main line duties. However, in later years these tended, for the most part to be 'handed down' from more important work — as in the case of the 'Saints' — while in the 1920s Moguls formed the 'top link'. There were also a few main line goods engines (though in earlier days there had been far more), some tank engines for local services, and the inevitable 0-6-0Ts. The allocation in 1947 was 51 engines.

At Hooton, on the joint line to Birkenhead, there was a double junction where the line from Helsby came in from the east and that from West Kirby from the west. Both lines entered Hooton from the Chester end, that from West Kirby joining the main line only about 200yd from the platform ends. Originally provided with bays behind the up and down platforms, the station was considerably enlarged in later years to have four lines separated by island platforms. A small engine shed, built by the Birkenhead Railway, on the up side, ceased to be used in about 1920 and was later converted to a goods shed.

The original main line terminated at Grange Lane, Birkenhead, where the Birkenhead Railway's engine shed and works were situated. An extension to Cathcart Street Junction (with the dock lines) was opened in 1850 for goods traffic. Situated on this extension were Canning Street goods station, the Cathcart Street goods station and private wharf, and the Morpeth goods station.

The main line was extended to a new terminus at Woodside station in 1878. Just under a mile long, the new line passed through Birkenhead Town station adjacent to the old engine shed and works. The latter dated from the opening of the railway in 1840, and were closed in 1878 when they were

Below:
Where it all ended — or began! Birkenhead Woodside station in April 1930, with 0-4-2T No 3571 leaving with a local passenger train, while an ex-LNWR superheated 4-6-2T (LMS No 6975) represents the interests of the other partner in the Joint Line. *J. A. G. H. Coltas*

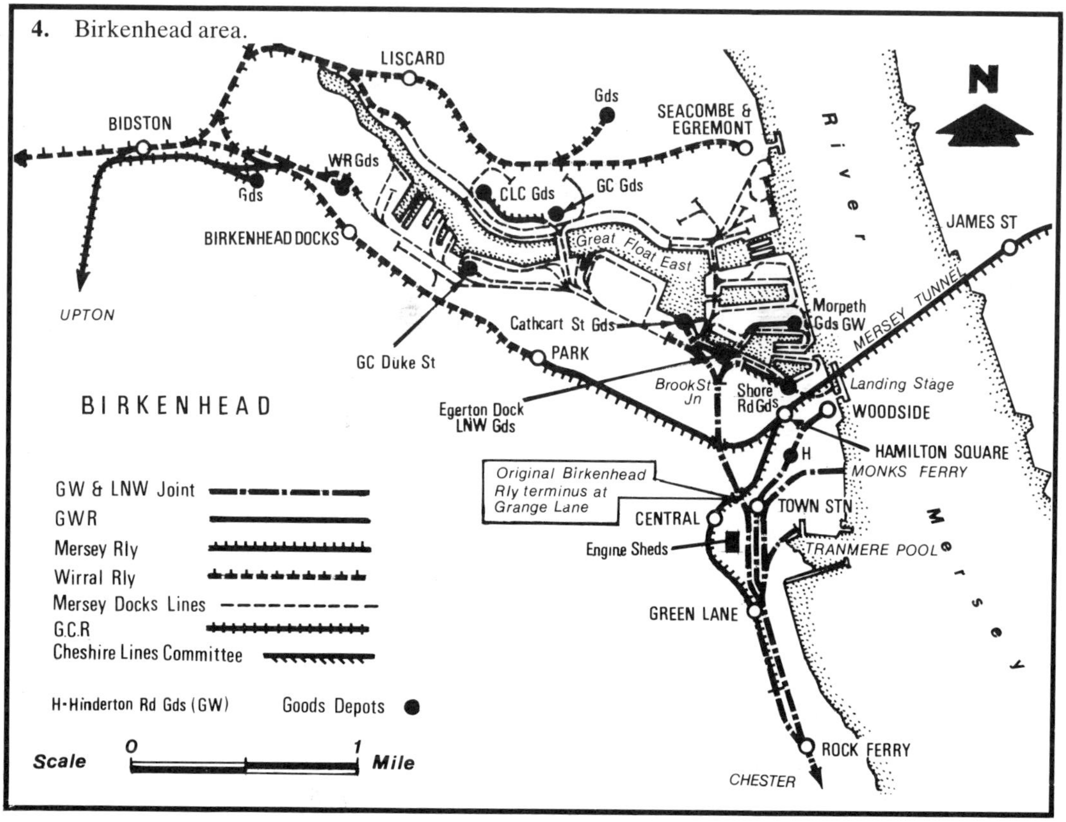

replaced by a new joint shed on the down side of the main line. The new premises consisted of two sheds side by side. Although of identical length and each having eight terminal roads, the LNWR shed had a pitched roof, with a raised vent over each road, while the GWR building had a northlight pattern roof. In latter years, Birkenhead housed mainly tank engines, for passenger work in the Wirral and for working over the dock lines. There were also a few main line goods and mineral engines. In 1947 there was an allocation of 42 engines.

Reached by means of a tunnel under the town, beyond which was Hinderton Road Goods Depot, Woodside had four platforms under an overall roof which was rather spoilt by having two arched spans of different sizes and curvature. Paddington was not likely to be unduly disturbed, for it never admitted that Woodside was the terminus. The GWR connected with the Mersey Railway at Rock Ferry, where all trains called; while for those who preferred fresh air, there was always the ferry boat to the landing stage. In its last hours, the GWR still defiantly insisted that the service over its northern main line was 'London, Oxford, Birmingham, Wolverhampton, Shrewsbury, Chester, Birkenhead and *Liverpool*'.

Below:
Birkenhead Woodside station. The driver of 2-4-2T No 3627 goes 'in over the top' to oil the motion before another turn of duty on a Paddington express as far as Chester. April 1930. *J. A. G. H. Coltas*

3 Standard Gauge Motley

With the amalgamation in 1854 the GWR acquired its first standard gauge engines; described by their new owners as being 'narrow gauge' — and thereby regarded as being undoubtedly inferior! The engines concerned may have been standard gauge; but they were in no respects 'standard', being a truly motley collection.

The company also inherited the locomotive works at Stafford Road, Wolverhampton, which were to play an important role in the GWR's affairs for the next 50 years; and in the person of Joseph Armstrong, the Locomotive Super-intendent in charge of the combined stock of the two Shrewsbury companies, it obtained the services of a first class engineer who was to follow Daniel Gooch in supreme command at Swindon. Lastly, but by no means least, there was Joseph's younger brother George, Locomotive Foreman of the S&CR, who was destined to become the virtually independent arbiter of the Northern Division's practice until the end of the century.

In their early days, both the Shrewsbury railways ordered engines from more than one firm, the general designs being according to the personal ideas of the respective Locomotive Super-intendents, but with a great deal left to the discretion of the builders. Though the companies worked in close partnership, with a common use of their engines, the latter were numbered in separate lists.

The earliest engines for the S&CR were ordered by their Engineer; at first they were under the care of Thomas Truss, the company's Carriage Super-intendent, but he was later succeeded by his assistant, Edward Jefferies. When the latter resigned in March 1853 Joseph Armstrong was placed in charge.

On the S&BR, Robert Stephenson was responsible for ordering the first locomotives, as the company's Engineer. William Marlow was the Locomotive Superintendent, although the stock

Below:
One of the first engines delivered to the Shrewsbury & Chester Railway in 1846, by R. B. Longridge & Co. No 5 was withdrawn in 1868, three years after being involved in the Rednal accident when it finished up in a field!
Ian Allan Library

was worked and maintained by Messrs Johnson & Kinder of Bromsgrove. The contract ended in 1853, whereupon the company took over the working themselves, the Hon Edmund Petrie being the Superintendent. The latter's resignation in 1854 resulted in Joseph Armstrong moving to Wolverhampton in command of both companies' affairs.

Shrewsbury & Chester Railway

When the line was opened in 1846, the company possessed four engines built by R. B. Longridge & Co, and two from Jones & Potts. According to the original description they were required to have six wheels, two pairs of 4ft 9in coupled wheels and the others 3ft 6in, cylinders 15in × 24in, Stephenson's patent boiler, and Dodd's patent expansion motion. Unless some were altered before delivery, a somewhat elastic interpretation of these requirements seems to have been allowed!

That the company had engines before its line was opened may be regarded as a portent of things to come, as there often appeared to be more than enough engines for the amount of work to be done. Early in 1846 Mr Truss was endeavouring to

Above:
S&CR No 14, built by Sharp Bros in 1848, is seen here at Wolverhampton Stafford Road, Lower Yard, c1880. Although withdrawn in December 1885, it was preserved in the Works until 1920. *Ian Allan Library*

Below:
S&CR No 15, built by Bury, Curtis & Kennedy in 1847, was a very early tank engine. Although rebuilt at Wolverhampton on three occasions, the old Bury firebox lasted until the engine was withdrawn in 1904! *Ian Allan Library*

postpone delivery of the other four engines until April 1847; this rather 'backfired' when the company had to approach the Birkenhead Railway for help with one or more of their engines within a few days of the line being opened!

The first four engines built by Longridge & Co were of three different types. No 1 was an 0-6-0 whose dimensions accorded with the requirements laid down, apart from having all wheels coupled. In common with the other three, it had inside frames and a 'long boiler' with Gothic firebox — ie all the wheels were in front of the firebox. In December 1863 it was renumbered 117, being rebuilt at Wolverhampton in 1866 as a saddle tank with a dome over the firebox, the tank extending from the back of the smokebox to the front of the dome. It was withdrawn from service in 1874.

No 2 conformed more strictly with the requirements, being a 2-4-0. It was rebuilt at Wolverhampton in 1868, on similar lines to No 117 (former No 1) but retained its original wheel arrangement. It was withdrawn in 1873. No 4 was

very similar and was rebuilt as a saddle tank in 1867, being withdrawn in 1870. There is some dispute about No 3, as A. L. Ahrons stated that it was originally a 2-2-2 with 5ft 9in driving wheels and it appears as such in an early GWR register. However, another GWR source shows it as a 2-4-0 with 5ft 0in coupled wheels. What is beyond dispute is that it was withdrawn in 1870.

Left:
Officially a rebuild of the old S&BR 0-4-2 tender engine (which had outside cylinders), No 40 emerged from Wolverhampton Works in 1862 — the 'rebuild' having taken four years! From March 1885 until it was withdrawn in January 1904, No 40 worked the Oldbury branch. *Ian Allan Library*

Below left:
Shrewsbury & Birmingham Railway 0-4-2 No 1 as GWR No 33. Built in 1849 as a 2-4-0 by Stephenson's, it had been rebuilt as an 0-4-2 by the time the GWR acquired it. Seen here at Chester, No 33 was the last survivor of the first lot of S&BR engines, not being withdrawn until December 1891. *Ian Allan Library*

Below:
Built by Fairbairn in 1854 as the Birkenhead Railway's No 31, No 107 was rebuilt at Wolverhampton in May 1873 according to GWR records — though the works plate on the engine states October 1873! Seen here as first rebuilt, without cab, number plates or engine brakes, No 107 was cut up in 1905. The unusual tender, with rear frame extension, appears to have been its original one. *Ian Allan Library*

Nos 5 and 6, also built by Longridge, were delivered after the line had been opened, commencing work in December 1846 and January 1847 respectively. They were similar to Nos 2 and 4. Both were withdrawn in 1868, No 5 having been involved in an accident at Rednal on 7 June 1865. An excursion train from Manchester to London left Chester with two engines, 28 carriages and two 'breaks'. Due to permanent way work, the engines ran off the road; the train engine, No 72, going to the right, and the leading engine, No 5, going to the left; each landing in a field, but on opposite sides of the line! Fourteen people were killed and many more seriously injured. Nos 7 and 8 were the Jones & Potts engines, being long-boiler 2-4-0s with outside cylinders; the original requirements did not, it appears, state where the cylinders should be located! They were of different appearances, No 7 having a Gothic firebox, while No 8 had an ordinary raised firebox with 'Crewe' type safety-valves. The driving wheels are reported to have been 5ft 6in, which certainly did not conform to the required 4ft 9in. Both engines had a fairly short life, being withdrawn in 1859.

A few weeks after the opening of the line, 13 more tender engines were ordered; seven from Sharp Bros and six from Bury, Curtis & Kennedy of Liverpool. The seven Sharp engines were all 2-2-2s, with double frames, six of them being the well known 'Sharp Singles'. No 9 had 5ft 0in driving wheels, while Nos 10, 13, 22 and 23 had wheels of 5ft 6in diameter; in each case the cylinders were 15in × 24in. No 14 also had 5ft 0in driving wheels, but smaller cylinders (14in × 20in); while No 21 was a slightly longer engine, with 5ft 6in driving wheels and 15in × 20in cylinders.

No 9 had been converted to a saddle tank by the

mid-1860s, and was withdrawn in 1873. Of the other 'Sharp Singles', No 10 was named *Prince of Wales* in November 1852, to act as pilot to a Royal Train from Chester to Wolverhampton, and was withdrawn in 1877. The train engine on that occasion was No 21, which was named *Victoria and Albert*: it was the first of the Sharp engines to be withdrawn, in 1870. The remainder were all withdrawn between 1873 and 1877, with the exception of No 14 which lasted until 1885 and was then preserved at Stafford Road Works — due, it is thought, to this engine having been a favourite of George Armstrong during his driving days — and was not cut up until 1920.

The six Bury engines had that firm's usual bar frames and domeless boilers with raised casing. They were of two types, there being four 2-2-2s with 5ft 6in driving wheels and 15in × 20in cylinders — these being Nos 11, 12, 19 and 20, delivered in pairs in September 1847 and September 1848. Nos 12 and 19 were reconstructed at Wolverhampton in 1860, receiving new plate frames and new motion, while the driving wheels were 6ft 0in and the cylinders 14½in × 22in. In this condition they lasted until 1869 and 1870 respectively. The other two were withdrawn unaltered, No 11 in 1865 and No 20 in 1869.

The second type consisted of two four-coupled engines, both delivered in 1849, with 5ft 0in wheels and 16in × 24in cylinders. They may have been built as 0-4-0s, but were described by Ahrons as being 0-4-2s, this being confirmed by the Swindon records in the case of No 17. Both were withdrawn in 1865.

There were also two 'branch engines', one of which was to have a long — and complicated — life story. This was No 15, an 0-4-0 saddle tank delivered by Bury in November 1847; it was thus one of the first tank engines. It had inside bar frames, wheels 4ft 0in diameter, and inside cylinders 15in × 20in, while the tank was over the barrel of the boiler. In 1866 it was partially rebuilt at Wolverhampton, with 4ft 2in wheels and 15in × 24in cylinders, splashers and a new domed boiler, though retaining the original firebox. In 1881 it was again rebuilt, new cylinders and another new boiler being fitted — but still with the old firebox! A new saddle tank, which extended to the front of the smokebox, was also fitted. More of the original engine disappeared in 1890, when it was rebuilt with 'new frames and stays complete'; however, the old Bury firebox lasted to the end, which finally came with withdrawal in 1904. It spent most of its long life in the Chester and Wrexham districts.

No 16 was a very different 'kettle of fish'. Although it was also an 0-4-0T engine, it had well

Below:
A sister engine to No 107, ex-Birkenhead Railway No 30 was rebuilt at Wolverhampton in 1875 and again in 1889 when its wheelbase was increased and outside frames fitted for the leading wheels. Its last years were spent on the Severn Valley line between Shrewsbury and Worcester. It is seen here at the latter station. No 106 was withdrawn in March 1900. *Ian Allan Library*

tanks only — two being fitted at the front end — and 4ft 4in wheels with 15in × 22in cylinders. It was built by Sharp Bros who provided access to the footplate on the left side only! In later years two additional well tanks were added behind the rear wheels. In 1872 it had the rare distinction for a Northern Division 'absorbed' engine of being rebuilt at Swindon, and emerged as a saddle tank. Its last days were spent working on the dock lines at Birkenhead, from where it was withdrawn in 1879.

From 1849 the locomotive history is rather confused owing to the close associations with the S&BR and the Birkenhead Railway. Nos 24-29 appear to have been used for engines obtained from one or other of these companies, but only Nos 25 and 28 were in stock in 1854; the other engines having been returned to their owners, the blank numbers were used for the next engines delivered. Some of these 'borrowings' were of a temporary nature and the engines were not numbered, while others stayed on the S&CR for some time. The company also lent some of its engines or exchanged them for others belonging to the other companies.

S&BR Nos 11 and 16 become S&CR Nos 25 and 28, both being long-boiler 0-6-0s built in 1849 by Longridge and Stephenson's respectively, and both remained with the S&CR until the amalgamation. From November 1851 until April 1853 the company worked the through goods trains to Birkenhead, engines Nos 2 and 4 being exchanged with the Birkenhead Railway for that company's Nos 11-14 — powerful 0-6-0s built by Hicks in 1849 — which presumably became S&CR Nos 24, 26, 27 and 29.

In 1852, more locomotives being needed, estimates were obtained for four powerful double-framed 0-4-2 tender engines to be built to Jefferies' specifications. Two of these, Nos 30 and 31, were ordered from the Vulcan Foundry in September, but were not delivered until the summer of 1853; the order for the other two was deferred. The coupled wheels were 5ft 0in, trailing wheels 3ft 6in, and cylinders 16in × 24in. The dome covers were painted and the safety valves were of polished brass. The boiler of No 30 exploded at Saltney in 1859, and the engine was replaced by a new No 30 built at Wolverhampton. No 31 was withdrawn in 1870.

No 32, known familiarly as the 'Flying Flogger', was a 2-2-2 inside-framed engine, built by Jones & Potts, and offered to the company for £2,000 in November 1852. The 15½in × 20in cylinders were inside the frames, but the steam chests and valve gear were outside! It had 6ft 6in driving wheels, a dome on a raised casing, and an old 'Crewe' type safety-valve on the centre of the barrel. Such an oddity could not be expected to last long, and it

was reconstructed at Wolverhampton in 1860, with 6ft 2in wheels and 14½in × 22in cylinders. The firebox — and probably the boiler — from the original engine was used, but No 32 now had 'Jenny Lind' type frames, with inside bearings for the driving axle and outside bearings for the other axles. The final appearance was very similar to three other engines, Nos 7, 8 and 30, built at Wolverhampton at about the same time. However, No 32 was not regarded as a 'renewal' — as it undoubtedly would have been a few years later. It was withdrawn in 1872.

A small tender engine was obtained from an unknown source in December 1852, being allotted No 33. Early in October 1853 the Board ordered that the 'Wrekin' engine be offered for sale and an advertisement appeared in the *Railway Times*. The engine was described as 'nearly new', with 14in × 18in cylinders, leading and driving wheels 5ft 0in and trailing wheels and tender wheels 3ft 6in — it was thus an 0-4-2 tender engine. No other S&CR engine of this description or dimensions has been recorded, so it is assumed that this was No 33. No trace of the disposal of this engine has ever been found.

In March 1853 two four-wheeled tender engines with intermediate crankshafts, said to have been built by Vulcan Foundry for T. R. Crampton in 1848, were offered to the company by the makers. Purchased and delivered immediately, they became Nos 34 and 35. The four coupled wheels were 5ft 3in diameter and the cylinders 16in × 2-4in. The dome covers were painted and the safety-valve covers of polished brass, this being the standard finish applied to engines built by Vulcan Foundry. Both engines were withdrawn in 1865, their demise being followed by the appearance of two new engine bearing the same numbers — which may have contained parts of the original engines.

The four Birkenhead engines were returned to their owners in April 1853, their numbers being filled by the last new engines delivered to the S&CR Nos 24 and 26 were built by the Vulcan Foundry and delivered in September 1853. They were identical to Nos 30 and 31. No 24 received new cylinders in 1865 and lasted until 1871, but No 26 was withdrawn, unaltered, in 1867. Nos 27 and 29 were double-framed 2-2-2s built by Sharp, Stewart & Co in 1853. Except that they had 14½in cylinders, they were identical with No 21. No 27 was withdrawn in 1870, while No 29 lasted until 1872.

Shrewsbury & Birmingham Railway
Twenty engines, all of the long-boiler type, were ordered in 1847, in readiness for the opening of the line; the order was equally divided between R. Stephenson & Co and R. B. Longridge & Co.

In October 1848 an order for a specimen engine and tender was placed with three firms — Bury, Curtis & Kennedy, W. Fairbairn & Co, and E. B. Wilson & Co. The first engines delivered were stored by the S&CR until they were required by their owners. On amalgamation, the existing S&BR stock, numbered 1-15 and 17-23, became GWR Nos 33, 36-56 in the same order.

Of the 20 engines ordered for 1848, several were ready for delivery in 1849. These included three passenger engines — one of which was 6in too long to turn on the 36ft turntables! — and one goods engine from Stephensons, and one passenger and at least two goods engines from Longridges. The passenger engines were not approved: Longridge agreed to 'alter' their remaining four from 'long boilers and outside cylinders to short boilers and cylinders' (sic); in the case of the Stephenson engines it was reported that they were 'very defective' and, upon learning that they had 'for the most part been made at a neighbouring factory', the company ordered that they be returned.

The Stephenson engines were 2-4-0s, with inside frames, 6ft 1½in wheels and 15in × 22in outside cylinders. There is considerable confusion in the records concerning these engines, as Stephenson's records suggest that they were returned and replaced by three different engines. However, in a S&BR report dated 4 March 1853 it is stated that Nos 1 and 2 were *altered* by Stephensons to 'single' engines: what is certain, is that all three were 2-2-2s by that date. In the same report, Nos 4 and 5 are described as 'made by Stephensons and not altered' and No 3 merely as 'made by Stephenson'. By the time they were taken over by the GWR all except No 3 had been reconstructed at Wolverhampton as 0-4-2 tender goods engines.

As the frames, wheels and cylinders were all new, little can have remained of the originals

Above:
Also acquired from the Birkenhead Railway was 0-4-2 No 105 (formerly Birkenhead No 29), built in 1853 by Sharp, Stewart & Co. Rebuilt at Wolverhampton in 1875, No 105 worked at Chester as seen here, until withdrawn in September 1886. Once again, there are no brakes on the engine! *Ian Allan Library*

Below right:
No 108, together with sister engine No 109, was built at Wolverhampton in 1866, parts of ex-Birkenhead Railway engines built by Benjamin Hicks & Sons, of Bolton, in 1849, being used in their construction. Note the wooden buffer beam and the absence of brakes on the engine. *Ian Allan Library*

except the shortened boilers. They now had 5ft 0in coupled wheels, 4ft 0in trailing wheels, and inside cylinders 15in × 24in. No 1 (GWR No 33) was rebuilt with a 'Metro' boiler in 1875, and in 1878 received new cylinders; it was even fitted with the vacuum brake in 1884, and was finally withdrawn from Chester in 1891. The remaining three engines (GWR Nos 36, 38 and 39) were never rebuilt and were withdrawn between 1870 and 1876.

No 3 (GWR No 37) was a 2-2-2 with Gothic firebox, delivered in February 1850. It had inside cylinders, but outside steam chests and valve gear — being similar in this respect to S&CR No 32. The inside frames, extending only to the front of the firebox, carried the driving axle; outside frames supported the leading and trailing wheels. The pumps were outside, worked by eccentrics from the end of the driving axle; while to add to the novelties, the driving wheels were flangeless! The latter were 6ft 1¼in diameter, and the carrying wheels 3ft 8in — according to Stephenson's records — though all railway records give them as being 5ft 6in and 3ft 6in respectively. At least Stephensons and the S&BR agreed that the cylinders were 15in × 22in! In June 1850 it had been considerably 'injured' in a collision at Shrewsbury and some modifications may have been made then. Like two of the S&CR engines, it enjoyed the distinction of being named, in this instance *Queen*, for the royal journey in November 1852. No 37 was withdrawn in 1870.

Nos 6-10 (GWR Nos 40-44) were the Longridge passenger engines, of which only No 6 was delivered in its original condition with long-boiler and outside cylinders. None of them gave much satisfaction either to the makers — who made many alterations to them *at Shrewsbury* after delivery — or to the Company. The fact that such work was done at Shrewsbury, prompts the question as to what facilities existed there, in view of there being no record of either of the Shrewsbury companies having engine sheds there.

No 6 was delivered in February 1849 as a 0-4-2 tender engine with single frames, outside cylinders, 4ft 4in coupled wheels, 3ft 6in carrying wheels, and a domeless boiler with a Gothic firebox. As No 40 it was taken out of service in June 1858 and completely reconstructed at Wolverhampton; indeed, so complete was the reconstruction that it did not emerge from the Works until March 1862, by which time it was a 0-4-2 saddle tank with *inside* cylinders! Ahrons stated that it 'contained absolutely nothing of the original engine', but the records state that the old boiler was used. The cylinders were 14½in × 22in and a short saddle tank covered the boiler only. In 1873 it was rebuilt with an '850' class boiler and 16in × 22in cylinders, and was again rebuilt in 1897

when it received another new boiler, wheels of 'H' section and new 15in × 22in cylinders. For many years it was a familiar sight on the Oldbury branch and was not withdrawn until 1904.

Nos 7-10 (GWR Nos 41-44) were delivered as 'short-boiler' engines, being 0-4-2s with inside frames, coupled wheels 5ft 0in, trailing wheels 4ft 0in, and inside cylinders 15in × 24in. They were not very successful, and were all withdrawn between 1868 and 1870. They were followed by five Longridge long-boiler goods engines, Nos 11-5, which were probably all delivered early in 1849; though the official dates show No 15 as January 1850, with Nos 12 and 14 entering stock in April 1852! They had inside frames, Gothic fireboxes, 4ft 9in wheels, and 15in × 24in cylinders. No 11 was sold to the S&CR, becoming their No 25. Nos 12-16 became GWR Nos 46-49. No 25, together with Nos 46, 48 and 49, was withdrawn unaltered, all going between 1868 and 1877; but No 47 had a much longer — and more varied — career.

In 1868 No 47 was rebuilt at Wolverhampton as a saddle tank, with new cylinders, the wheelbase being extended between the second and third axles by 7in. The new boiler had a tubular iron firebox with a Cornish flue — a most unusual feature, at least on the GWR — while the grate area was 17.41sq ft compared with the previous 10.2sq ft (!) It was again rebuilt in 1875, with a domed boiler and ordinary firebox. Its final duties were on the Shipston-on-Stour branch during the first few months of that line being opened to traffic in 1889, and it was withdrawn that year.

The five goods engines from Stephensons, Nos 16-20, were also delivered in 1849, but the dates at which they were taken into stock extended to 1851. These were also long-boiler engines with

inside frames, having boilers with a dome on the middle ring and an ordinary raised casing. The wheels were 4ft 9in, with the middle pair flangeless — a feature in vogue at Stephensons at that time — and the cylinders were 15in × 24in. In 1854 No 16 was working on the S&CR as their No 28 (becoming GWR No 28). The others became GWR Nos 50-53, and all were withdrawn between 1869 and 1877.

The 'one specimen locomotive and tender each' from the three firms of Bury, Curtis & Kennedy, Fairbairn, and E. B. Wilson, in 1848, were all 2-2-2 express passenger engines, but were of very different designs. No 21 *Salopian* was a large 'Jenny Lind' type delivered by Wilsons, probably in April 1849. The driving wheels were 6ft 6in and carrying wheels 4ft 0in, while the cylinders were 15½ × 22in. The boiler was domed, with a raised casing, and the firebox had a longitudinal midfeather. The engine weighed 28 tons.

No 23 *Vulcan* was by Fairbairns, and was probably delivered in July 1849. It had double frames and a boiler with the dome on the middle ring, being described by Ahrons as 'an enlarged copy of the famous Sharp singles'. The wheelbase was slightly longer than that of the Wilson engine, with the driving wheels 5ft 8in and the carrying wheels 3ft 6in. The cylinders were 16in × 21in and

the engine weighed 22ton 8¼cwt, considerably less than the Wilson engine.

No 23 *Wrekin* was one of the last engines built by Bury, Curtis & Kennedy. The official date is July 1850, though a month earlier it was reported as being in a collision at Shrewsbury, and it was also used, together with *Salopian,* on the first Shrewsbury to Wolverhampton train on the occasion of the opening of the line on 12 November 1849. It had Bury's usual bar frames and domeless boiler with raised casing. It was much the longest of the three engines, and the wheel diameters were all different: leading wheels 4ft 3in, driving 5ft 9in and trailing 3ft 6in. The cylinders were 15in × 20in (the same size being given in GWR records for the Fairbairn engine), and it weighed 22tons 13cwt.

The three engines became Nos 54-56 in the same order. *Vulcan* appears to have been the most successful, lasting until 1872; the others were withdrawn in 1869 and 1871 respectively.

The only other engine owned by the company was a small 0-4-0WT ordered by Messrs Johnson & Kinder from Sharp, Stewart & Co. and delivered on December 1853. It took the number 11 (vacant by the sale of the Longridge goods engine to the S&CR). As GWR No 45 it had 3ft 9in wheels, cylinders 15in × 22in, and a boiler with the dome

on a raised casing. In about 1860 it was converted to an 0-4-2ST by the addition of a short saddle tank and 2ft 6in carrying wheels. It was withdrawn from service in 1877.

The Birkenhead Railway

When the Birkenhead Railway was vested in the GWR and LNWR on 1 January 1860, its 42 engines were equally divided; though the two companies did not take possession of them until 20 November. Two goods engines already on order were delivered direct to the GWR in 1861. Including the latter two engines, the GWR share was numbered 95-116 and 118; apart from keeping engines of the same class together there appears to have been no principle upon which the numbering took place, as it was neither in the Birkenhead numerical order, order of age, or order of wheel arrangement!

Only one of the first lot of engines delivered to the C&BR lasted long enough to be acquired by the GWR in 1860. Birkenhead No 3 *Touchstone* had been built in 1840 by Mather Dixon, being a 2-2-2 with outside frames, 5ft 6in driving wheels, 3ft 6in carrying wheels, and 12in × 18in cylinders. In March 1853 it had been rebuilt with 'new boiler and motion', which probably accounted for its survival. At first GWR No 114, it became No 1 in December 1863 — to allow Nos 111-114 to be used for the first four 2-4-0s built at Wolverhampton — and was withdrawn in 1873.

Two other 2-2-2s, built by C. Tayleur in November 1845, which were C&BR Nos 9 *Victoria* and 10 *Albert*, became GWR Nos 115 and 116. They were long-boiler engines with double frames, having driving wheels of 5ft 6in and carrying wheels of 3ft 6in, while the cylinders were 13in × 18in. In 1856-58 they were 'renewed' with new boilers and motion, the dome being just behind the chimney, and the driving wheels were now 5ft 3in. No 115 was withdrawn in 1876 and sold to the Severn Tunnel Railway. No 116 was withdrawn in 1872, but according to Ahrons it was still standing in a scrap siding at Swindon in 1886!

The remaining engines were ordered by the Birkenhead, Lancashire & Cheshire Railway.

Left:
Nos 108 (right) and 109 (left) at Chester after being withdrawn from service at the end of 1887. The difference in the shape of the cabs and smokebox wingplates should be noted, also the fact that whereas No 109 was fitted with a vacuum brake, No 108 had only a hand brake on the tender. The wooden buffer beams appear to be somewhat cracked on both engines! *Real Photos*

Nos 11 and 12, named *Birkenhead* and *Chester* — but later renamed *Blazer* and *Gnome* — became GWR Nos 108 and 109. Built by Benjamin Nick & Sons, of Bolton, they were among the first inside-framed standard gauge 0-6-0s to have the firebox between the driving and trailing axles. The wheels were 5ft 0in and cylinders 16in × 24in, while they weighed about 25 tons. The motion is believed to have been of the old gab fork pattern, but this had been replaced by Dodds wedge motion before 1860. In order to clear the smokebox, the overhung leading springs were inverted and placed to the rear of the axle box centre line; the necessary connection between the axle box and spring pillars being made by a lever. In place of trailing springs of the usual type, a large single transverse spring was fitted.

These were two of the four engines handed over from November 1851 to April 1853 to the S&CR in exchange for that company's Nos 1 and 4. They received new names on their return to Birkenhead stock — the old ones probably having been removed by the S&CR. Both were partially rebuilt with new cylinders, smokeboxes and fireboxes at the Vulcan Foundry in 1856 and 1857. No 11 became a 2-4-0 and was converted from coke to coal burning by the same firm in 1860; however, it did not work well in its new form and was reconstructed at Wolverhampton between April 1861 and April 1862. In February 1865, its boiler exploded at Leominster and it was withdrawn from service, as was No 109; parts of both engines being used in the construction of new engines with the same numbers.

Six 2-2-2 passenger engines were delivered by Hick & Son in 1851, Nos 15-20, of which Nos 16-19 were acquired by the GWR (Nos 110-113). They had inside frames and outside cylinders, low-pitched domeless boilers with a raised casing, and Stephenson's link motion. The driving wheels were 6ft 0in, carrying wheels 3ft 6in, and cylinders 15in × 22in. By the time these engines were withdrawn, in 1862 and 1863, Nos 111-113 were recorded as being 0-4-2 tender engines with 16in × 24in cylinders!

Nos 25 *Birkenhead* and 26 *Weaver* were 2-4-0 passenger engines, with inside frames and cylinders, built by Stephenson & Co in January 1853. They became GWR Nos 99 and 100, having coupled wheels of 5ft 6in diameter, leading wheels 4ft 3in, and cylinders 14in × 20in; the boilers had a dome on the middle ring and a raised casing. Both were withdrawn in 1880.

Nos 28 and 29 were 0-4-2 tender engines with inside frames and cylinders, delivered in April and May 1854 by Sharp, Stewart & Co. Their coupled wheels were 5ft 0in, trailing wheels 3ft 6in, and cylinders 16in × 22in; while their boilers had a dome on the front ring and a raised casing. As

GWR Nos 104 and 105 they were rebuilt in 1875 and 1874 respectively, with boilers having a small dome on the middle ring and a flush casing, and at the same time the cylinders were reduced in diameter to 15in. These remained Chester engines until withdrawn in 1886 and 1887 respectively.

Two other 2-4-0s, of similar appearance to Nos 28 and 29, were built by Fairbairns in 1854. Apart from the leading wheels being 3ft 4in, their dimensions were the same as for the Sharp, Stewart engines. As GWR Nos 106 and 107, they were rebuilt in 1875 and 1873 respectively, with boilers identical to those provided for Nos 104 and 105, and with 3ft 6in leading wheels. In 1889 the latter were replaced by the new standard 4ft 0in wheels, with outside bearings, and the wheelbase increased by one foot. No 107 was again rebuilt at Wolverhampton in 1896, when it received a '517' class boiler with dome on the middle ring and a raised casing.

After their rebuilding both engines spent many years at Chester and then at Shrewsbury, where they were employed on working over the Severn Valley line to Worcester. No 106 was withdrawn in 1900, but No 107 lasted longer through being loaned to the Bishop's Castle Railway; although the official date for withdrawal was recorded as December 1902, it had a general overhaul at Shrewsbury early in 1904 and was not cut up until March 1905!

A pair of 2-4-0 side tanks, Nos 32 *Volante* and 33 *Voltigeur* (GWR Nos 97 and 98) were delivered by Stephenson & Co in January and February 1856. Their coupled wheels were 5ft 3in, leading wheels 3ft 8in, and cylinders 14in × 20in. They appeared to have retained their names for some years after coming into GWR stock. Another distinction was that they visited London, being used during the 1860s on a long-forgotten service between Victoria (London, Chatham & Dover Railway) and Southall — furthermore, they worked from the Chatham's Longhedge shed at Battersea! After this unexpected and exciting migration, they returned to their more familiar surroundings at Birkenhead; though No 98 was withdrawn from Shrewsbury. They were withdrawn in 1878 and 1880 respectively.

Below:
Two small saddle tanks built for the Birkenhead Railway by Sharp, Stewart & Co in 1856-7, and later GWR Nos 95 and 96, had very long lives indeed. No 96, seen here at Wolverhampton in original condition, was rebuilt in 1888 and was not withdrawn until 1935. *Ian Allan Library*

Right:
Ex-Birkenhead Railway No 6 in its better known guise as GWR No 95, and as rebuilt at Wolverhampton in 1872. It lasted until 1924. *Ian Allan Library*

Nos 37 *Thunderer* and 40 *Dreadnought* were two six-coupled tender goods engines with double frames; built by Stephenson's as part of an order for the Midland Railway, they were instead delivered to the Birkenhead Railway in August and September 1856. They had 5ft 0in wheels and 16in × 24in cylinders, while they weighed 31ton 14cwt, which was quite heavy for the time. They were very similar to several engines inherited by the GWR from the West Midland Railway in 1863. They became GWR Nos 101 and 102. In 1865 the former's boiler exploded at Chester, with spectacular results; following which, the engine was rebuilt in 1866, the new boiler having a small painted dome on the middle ring — and Armstrong's large safety valve cover. Both engines received new 17in cylinders (in 1873 and 1875), and although No 101 lasted until 1888 — outliving all the ex-WMR engines of similar design — No 102 was withdrawn in 1878.

Two small 0-4-0 saddle tanks, built by Sharp, Stewart & Co in 1856 and 1857, were Birkenhead Nos 39 *Cricket* and 6 *Grasshopper* (GWR Nos 96 and 95). As built, they had the dome on the firebox, while the short tank covered the barrel only, and access to the footplate was on the left-hand side only — a feature shared by S&CR No 16, also built by Sharp, Stewart's. Their wheels were 4ft 0in and cylinders 14in × 18in. No 96 was rebuilt at Wolverhampton in 1888, the new boiler having a dome on the middle ring; while the saddle tank now extended to the front of the smokebox. No 95 was rebuilt in a similar fashion in 1890; however, to enable it to work through a low tunnel in the Croes Newydd area, the chimney and dome were cut down, the roof and back of the cab removed, and 3ft 6in wheels were fitted.

No 96 lasted until 1935, with 79 years of service, nearly all of which was spent in the Northern Division; with new fireboxes and retubings, the 1888 boiler lasted to the end. No 95 deserted the Chester area in 1899, being in South Wales for three or four years. It then returned north where it stayed until 1922, when it went south for a second and last time; it was withdrawn in 1924.

The final two engines received by the GWR never ran on the Birkenhead Railway: ordered from R. Stephenson & Co in June 1860, they were not delivered until November and December 1861, when the GWR numbered them 103 and 118. They were double-framed 0-6-0s with sloping Cudworth fireboxes, a patent design by the Locomotive Superintendent of the South Eastern Railway, and had Giffard injectors; thus providing the GWR with two new novelties! Their wheels were 5ft 0in and cylinders 16in × 24in; while they weighed no less than 33ton 10cwt, being the heaviest 0-6-0s on the GWR during the 19th century. Their grate area of 21sq ft was also the largest. However, they did not find much favour, as neither was rebuilt, and both were withdrawn in 1879.

By the time they were withdrawn, the company had well over 300 modern 0-6-0s of Armstrong's own designs, as well as the 30 truly splendid Beyer, Peacock engines and over 50 earlier engines built under Gooch's direction. With such alternative power available, few absorbed goods engines enjoyed an extended life.

4 Some Northern Division Locomotives

The 'Standard Gauge Motley' acquired by the GWR in 1854 and 1860 was increased both in numbers and variety by the stock of the West Midland Railway in 1863. Many of these engines were far from satisfactory, and a decision was made to scrap most of them when their cylinders or fireboxes wore out: they were to be replaced by new engines having features and dimensions in common with the newer engines on the broad gauge.

Wolverhampton Works not being able to undertake such a programme of replacement, Swindon — the 'temple' of the broad gauge — had to suffer the indignity of building engines for the 'narrow gauge' which it so despised! Two or three pits in the Erecting Shop were adapted for this work, but there was no track on which the engines could run. Swindon was thus in the position of many private firms who had built engines for the broad gauge! The first engines were sent north to Wolverhampton on specially constructed broad gauge wagons, their running trials taking place after delivery.

The first engines built, in 1855, were a dozen 0-6-0 goods engines (Nos 57-68) designed by Daniel Gooch, with outside sandwich frames (part-length inside frames extended from the cylinders to the firebox front). They had 5ft 0in wheels, 15½in × 22in cylinders, and Gooch valve gear; while the boilers were domeless, as on broad gauge engines, and compensating levers were fitted to the suspension. The majority spent their entire lives in the north, all being 'renewed' at Wolverhampton between 1873 and 1890; however, little of the original engines remained, as new full-length inside plate frames were fitted and the Gooch valve gear was replaced by Stephenson's link motion. At this renewal Nos 60 and 67 became saddle tanks, though both were later reconverted to tender engines. For no apparent reason, three brand-new engines of the same design, Nos 316-318, were built at Wolverhampton in 1890-91, taking the numbers previously carried by

Below:
No 30 was the third engine to be built at Stafford Road Works, in 1860, and was designed by Joseph Armstrong. Withdrawn in December 1883, it was officially 'renewed' as a 2-4-0 of the '111' class — though the latter engine did not appear until November 1886! *Real Photos (15126)*

Above right:
No 1009 was one of Joseph Armstrong's '111' class 2-4-0s, being built at Wolverhampton in August 1866. It is seen here as running c1870, with copper-capped chimney and painted number at Stafford Road. *Ian Allan Library*

engines of the similar '131' class which had been scrapped! These were the last new tender engines to be built at Wolverhampton. The class was withdrawn between 1908 and 1927, No 316 enjoying the distinction of being the last sandwich-framed 0-6-0 to remain at work.

Gooch also designed some Singles of the 2-2-2 type — again with his link motion and the usual broad gauge features, though the sandwich frames were outside. Eight of these engines, Nos 69-76, were built by Beyer, Peacock & Co, Manchester, the first four being the first engines to be built by that firm. Delivered during 1855-56, these engines had 6ft 6in wheels and 15½in × 22in cylinders, their boilers being of the same design as those on the 0-6-0s. For their first few years they were in charge of the principal express trains north of Wolverhampton, but when the standard gauge reached Paddington they were transferred to the London and Wolverhampton service. Although they were 'renewed' at Wolverhampton between 1872 and 1875, little of the original engines remained, as new sandwich frames and Stephenson link motion were incorporated. Indeed, the first two, Nos 70 and 74, were officially new engines and received Wolverhampton works numbers! All were converted to the 'River' class 2-4-0s in the 1890s.

Next to appear, in 1857, were two unusual goods engines, Nos 77 and 78, supplied by Beyer to their own design, but with boilers made to Gooch's drawings — a combination delightfully described by Ahrons as 'Gooch designed the coat and Beyer the trousers'! Inside-framed engines, with Stephenson link motion, they had 5ft 0in wheels and 16in × 24in cylinders. Apart from their boilers, they looked as little like a typical GWR engine as possible! A further four engines,

Nos 167-170, were delivered in 1861 (having been ordered by the Shrewsbury & Hereford Railway). On these engines, Beyer designed 'both coat and trousers', as the boilers were to their design with a plain brass dome on the middle of the barrel and a normal safety-valve cover. They were also built to be driven from the left-hand side, an abhorrence to all right-thinking GWR men down to 1947 and beyond! All were given new boilers of Wolverhampton design; while one at least, No 169, was altered to right-hand drive. They spent their entire lives in the Northern Division, being withdrawn, between 1902 and 1904.

Twelve more 0-6-0s from Swindon, Nos 79-90, were built in 1857-58, followed by another dozen, Nos 119-130, built in 1861-62. Intended for mineral traffic, they were very similar to the '57' class, but had smaller wheels (4ft 6in) and larger cylinders (16in × 24in). Originally stationed at Chester and Birkenhead, they were later put to work on coal trains between Pontypool Road and Birkenhead, working from the latter shed. Between 1877 and 1880 they were 'renewed', all of the second series (except No 122) becoming tank engines; while those renewed as tender engines (with the exception of Nos 81 and 85) had condensing apparatus fitted in their tenders for feed water heating, pumps being fitted instead of injectors. Both the pumps and the condensing gear were removed within a few years. The tender engines were withdrawn between 1905 and 1918, by which time several of them were in South Wales, as were those converted to tank engines.

In 1857 two small engines were delivered by Beyer, Peacock & Co, one of which was destined to have a life of extraordinary longevity. Intended for work in the North Wales coalfield, Nos 91 and 92 were 0-4-2 saddle tanks with inside frames,

Above:
Also a member of the '111' class, No 112 is seen as rebuilt at Wolverhampton in 1881. Most engines of this class spent many years working local and main line trains in the Chester area. No 112 was withdrawn in October 1904. *Ian Allan Library*

Below:
Wolverhampton's first passenger tank engines were a dozen 2-4-0Ts, with back and well tanks, built between 1864 and 1866. All were later rebuilt as saddle tanks, No 346 was withdrawn in January 1888: all had gone by 1893. *Ian Allan Library*

inside cylinders, and open splashers. The boiler was low-pitched and had no dome, while the safety-valve cover was on a raised firebox casing. The tank covered only the boiler barrel, and there was no attempt to provide any sort of cab. They had 4ft 0in wheels and 13in × 20in cylinders.

No 91 lasted only until January 1877 when it was 'cannibalised', the frames and cylinders being used to repair No 92 two months later. In December of the following year No 92 was reconstructed and 'amputated' at Chester, emerging from this operation as a 0-4-0ST. In 1893 it underwent further surgery, with another reconstruction, this time at Wolverhampton, from which it emerged with a shortened wheelbase, new wheels having 'H' section spokes, modified framing, closed splashers, and a new boiler. No 92 now had a cab consisting of a roof supported by front and back spectacle plates. Apart from its number, it is difficult to see what remained of the original No 92!

After spending most of its life in the Wrexham colliery district, it was sent to South Wales in 1936, but returned north in July 1942 to become a stationary engine at Wellington. Although officially withdrawn at that time it remained intact for several years. No 92 was not cut up until it was about 90 years old, at least its number was that age!

The opening of the Herbert Street goods depot, adjoining the Victoria Basin at Wolverhampton, in

1858, enabled the original S&BR goods yard to be closed and the works to be extended. An erecting shop was built on the site of the original engine shed in the works, using two of the former repair roads which were served by a traverser. Thus Joseph Armstrong was able to start on the design of his first new engine.

The first new engines to be built at Wolverhampton appeared in 1859, these being two Singles, 2-2-2s No 7 and 8, which replaced ex-S&CR engines which had been scrapped. Originally they had 14½in × 22in cylinders (later increased to 16in diameter) and 6ft 2in driving wheels, domeless boilers with a raised firebox, and plate frames. The leading and trailing wheels had outside bearings, those for the driving wheels being inside (a combination later known as the 'Jenny Lind' type). A third engine, No 30, built in 1860, differed in having a manhole cover on the boiler barrel, 6ft 6in wheels and 15in dia cylinders. All three engines had large safety-valve covers on the casing, instead of the usual GWR Gooch pattern.

Two years later, No 110 appeared; however, this engine had outside bearings for all axles and 6ft 0in driving wheels, though its cylinders were the same size as those on No 30. All four engines were withdrawn between 1876 and 1883, having worked from Shrewsbury shed. Nos 30 and 110 were supposedly 'renewed' as 2-4-0s, but as the old No 30 was withdrawn three years before the new

Above:
Very similar in appearance to the 2-4-0Ts as rebuilt, apart from having domed boilers, were the first 54 engines of the '517' class as built during 1868-9. However, all were later rebuilt as side tanks. No 556 is seen c1877: rebuilt as a side tank in 1879 and given a longer wheelbase in 1911, it was not withdrawn until September 1933. Note the disc and crossbar signal. *Ian Allan Library*

No 30 appeared, there can have been little connection — apart from the number!

The first standard gauge 0-6-0Ts, fore-runners of the vast army of such engines on the GWR, were Nos 93 and 94, built at Swindon in 1860. They had the usual Gooch features, with inside frames, 4ft 0in wheels and 15in × 22in cylinders. Used on shunting duties at Chester and Wolverhampton, both were completely 'renewed' as saddle tanks of the '850' class. In their original form they had both side and back tanks.

Stafford Road Works and Swindon both being hard pressed to keep the growing number of engines under repair, the GWR was forced to place orders with outside firms to construct some of the engines needed. When an additional 18 goods engines were built in 1862, only six (Nos 131-136) were Swindon products, the remainder Nos 137-148 being built by Slaughter Gruning & Co of Bristol.

Although ordered by Gooch, the '131' class had Stephenson link motion and the compensating levers were omitted. These changes were probably made at the behest of Joseph Armstrong. A further 10 engines, Nos 310-319, were built at Swindon in 1864-65. All were later fitted with 17in cylinders in place of the original 16in × 24in ones, and a few years later cabs were fitted. They were mostly to be found in the Chester and Birkenhead area. Three engines, Nos 132, 135 and 314, were 'renewed' in the normal manner in 1877-78 (No 135 having condensing apparatus in the tender), and 12 others were withdrawn and scrapped between 1879 and 1893. Renewal No 314 was withdrawn in 1894, in which year No 132 achieved the unique distinction of being 'renewed' a second time! It later achieved another unique status, that of being the only sandwich-framed 0-6-0 to carry a superheated boiler: this was fitted in May 1922, and No 132 appears to have been

Above:
Goods engines for the Northern Division were built either at Swindon or by outside contractors. No 136, a member of the '131' class, was built at Swindon in 1862 and is seen here in its original condition. 'Renewed' in 1886, it remained in service until 1921. *Ian Allan Library*

Below:
No 78 was one of a pair of inside-framed 0-6-0s built by Beyer, Peacock in 1857. It is seen here at Chester as fitted with a rounded cab during the 1870s, but prior to receiving number plates. The left-hand side reverse should be noted. It was withdrawn in March 1903. *Ian Allan Library*

unable to stand the strain as it was withdrawn in August 1924! The third 'renewed' engine, No 135, lasted until 1906.

The remaining 13 engines were also 'renewed',

but were termed 'special renewals': one of them was an addition to stock, the old No 146 having been withdrawn seven years previously. However, it did not receive either a lot number or a works number; whereas the other 12 were lot K2. They were built in numerical sequence and all were uniform, which was something quite 'special' as far as Wolverhampton renewals were concerned! Although the first of the 'special renewals' was withdrawn as early as 1905, several of them soldiered on until after World War 1. Indeed, five of them went on war service, being lent to the LNWR in 1917 to work in Lancashire. The last survivor was No 146, the addition to stock and one of those loaned to the LNWR, which was withdrawn from Wellington in 1925.

In 1862 George England & Co, of Thatcham Ironworks, Kent, built the GWR's first 2-4-0s for the standard gauge. Nos 149-156 were of Gooch's design, with the usual sandwich frames and domeless boilers, but had Stephenson's link motion. At this time, Singles were generally preferred for express work and it was to be 10 years before any more express engines of this type were built for the GWR. The coupled wheels were 6ft 6in, leading wheels, 4ft 0in, and the cylinders 16in × 24in. They were all stationed at Wolverhampton, working mainly to Chester.

As was usual with engines of this construction, the whole class was 'renewed' between 1878 and 1883, but the renewals contained little or nothing of the originals. They now had 17in cylinders, though both the wheelbase and wheel diameters were as before. The boilers were of the standard Wolverhampton pattern, with flush firebox casing and domes on the middle ring. Initially, there were two large slots in the splashers, but these were later closed in; while new cab sides of a peculiar shape were fitted and the wheel diameters increased by fitting thicker tyres — the driving wheels now being 6ft 8½in. When first 'renewed' Nos 149, 151 and 154 had condensing apparatus in their tenders. No 154 was named *Chancellor* in honour of Sir Stafford Northcote who visited Stafford Road Works while it was undergoing renewal in November 1878.

The renewals at first performed the same duties, but in 1888 Nos 149-152 were sent to Shrewsbury for express work over the newly-opened 'North to West' route via the Severn Tunnel. In later years they worked mainly on local and branch services. Nos 149 and 153 were withdrawn early in this century but the remainder lasted until after World War 1 — No 155, the last survivor being withdrawn in May 1920. All ran at least a million miles, with No 154 reaching the impressive total of 1,300,000.

A few months after the '149' class had entered service, another class of 2-4-0 was introduced; however, these were designed by Joseph Arm-strong and built at Wolverhampton, having double plate frames and outside bearings for all the wheels. The domeless boilers had raised firebox casing on which was placed a large safety-valve cover. Six engines were built in 1863-64, being numbered 111-114, 1004 and 1005 (the last two being numbered 115A and 116A until September 1866): the numbers above 1000 were part of a series allocated for new engines built on the Renewal Account and for which no blank numbers existed in the ordinary list.

A further dozen engines were built in 1866-67, Nos 372-77 and 1006-11 (Nos 1006-9 were Nos 5A-8A until September 1866). These engines had flush firebox casings and a small painted dome on the middle ring of the boiler. They were noteworthy in probably being the first GWR *standard gauge* engines to be built with copper-capped chimneys — a distinction hitherto reserved for the broad gauge! These were George Armstrong's first new engines after assuming command at Wolverhampton.

All these engines were employed on secondary trains. The majority of the class were shedded at Chester, working mainly to Birkenhead and Manchester, but also to Wolverhampton — where some of them were shedded. There were also a few at Hereford, which also worked to Chester and to Birmingham. In 1886-87, two additional engines appeared, Nos 30 and 100 being 'renewals' of the two Singles built in 1860 and 1862: both were shedded at Wolverhampton. The entire class was withdrawn prior to 1914.

Apart from numerous 'renewals', these were the last tender engines to be built at Wolverhampton for more than 20 years. It was therefore a great surprise when in 1889 a class of 2-4-0 tender engines appeared: equally surprising was the fact that the design was simply a modified version of the '111' class — indeed, it was originally proposed to number them 104-109, and the first engine is reported to have run as No 104 for about a week. However, they were numbered 3226-31, being known as the '3226' class. The first three engines went to the West Midland Section, but the last three worked mainly between Chester and Wolverhampton, being joined at a later date by No 3227. They were withdrawn between 1914 and 1922, No 3231 being one of the many 2-4-0s whose last work was done on the Crewe branch.

The first of the small passenger tank engines, for which Wolverhampton became well known, appeared in 1864; a total of 12 being built by 1866. Although designed by Joseph Armstrong, his brother George was in command by the time the first of them appeared. They were 2-4-0Ts, a type otherwise associated with Swindon Works. Although not alike in all respects, all had inside frames, domeless boilers with a raised firebox casing, and well and back tanks. The cylinders were 14½in × 22in, leading wheels 3ft 6in and coupled wheels 5ft 0in. Their numbers were 11, 17, 18, 227, 344-349, 1002 and 1003 (Nos 17 and 18 were Nos 1A and 2A until July 1865: Nos 1002 and 1003 were Nos 3A and 4A until September 1866; while No 227 was first No 117 — until August 1867 — and then No 238 until July 1870!). After a few years all were fitted with saddle tanks covering the barrel only, thus resembling the earliest engines of the 0-4-2T type. Five of the class were sent south, but the remainder stayed in the Northern Division, working on local and branch duties from Wellington and in the Wrexham area. All were withdrawn between 1883 and 1893.

Four years after the appearance of the GWR's first 0-6-0Ts, eight much larger engines entered service in 1864-65. Nos 302-309 were built at Wolverhampton to Joseph Armstrong's design, though after his departure. They were the first of the many hundreds of large 0-6-0Ts and had double frames. As built, short saddle tanks were fitted which covered only the barrel of the boiler — which was domeless and had a raised firebox — while the chimneys were of the Gooch pattern. The wheels were 4ft 6in and the cylinders 16in × 24in. All eventually migrated south, mostly to South Wales. The last of the class was not withdrawn until 1932.

In November 1864 an additional shunting engine was acquired, this being a small 0-4-2ST which became No 342. It had been built by Beyer for the Commissioners of Chester joint station — though why those gentlemen should have needed an engine of their own is a mystery! It was similar to Nos 91 and 92, but had wrought iron wheels. Its history was also like that of No 92, as it was rebuilt at Chester in 1881 as a 0-4-0ST and again rebuilt at Wolverhampton in 1897, when it received a domed boiler, new saddle tank, and a new cab — all similar to those on No 92. However, unlike the latter engine it did not have 'H' section spokes in its wheels. Most of its life was spent at Chester or Wrexham, and it was withdrawn in 1931 after 75 years in service.

Wolverhampton's enthusiasm for 'renewing' engines may have been kindled in 1866 when the two peculiar 0-4-0s with intermediate crankshafts, inherited from the S&CR, were taken in hand. These emerged as long-boiler 0-6-0s, all the wheels being in front of the firebox. The boilers, which were domeless, were of the same design as those on the old engines, being low-pitched and having raised firebox casings. Their appearance was not improved by the bunching together of the two rear axles, so that the wheelbase was 7ft 2in+4ft 9in. Both spent their lives in the north, No 34 being in the Chester area, and they lasted until 1888-89.

Shortly after reconstructing Nos 34 and 35,

Wolverhampton dealt with another pair of absorbed engines, Nos 108 and 109, inherited from the Birkenhead Railway. Built as 0-6-0s, they had been rebuilt as 2-4-0s and were 'renewed' as such. Both worked in the Chester district on local trains and both were withdrawn at the end of 1887, by which time No 109 had been fitted with a vacuum brake. All four of these engines were counted as being new constructions and received Works Numbers.

Armstrong obtained 30 very handsome and successful double-framed 0-6-0s from Beyer, Peacock & Co between 1864 and 1866, these being numbered 322-341 and 350-359. Six were rebuilt as saddle tanks between 1878 and 1885, and it was apparently the intention to convert the entire class. Most of them were Northern Division engines for much of their long lives, many being at first employed between Pontypool Road and Birkenhead on mineral traffic, with the majority shedded at the former place: for many years, Pontypool Road was in the Northern Division!

Armstrong's own 0-6-0 goods engines were all built at Swindon, though a considerable number spent the greater part of their lives in the north. The first dozen engines, delivered in 1860, differed from the later ones in having their outside plate frames slotted out to form solid tie bars. The '360' class worked between Chester and Birmingham when first built (though No 362 was in South Wales), and the majority continued to work in the north for many years. Originally Nos 360-371, the last two engines were later renumbered 1000 and 1001 — while the former was again renumbered to 1015. Just to confuse matters, numbers 370 and 371 were then used for new 0-6-0s of the 'Standard Goods' class! Although No 1001 was withdrawn in 1912, No 363 lasted until March 1924.

A veritable flood of the 'Standard Goods' engines followed hard on the heels of the '360' class, over 300 being built between 1866 and 1876. About 85 of the class were permanently attached to the Northern Division during the 19th century, and these became as different as possible from those in the south; not least by reason of the Wolverhampton boilers with which they were rebuilt.

Armstrong followed Gooch's example when he designed a smaller-wheeled version of his goods engines specially for mineral traffic, these being the '927' class — popularly known as 'Coal Engines'. The 20 engines, Nos 927-946, were all built in 1874, with the same boilers and cylinders as the 'Standard Goods' class, but with 4ft 6in wheels in place of the latter's 5ft 0in. In common with the other 0-6-0s they had no cabs or even side sheets when first built. The name 'Coal Engines' was bestowed because they were used between Pontypool Road and Birkenhead on coal trains,

Above:
The famous No 92, originally an 0-4-2ST built in 1857 by Beyer, Peacock, and which passed through several rebuildings as an 0-4-0ST. Seen here at Wolverhampton in 1935, it was not withdrawn until 1942 — and even then lasted as a stationary boiler for several years! *H. Wheeller*

most of them being shedded at Birkenhead. As late as 1919 most of the surviving engines were still in the Birkenhead area, and at least 15 of the class were broken up at Wolverhampton between 1919 and 1928 — when the last survivor, No 934, was withdrawn from Stourbridge.

North of Wolverhampton, main line passenger engines normally had coupled wheels; and in 1868 Swindon built six 2-4-0s for secondary duties on the main line, these being Nos 439-444, of the '439' class — though better known as the 'Bicycles' because of their peculiar framing. They had inside frames — a departure from Armstrong's previous practice — with platforms which curved over the coupled wheels to form splashers. The leading wheels were 4ft 0½in and coupled wheels 6ft 1in (Swindon having begun to use thicker tyres), while the cylinders were 16in × 24in. The boilers had flush firebox casings and a small painted dome on the middle ring. Only weatherboards were fitted at first, but later side sheets and, eventually, cabs were fitted. They were always exclusively Northern Division engines, working between Wolverhampton and Chester; though the '149' class remained the premier express passenger engines.

All the class was 'renewed' in 1885-86, being the only engines of Joseph Armstrong's design to be so dealt with. The resulting engines were all new, apart from the old wheel centres. The platforms were only slightly raised over the coupled wheels and had a deep valance extended at the front end to form outside bearings for the leading wheels.

This was a Wolverhampton design feature of that period, and was copied from Swindon's use of such frames on the '717' and '806' classes. The coupled wheels had closed splashers bearing a metal coat-of-arms, while the cylinders were now 17in × 24in and the coupled wheels 6ft 2in. They continued to work on the same duties as the old engines with the same numbers.

In 1895, a surprising addition to the class arrived in the 'renewal' of No 20, a member of the smaller '481' class; the only difference between No 20 and the others being that it had a raised firebox casing — a feature of Wolverhampton engines during the 1890s. No 20 was shedded at Leamington in 1901, being that shed's only tender passenger engine. In their later years all the class worked on local trains, Nos 20 and 443 being at Chester. However, the duties of Nos 439, 441 and 442, at Shrewsbury, included piloting heavy expresses over the 'North to West' route between Shrewsbury and Hereford. No 444 was the first to be withdrawn, in 1907, and the remainder went between 1916 and 1918. No 442 ended its days at Wolverhampton; while No 443 was withdrawn from Shrewsbury.

Only three of the smaller engines of the '481' class went to the Northern Division, and all were reboilered between 1880 and 1890 with typical Wolverhampton boilers. In addition, No 12 had modified framing and closed splashers with metal coats-of-arms; though Wolverhampton can hardly have considered it to be an express engine — especially as, with No 19, it spent over 30 years working on the Crewe branch! When rebuilt, No 19 was not altered to have modified framing. As already recorded, No 20, which had also worked on the Crewe Branch since 1869, was 'renewed' in 1895 and emerged as a member of the '439' class. Nos 12 and 19 were withdrawn in 1903 and 1906 respectively.

1867 saw the construction at Wolverhampton of the first members of a class of 60 double-framed 0-6-0STs, the '1016' class; however, the first engine to be built was No 1017 (in January), while the second engine (built in February) was numbered 238 until the following August when it became No 1016 — by which time Nos 1018-25 had been built (Nos 1012-16 having been left unused!). Like the earlier '302' class, they had very short saddle tanks, but the boilers had a small dome on the middle ring and flush-top fireboxes. Wheels and cylinders were identical with those of the earlier engines. The final dozen appeared in 1871, after which Wolverhampton built no more double-

Above:
The earlier 0-6-0STs built at Wolverhampton all had short tanks. No 1051 still retained the short tanks when this photograph was taken at Newport, Bolt Street — for some years this shed was in the Northern Division! No 1051 became a pannier tank in 1917, and was withdrawn in July 1930. One wonders if the boy cleaner ever became a driver?!
Ian Allan Library

Right:
The '2021' class was built at Wolverhampton between 1897 and 1905. No 2028 was one of the first engines of the class. Fitted with a domeless boiler in 1925, it retained this, together with its saddle tank, until withdrawn in 1938. Seen here inside Shrewsbury shed in August 1935.
H. Wheeller

framed tank engines. The class was fairly evenly distributed between the two Divisions; and from 1911 onwards pannier tanks replaced the saddle tanks on all except about a dozen members of the class. Four of the remaining saddle tanks were withdrawn prior to 1914, but the rest lasted longer, being withdrawn between 1925 and 1935 — most of them having a mileage of well over a million.

A few months after commencing to build the '1016' class, there appeared the first of a class of small passenger tank engines which were to be built over a period of 18 years, reaching a total of 156 engines. This was No 1040, better known by its later number, 517. It was a 0-4-2ST with 15in × 24in cylinders, 5ft 0in coupled wheels and 3ft 6in trailing wheels. Until 1870, the first 60 engines, later Nos 517-576, bore the less-familiar numbers 1040-87 and 1100-11. The final numbers of the entire class were: 202-205, 215-222, 517-576, 826-849, 1154-1165, 1421-44 and 1465-88. They were the first engines built at Wolverhampton which owed little or nothing to Joseph Armstrong.

As might be expected, from such a long period of construction, there were numerous developments in the design. The first 54 engines had short saddle tanks, bell-mouthed chimneys and painted dome covers — though brass safety-valve covers were fitted. The only protection for the engine men was a spectacle sheet, but soon afterwards additional protection was provided in the form of a spectacle plate at the front of the bunker. Nos 553-570 of this series were longer engines; while Nos 571-576 not only had an even longer wheelbase, but were side tanks. From 1876, the saddle tanks were gradually rebuilt as side tanks, the first 36 engines also being given a longer wheelbase.

Beginning with No 1453, built in 1877, open-backed cabs were fitted; while the last six engines, Nos 1483-88, built in 1885, had outside axleboxes for the trailing wheels. By this time, 16in cylinders were being fitted (increased to 16½in from 1896 onwards). Many of the class worked in the Southern Division, so Swindon as well as Wolverhampton was responsible for rebuildings, and an incredible variety was the result! There were differences in wheelbase and length of frames; engines with a short wheelbase retained inside bearings for the trailing wheels, but those with the longer wheelbase had outside bearings; the shape and size of the bunkers varied from engine to engine; in this century, some engines received all-over cabs, but others retained their open cabs; some engines had raised firebox casings, while others had flush casings, and some were given Belpaire boilers; and, lastly from 1904 onwards some engines were auto-fitted!

During the 19th century, about half the class were in the Northern Division being employed on most of the branches, on local trains on the main line, and on suburban services around Birmingham. Withdrawal was spread over a period of 40 years; although the first two engines, Nos 849 and 202, were withdrawn in 1904, No 1159 almost outlived the GWR (being withdrawn in August 1947).

A few more 2-4-0s arrived from Swindon in the 1870s, these being four engines of the '806' class built in 1873, which were Armstrong's last 2-4-0 design and the first intended for express passenger work. Nos 806, 807, 810 and 821 were shedded at Stafford Road for working to Chester on the most important express trains (though No 807, at least, was later shedded at Chester), joining the '149' class engines on these duties. In later years, after being replaced on the express workings, they remained in the north. No 810, which lasted until December 1926 working on the Crewe branch, was the 'odd man out' among all the Northern Division 2-4-0s in never carrying a Wolverhampton boiler: it was also the only one of the quartet not to be cut up at Wolverhampton.

The '806' class engines were the last new express passenger engines to be sent to the Northern Division for 20 years, the next to arrive being a handful of the '3232' class — the very last GWR 2-4-0s built in 1892-3, which were used for a few years between Wolverhampton and Chester as well as from Shrewsbury on the 'North to West' services. Although Singles were not normally used north of Wolverhampton, three of Armstrong's 'Sir Daniel' class 2-2-2s, Nos 378 *Sir Daniel*, 473 and 578, were permanently allocated to the Northern Division: from the introduction of the new fast train, the 'Zulu' in 1880, they had the exclusive haulage of the up and down trains between Wolverhampton and Birkenhead. As was to be expected, they were rebuilt with Wolverhampton boilers and cabs which differed from those on the rest of the class. They also had another unique feature, the distinction of carrying brass coats of arms on the splashers when they were closed in.

Above:
A Wolverhampton conversion was that of six engines of the '322' class, built by Beyer, Peacock & Co as 0-6-0s. No 323 was originally No 359 and was rebuilt as a tank engine in 1879. Becoming a pannier tank in 1925, it remained in service until July 1932. *Ian Allan Library*

Below right:
Wolverhampton's rebuilds always tended to be different in appearance, even when of the same class. No 12 of the '481' class, built at Swindon in 1869, was rebuilt in 1890 when it received a modified form of framing and brass figures instead of number plates. It was withdrawn in 1903 after spending its entire life working on the Crewe Branch. *Bucknall collection*

In 1871 George Armstrong and Wolverhampton inaugurated the era of the inside-framed 0-6-0T. The initial dozen, Nos 633-644, were side tanks — the only 0-6-0Ts built at Wolverhampton which did not have saddle tanks — and were always in the South. Immediately afterwards, further engines having the same dimensions — 16in × 24in cylinders, 4ft 6½in wheels and 140lb/sq in pressure — but fitted with saddle tanks, began to appear from the Works. Between 1872 and 1881 a total of 108 engines was built, divided into two classes: the only difference between the '645' and '1501' series being that the former had short saddle tanks, while the latter had full-length tanks and were 6in longer. Their numbers were 645-656, 757-775, 1501-60 and 1801-12 (five other engines being sold direct from Works to minor railways in South Wales).

Over the years, rebuildings resulted in different boilers being fitted, and some of the series had their frames lengthened to conform with the later '655' class while all except eight engines later carried pannier tanks. Eight of the '1501' series lasted long enough to see service during World War 2, the last one, No 1542, not being withdrawn until 1951.

Over 10 years elapsed before further engines of this type appeared from Wolverhampton, until in February 1892 Nos 655 and 767 entered service — carrying the numbers of two of the earlier engines which had been sold out of service. They were followed by another 50 engines, Nos 1741-50, 1771-90 and 2701-20, during the next five years. In 1892 a change was made to building engines in Lots of 10 (as had been the practice at Swindon since 1866) instead of the previous custom of turning out dozens or half-dozens. As with the previous class, Belpaire boilers were fitted in later years; and all except No 1778 finished their lives as pannier tanks. The last of the class was withdrawn in 1950.

However, Wolverhampton had been building 0-6-0Ts during the intervening years, but these had been much smaller engines with 4ft 0in wheels and 15in × 24in cylinders, with a compact wheelbase of only 13ft 8in. The first of these engines, the '850' and '1901' classes, were Nos 850-861, built in 1874, and there were eventually 170 of them. They owed nothing to Joseph Armstrong or to Swindon. The first 36 engines, Nos 850-873 and 987-998, had boilers with raised fireboxes on which the domes were mounted, surmounted by lock-up safety-valves. Full-length saddle tanks were fitted and spectacle plates provided. As built, they had bell-mouthed chimneys and brass covers for the dome tops which looked like very deep safety-valve brasses, while the wheels had wrought-iron centres. Only eight of these engines remained in the Northern Division, the remainder going south. Cabs were fitted from about 1880, and the engines in the north received roll-top chimneys; though those in the south had the Dean type fitted.

Another 12 engines, Nos 1216-27, built in 1876-77, had normal boilers with domes on the barrels, and 16in cylinders. The wheel centres were cast iron, with 'H' section spokes (as used on the LNWR), which were unique to this class, except for three small tank engines, Nos 40, 45 and 92. To this dozen were added Nos 93 and 94, the 'renewals' of the old Swindon-built side tanks designed by Gooch.

Commencing with No 1901, built in 1881, a further series had cabs, but retained the wheels with 'H' section spokes. A considerable number of these also went south. With their short wheelbase they were in great demand, especially in dock areas. As with the larger 0-6-0STs, most were later fitted with pannier tanks; though Nos 1925 and 2007 remained as saddle tanks until withdrawn in 1951 and 1949 respectively. Three engines were sold out of service prior to 1914; but withdrawals did not commence until 1928, and 43 of the class outlived the GWR. Some quite remarkable mileages were achieved for such small engines, with No 1903 reaching 1,288,742 miles! No 2012 was the last to be withdrawn, in 1958.

In 1895, a further class of 0-4-2Ts appeared, after an interval of 10 years. Nos 3571-80 were a development of the '517' class, with 16½in cylinders and larger grates (though the boiler pressure remained at 140lbs). They were later rebuilt with Belpaire boilers having 165lb/sq in

pressure, as were many of the older engines. The outside framing for the trailing wheels was continuous with the valance, a feature which had appeared on No 1477 when rebuilt in December 1894 and which meant that the axleboxes and springs were in a singularly inaccessible position! Although the first nine engines were built between May and December 1895, No 3580 did not appear until January *1897* — when it was built between the 19th and 20th engines of the final lot of large 0-6-0Ts!

Most of the class spent much of their lives in the north; though Nos 3576-78 spent a few years at Pontypool Road, and No 3576 remained in the south until the 1920s. The majority spent many years working between Chester and Birkenhead; however, in 1901 six were at Corwen for the Ruabon to Dolgelley line, while No 3577 was

Above:
Of the same class as No 12, but of very different appearance, No 19 retained its original framing when rebuilt at Wolverhampton in 1886 and 1896. Also employed on the Crewe branch, No 19 was withdrawn in 1906. *Real Photos (15175)*

Below:
A Wolverhampton number plate which still retains the building date etc: long after such details had supposedly been removed from all GWR engines. No 1744 was photographed at Croes Newydd in August 1935. *H. Wheeller*

working from Bordesley Junction shed. Two of the class, Nos 3572 and 3576, were withdrawn in 1928-29, both from Birkenhead, but the remainder lasted much longer — the last four being withdrawn in 1949.

Immediately after building the last of the large 0-6-0STs, No 2720, in January 1897, Wolverhampton turned once again to the production of small 0-6-0Ts. The new engines, the '2021' class, were a foot longer than the '850' class, due to the fitting of a longer firebox, and had wheels with normal spokes. The class numbered 140 engines, divided into two distinct series; the '2021' class built up to 1901 having boilers with raised round-top fireboxes, a dome on the front ring, and short smokeboxes; and the '2101' class having domeless boilers with raised Belpaire fireboxes and 165lb/sq in pressure (the earlier engines worked at 150lb), and safety-valves placed on the boiler barrel — the covers protruding through the saddle tanks! Both series had 16½in cylinders and 4ft 1½in wheels. The '2101' series were built between 1902 and 1905. Wolverhampton's autonomy was over: George Armstrong had retired in 1897 (at the age of 75!) and the '2101' series was a visible sign that new ideas were being imposed from Swindon.

The majority were converted to pannier tanks, though No 2028 was still a saddle tank — with a domeless Belpaire boiler off one of the '2101' series — when withdrawn from Shrewsbury in 1938. Some of the '2101' series retained their domeless boilers when rebuilt as panniers, Nos 2048 and 2089 keeping them until 1948. Although built with open cabs, many engines later received the enclosed pattern; while a number were fitted for auto-working. Apart from two engines sold to collieries in South Wales when only a few years old, only three were withdrawn prior to 1939: 120 of the class outlived the GWR, No 2069 not being withdrawn until 1959. Most appropriately, but sadly, No 2160, the last engine of Wolverhampton *design* to be built, was also the last Wolverhampton-built engine to be cut up at that works, in 1957.

5   Paddington to the North

Above:
The first standard-gauge 2-4-0s built for the GWR were the eight engines of the '149' class, which were used on express passenger trains between Wolverhampton and Chester. No 155 is seen in its original 1862 condition. The small 'GWR' plate should be noted — this appears to have been unique to this engine. *Ian Allan Library*

Having acquired a second main line, the GWR did little or nothing towards providing a fast or frequent train service to Chester and Birkenhead. The main emphasis was always upon the section south of Wolverhampton, though even Birmingham suffered from chronic neglect for years on end during the 19th century. As MacDermott remarked, 'No inducement was offered to Birmingham passengers to use the longer Great Western route, while beyond Birmingham all competitive traffic was patiently resigned to the LNWR'.

While all classes suffered from this neglect, the third class was the most affected. In the late 1850s their only train was the 'Northern Cheap' which left Paddington at about 7.40am for stations beyond Birmingham, though this train was often combined as far as Didcot with the 'Cheap' which was supposed to leave about 7.00am for GWR stations in general. Stopping at every station, it took 7hr to reach Birmingham; while the unfortunate Chester passengers eventually reached that city after travelling for 12hr! In 1861, the last year in which passengers had to change trains — and gauge — at Wolverhampton, Chester was being reached in just over 6hr by the fastest trains. The service provided after through working commenced consisted of five trains in each direction.

It was not until July 1880 that the first fast train from Paddington to Birkenhead was introduced, this being the 4.45pm; Chester was reached in 4hr 50min, and Birkenhead in 5hr 10min. The new service involved an acceleration of more than an hour as far as Chester and Birkenhead were concerned! The new up train, leaving Birkenhead at 11.45am, was not so fast, taking 38min longer. These trains were known, north of Didcot, as the 'Zulu'; though they were generally known at Paddington as the 'Northern Zulu' to distinguish them from the West of England trains which had been so named by the staff. The 4.45pm was still known as the 'Zulu' in 1905, and was recorded as such in the Block Telegraph Register at Madeley Junction Signalbox. On Monday, 6 November, it was entered as having passed out of section at 8.20pm.

Leaving Wolverhampton at 7.51pm, the down

train called at Wellington and arrived at Shrewsbury at 8.33pm. It then stopped at Gobowen and Wrexham — where the Chester portion was detached — after which it ran non-stop to Birkenhead, arriving at 10.02pm. The Wellington stop was later omitted and it ran non-stop from Shrewsbury to Chester, to arrive at Birkenhead at 9.33pm. In 1888 the Wellington stop was restored and the train stopped in Chester cutting to detach the Chester carriages. The up train now departed from Birkenhead at 11.50am and avoided Chester, stopping only at Wrexham and Ruabon before arriving at Shrewsbury.

One bright feature was that all trains now carried third-class passengers and there were no express fares charged (unlike the West of England service). Between Shrewsbury and Birkenhead the service was augmented in 1888 by the introduction of through carriages (TC) to and from Bristol and South Wales, these being part of the GWR's first cross-country service over the 'North to West' route. However, in some instances, the TC were attached to the existing London trains. In 1891 the whole service was revised and somewhat improved, and in March 1892 the GWR's first corridor train (and the first in Great Britain), gangwayed throughout and heated by steam, was introduced between Paddington and Birkenhead.

While it was some years before all the absorbed engines were withdrawn from service, they were soon supplanted by the Beyer, Peacock 2-2-2s, Nos 69-76, which were responsible for the more important trains for six years, during which time they were isolated north of Wolverhampton by the break of gauge. When through services between Paddington and Merseyside (though not, alas, to Liverpool!) commenced in 1861, the change of engine continued to be made at Wolverhampton.

The Beyers were now used exclusively south of that point, coupled engines normally being used between Wolverhampton and Chester (and anything which was available between Chester and Birkenhead!). This meant that some of the absorbed engines made a re-appearance on express duties. A year or so later, the eight 2-4-0s of the '149' class arrived to take charge of this work on which they remained for the next 10 years.

From 1873 until the early 1890s, the top-link express engines were the four '806' class engines, Nos 806, 807, 810 and 821. Ahrons mentioned that No 807 had a monopoly of the 1.30pm express from Chester as far as Shrewsbury, except when it was under repair and another engine of the same class took its place: this suggests that some engine changing was taking place at Shrewsbury. After 'renewal' between 1878 and 1883 the '149' class engines continued to work alongside the '806' class quartet, but from 1892 some of the '3232' class took over the most important duties and both the '149s' and '806s' were relegated to a minor role. Among the members of the '3232' class in the North at an early date were Nos 3237, 3238, 3240, 3244 and 3246, all of which except No 3238 were still there in 1921.

Below:
The six engines of the '439' class, built at Swindon in 1868, supplemented the double-framed '149' class engines. No 444 is seen at Chester, c1890, after the whole class had been 'renewed' at Wolverhampton during 1885-6. It was the first member of the class to be withdrawn, in March 1907. *Ian Allan Library*

1902

DOWN		C		C	C		
Paddington, dep	12.15am	6.30am	9.45am	9.50am	2.10pm**	4.55pm	6.50pm
Wolverhampton, dep	4.15am	11.15am	2.05pm	1.12pm	5.05pm	7.57pm	11.02pm
Wellington	—	12.00 noon	2.48pm*	1.43pm	SC	SC	all stations
Shrewsbury, arr	4.55am	12.16pm	3.05pm	1.59pm	5.45pm	8.33pm	12.08am
dep	5.05am	12.35pm WE	3.10pm	2.13pm	5.55pm	8.36pm‡	—
No of stops	2	—	4	3†	3	3	
Chester, arr	6.10am	1.32pm	4.33pm	5.33pm	7.10pm	9.42pm D	
Birkenhead	6.43am	2.07pm	5.06pm	4.14pm	7.45pm	10.02pm	

C   Corridor Train
D   Train divided, Birkenhead portion non-stop from Chester cutting
WE TC from West of England and Cardiff to Birkenhead attached — 'West of England Express'
*   TC Paddington to Manchester (London Road) detached
†   TC Paddington to Barmouth detached at Ruabon
‡   TC Weston-super-Mare to Birkenhead attached
**   TC Bournemouth to Birkenhead attached at Birmingham
SC Slip carriage(s)
The 2.10pm was the 'Birmingham and North Corridor Express'

As mentioned in Chapter 4, one exception to the use of coupled engines was the 'Zulu', for which the three 'Sir Daniel' class 2-2-2s were used. Shedded at Birkenhead, they had two turns: on the first of these they worked the 'Zulu' to Wolverhampton, returning on the down train; while on the second they worked to Chester and Manchester (Exchange) via Warrington.

In 1902 the timetables were headed 'London, Oxford, Birmingham, Wolverhampton, Shrewsbury, Chester, Liverpool and Manchester' (there being no mention whatever of Birkenhead!). Three of the six trains in each direction were shown in the tables as being Corridor Trains. All trains stopped at Shrewsbury — some for a considerable time — and most of them also stopped at Wellington, Gobowen, Ruabon and Wrexham, as well as at Chester.

The 4.15pm from Birkenhead and the 10.00am from Shrewsbury were also shown as Corridor Trains in a special list of such trains, though not in the Tables themselves! An additional train to Paddington commenced from Wellington at 8.55am, calling at all stations to Wolverhampton (arr 9.45am) and arriving at Paddington at 1.58pm.

In addition to the Paddington trains there were

UP	C		C		WE	C	
Birkenhead, dep	6.15am		9.30am	11.47am	12.00 noon	2.25pm	4.15pm
Chester, dep	6.48am		10.07am	12.15pm	12.40pm	3.00pm	5.10pm
No of stops	2		1	2†	4	3	3‡
Shrewsbury, arr	8.05am	—	11.05am	1.27pm	2.03pm	4.20pm	6.26pm
dep	8.09am	10.00am	11.07am	1.33pm	2.15pm	4.25pm	6.30pm
Wellington	8.28am	10.17am	—	—	2.39pm	4.46pm	6.50pm
Wolverhampton, arr	8.57am	10.44am	11.49am**	2.13pm	3.23pm*	5.15pm	7.18pm
Paddington, arr	12.15pm	2.10pm	3.30pm*	5.20pm	7.32pm	8.45pm	10.50pm

C   Corridor Train
**   TC Birkenhead to Bournemouth detached at Oxford
†   TC Barmouth to Paddington attached at Ruabon
WE TC Birkenhead to Cardiff and West of England, detached at Shrewsbury
‡   Llangollen to Wolverhampton attached at Ruabon
*   TC Manchester (London Road) to Paddington attached from Wolverhampton

several short-distance semi-fast trains, of which both the up examples ran ahead of Birkenhead to Paddington trains to collect passengers from stations at which the expresses did not call. The only down example was a semi-fast train leaving Wolverhampton at 9.00am (the 7.30am from Leamington) which called at the principal stations to Chester (arr 11.30am), reaching Birkenhead at 12.08pm. The 8.15am from Birkenhead (Chester dep 9.00am) called at the principal stations to collect passengers for the 9.30am corridor train and also conveyed the Manchester to Paddington TC from Wellington Wolverhampton (arr 11.39am); while the 3.38pm from Birkenhead (Chester dep 4.20pm) performed the same office in connection with the 4.15pm corridor train.

Although the principal 'West of England Express' was combined with the 6.30am from Paddington between Shrewsbury and Birkenhead, two trains on the 'West to North' service ran through to Birkenhead. The 4.00pm from Shrewsbury, with TC from Cardiff, arrived at Chester at 5.03pm (Birkenhead arr 5.41pm); while the 7.23pm 'West of England Express', also with TC from Cardiff, arrived at Chester at 8.30pm (Birkenhead arr 9.11pm). Part of this train commenced from Birmingham at 5.55pm (having originated as the 4.20pm 'stopper' from Leamington). From Birkenhead the 'West of England Express' left at 10.35am (Chester dep 11.10am) reaching Shrewsbury at 12.10pm; while TC for Cardiff were attached to the 12.00 noon to Paddington. A second through train left at 2.55pm (Chester dep 3.32pm) from which TC for Barmouth were detached at Ruabon, Shrewsbury being reached at 4.50pm, and part of this continued to Leamington (arr 8.06pm).

The service on Sundays was sparse indeed! The overnight train from London ran as on other days, but the only through train during the day left Paddington at 9.00am and called at every station between Reading and Chester (arr 6.45pm) Birkenhead not being reached until 7.55pm! There was also the 3.20pm from Paddington to Shrewsbury (arr 8.58pm), which was 'all stations' from Wolverhampton (dep 7.38pm). The up service consisted of the 8.50am from Shrewsbury, another 'all stations' to Wolverhampton (arr 10.12am), which arrived at Paddington at 3.50pm, and the 8.35pm from Birkenhead (Chester dep 9.40am). The latter called at all stations to Wolverhampton (arr 12.50pm), then all stations to Leamington, the principal stations to Oxford, all stations to Reading, Maidenhead and Westbourne Park, before finally coming to rest at Paddington at 6.15pm. Birkenhead and Chester passengers with any sense obviously travelled by the LNWR on Sundays!

The opening of the new and much shorter route between Paddington and Birmingham, via Bicester, in July 1910, resulted in a considerable reduction in the journey time between London and places north of Wolverhampton. The mileage was reduced by no less than 18¾ miles, though a few trains in each direction still ran via Oxford. The best down train was now the 9.10am, with luncheon car, which took 4hr 13min to reach

Below:
Four of Joseph Armstrong's last design of 2-4-0, the '806' class built in 1873, spent their lives in the Northern Division where they were the 'top link' engines for over 20 years. All were rebuilt at Wolverhampton, when the open splashers were covered over. No 806 was withdrawn in 1918.
Ian Allan Library

Chester. There were five trains daily in each direction.

Another of the GWR's new routes was that from Birmingham to Cheltenham via Honeybourne, which was used by a new service from Birkenhead and Weston-super-Mare. As there were already two through trains in each direction between Birkenhead and the West of England via the 'North to West' route, the company provided what was, in effect, a competing service! Prior to World War 1 there were also daily through services between Birkenhead and Bournemouth and Portsmouth, and between Birkenhead and Folkestone.

In contrast with other main lines, there was little change in locomotive working until well into the first decade of this century. Until 1900 the turntables at Stafford Road (where three of the shed buildings were turntable sheds) were not large enough for anything longer than a six-wheeled engine! So the 2-2-2s continued to work between London and Wolverhampton, and the 2-4-0s between Wolverhampton and Chester.

Gradually, the 'Badminton' and 'Atbara' 4-4-0s, which from 1900 had worked with the Dean 7ft 8in Singles between Paddington and Wolverhampton, became responsible for much of the express working to Chester. Within a few years they were joined by the 'Cities', though some turns were also worked by the smaller-wheeled 'Bulldogs'. In 1909-11 the four lovely 7ft 0in 4-4-0s of the 'Armstrong' class also arrived in the area, though their large wheels were not ideal for that line! Nos 7 *Armstrong* and 8 *Gooch* spent their last years before being rebuilt with 6ft 8in wheels in 1923 on station pilot and local work at Wolverhampton.

Although used extensively on the 'North to West' services from Shrewsbury, the outside cylinder 'County' class 4-4-0s do not appear to have been used regularly on the main line north of

Above:
A few of the final design of GWR 2-4-0s, the '3232' class of 1892-3, including No 3237, were the premier express passenger engines north of Wolverhampton during the 1890s. Most of these remained in the north for their entire lives, and No 3237 was withdrawn in 1929 from Stafford Road where it had been shedded for most of its existence. Note the double water crane.
Ian Allan Library

Wolverhampton. The introduction of the various classes of 4-4-0s saw the rapid demotion of the 2-4-0s to branch work, many of them soon being withdrawn from service. As early as 1901, No 806 had ceased to be used on express work, being by then shedded at Bordesley Junction. However, wartime shortages of engines sometimes resulted in the employment of some most unusual types on express passenger duties, as in 1918 when 'Standard Goods' No 700 was regularly used on one turn which involved working an express train from Chester to Shrewsbury: the experience seems to have been too much for the engine, which was withdrawn at the end of the following year!

In 1921 there were eight 'Counties', four 'Cities' and five 'Flowers' at Wolverhampton (though some may have been in Stafford Road Works); while the allocation at Shrewsbury was three 'Counties' — Nos 3811 *County of Bucks*, 3824 *County of Cornwall* and 3827 *County of Gloucester* (used on the 'North to West' trains); 'City' class No 3707 *Malta*; and three 'Flowers' — Nos 4111 *Marlborough*, 4134 *Sir Redvers* and 4157 *Lobelia*. The only express passenger engines at Chester were a couple of 'Cities', Nos 3710 *City of Bath* and 3711 *City of Birmingham*, and No 4163 *Marigold* of the 'Flower' class. However, there were no less than 17 Moguls at Chester, whose duties included working many of the Paddington

trains: on occasions, two Moguls would take over at Wolverhampton from the 'Saint' or 'Star' which had worked from Paddington.

The eventual successors to the four-coupled engines were the immortal 'Saints'. Although there were 11 of the class at Stafford Road in 1913, there was little or no regular use of them north of Wolverhampton. During World War 1 they began to be used on the 'North to West' route, Nos 2926 *Saint Nicholas* and 2981 *Ivanhoe* being shedded at Shrewsbury in 1921: however, their number was not increased, and there was only one 'Saint' there in 1932, though by then there were no less than 11 'Stars' shedded there.

By 1921, Wolverhampton's allocation of 4-6-0s had been drastically reduced, and there were only 'Saints' Nos 2923 *Saint George*, 2924 *Saint Helena* and 2990 *Waverley*, and 'Stars' Nos 4043 *Prince*

1932

DOWN	A		RC B	RC C	RC D	E	F
Paddington, dep	MX 12.10	1.30	9.10am	11.10am	2.10pm	4.10pm	6.10pm
	via Oxford : via Bicester						
	combined at Birmingham						
Wolverhampton, dep	4.42am		11.40am	1.40pm	4.40pm	6.40pm	8.40pm
Wellington	set down only		12.05pm	—	5.06pm	7.06pm	9.11pm
Shrewsbury, arr/dep	5.23/35am		12.19/24pm	2.15pm	5.21pm	7.18pm	9.24pm
				2.20pm‡	5.25pm‡	7.28pm	9.30pm
No of stops	3		2*	3*	1	2	3
Chester, arr	6.49am		1.27pm	3.26pm	6.23pm	8.34pm	10.37pm
Birkenhead, arr	7.35am		1.57pm	4.00pm	7.00pm	9.10pm	11.15pm

A   'Isle of Man Boat Express'
B   'Birmingham and North Express' and 'Isle of Man Boat Express'
C   'London to Birmingham and North Express'
D   'London to Birmingham, Aberystwyth and North Express'
E   'London to Birmingham and North and Belfast Boat Express'
F   'London to Birmingham and North Express'
RC   Restaurant Car
‡   Restaurant Car and TC Paddington to Aberystwyth detached
MX   Mondays Excepted
*   TC Paddington to Pwllheli detached at Ruabon

UP	A	B	C	D	
Birkenhead, dep	6.30am	9.05am	11.45am RC	2.40pm	4.35pm
Chester, dep	7.10am	9.40am	12.20pm	3.15pm	5.10pm
No of stops	ps	3†	3*	3*	3
Shrewsbury, arr	8.33am	10.48am	1.38pm‡	4.28pm‡	6.18pm
dep	8.40am	10.53am	1.43pm	4.33pm	6.26pm
Wellington	9.00am	—	—	4.55pm	6.47pm
Wolverhampton, arr	9.27am	11.30am	2.23pm	5.23pm	7.14pm
	LR	RC attached		divided at Birmingham	divided at Birmingham
Paddington, arr	12.05pm	2.00pm	5.05pm	8.05pm DC 9.20pm via Oxford	10.05pm DC 10.55pm via Oxford

* TC Pwllheli to Paddington attached at Ruabon
† TC Birkenhead to Aberystwyth detached at Gobowen
‡ TC Aberystwyth to Paddington attached
RC Restaurant Car
DC Dining Car
LR Light refreshments available from Birmingham
ps Calls at principal stations
A 'Birkenhead, Birmingham and Leamington Spa Express'
B 'Belfast Boat Express' and 'Birkenhead, Birmingham and Leamington Spa to London Express'
C 'Birkenhead, Birmingham and Leamington Spa to London Express'
D 'Birkenhead, Birmingham and Leamington Spa Express' and 'Isle of Man Boat Express'

Above left:
The 'Barnum' class sandwich-framed 2-4-0s were still used on express trains in the 1920s, albeit between Birkenhead and Chester. No 3221 is seen on an up express at Hooton — with quite an assortment of carriages. *Ian Allan Library*

Henry, 4049 *Princess Maud* and 4054 *Princess Charlotte*. However, by 1932 the number of 'Saints' had increased to seven; while there were also seven of the class at Chester. Thus, during the 1920s, the 'Saints' had taken over the majority of the express passenger workings, a role they retained for the next 20 years. Although Chester had two 'Castles' in 1932 (though none was shedded at Shrewsbury until 1935), this proved to be a brief allocation, none being shedded there again until the last days of the GWR.

On 25 March 1927 the GWR ran two excursion trains to Birkenhead in connection with the Grand National at Aintree. The third-class special left Paddington at 7.50am behind No 4081 *Warwick Castle*, and after calling at Ealing Broadway ran non-stop to Shrewsbury where No 2952 *Twineham Court* took over for the remainder of the journey — non-stop to Birkenhead, which was reached just four hours after leaving Ealing. The first-class special departed at 8.25am with No 4097 *Kenilworth Castle* in charge for the non-stop run to Shrewsbury where No 2948 *Stackpole Court* took

over for the second stage — Birkenhead being reached at 12.25pm. The inclusive return fares, including all meals on the trains, were first class £2-14s-6d and third class £1-17s-0d! The first train was 9min early in arriving at Birkenhead, while the second was 10min early.

In the 1932 summer timetables, the service was headed 'London, Banbury, Leamington Spa, Birmingham, Wolverh'mpt'n, Shrewsbury, Chester and Liverpool'. There was still no mention of Birkenhead, though Manchester had disappeared as there were no longer TC to and from Paddington. There were still six trains from Paddington (as in the 1860s); while a seventh ran as far as Shrewsbury. However, there were now only five up trains from Birkenhead, though another two commenced from Shrewsbury. The 'regular departure times', inaugurated in 1924, meant that down trains now left Paddington at 10min past the hour.

The down train terminating at Shrewsbury was the 7.10pm, leaving Wolverhampton at 9.55pm (Shrewsbury arr 10.50pm). The up trains from Shrewsbury were at 7.40am and 9.55pm, the arrival times being 1.00pm and 4.15am: the 9.55pm ran via Oxford and provided the only overnight service from the north.

During the summer months there were several other services, most of which ran on Fridays and Saturdays only. The Birmingham to Birkenhead SO 'Isle of Man Boat Express' (Tyseley dep

7.00am), which left Wolverhampton at 7.43am, ran non-stop from Shrewsbury to Birkenhead (arr 9.48am); while the FSO 'Birmingham to Aberystwyth Express' (Snow Hill dep 9.10am), departing from Wolverhampton at 9.35am, called at Wellington and then ran non-stop to Welshpool (arr 11.00am). A similar working, avoiding Shrewsbury station, was the SO Paddington to Aberystwyth 'Cambrian Coast Express', leaving Wolverhampton at 12.50pm and shown as running non-stop to Aberystwyth! In the case of the latter trains, 'Duke' class 4-4-0s were used from Birmingham and Wolverhampton respectively.

The precursor of the 'Cambrian Coast Express' first ran in July 1921, as a restaurant car train leaving Paddington at 9.50am, with portions for Aberystwyth and Pwllheli (divided at Dovey Junction). The name 'Cambrian Coast Express' was adopted in 1927, but by then it ran FSO. Throughout the years the departure time from Aberystwyth had been at about 12 noon.

A daily 'Bournemouth and Southampton to Birkenhead and Manchester Express', including TC from Portsmouth to Manchester via the Crewe branch, left Wolverhampton at 2.47pm and arrived at Chester at 4.48pm (Birkenhead arr 5.29pm). There was also a FSO Portsmouth to Birkenhead service leaving Wolverhampton at 2.00pm and arriving at Chester at 4.05pm (Birkenhead arr 4.52pm). The 'Through Express, Deal, Dover, Folkestone, Ramsgate and Margate to Birkenhead' left Wolverhampton each day at 4.42pm, arriving at Chester at 5.35pm (Birkenhead arr 6.15pm). The last remnant of the through service between South Wales and Birkenhead was the SO 'Holiday Ticket Train' leaving Shrewsbury at 1.55pm and arriving at Birkenhead at 3.54pm.

There were three semi-fast trains. The 7.30am from Leamington still ran, leaving Wolverhampton at 8.52am (in 1902 it left at 9.00am) and arriving at Chester at 10.31am (in 1902 it did not arrive until 11.30am); while two trains from Shrewsbury provided connections from the 'west to north' services — at 1.10pm and at 5.40pm,

Above left:
'City' class 4-4-0 No 3717 *City of Chester* leaving Shrewsbury station c1928 — most appropriately for Chester. The 'Cities' spent their final years on such duties. *W. Potter*

Left:
'Bulldog' class 4-4-0s did much express passenger work to and from Chester for many years. No 3410 *Colombia* is seen on the down 'Zulu' at Chester in 1920. The engine on the right is an LNWR 'Special Tank'. *H. G. Tidey: Real Photos (T6675)*

arriving at Chester at 2.50pm and 6.35pm respectively.

The up Birkenhead to Margate (and other resorts!) train left at 8.00am (Chester dep 8.35am) and arrived at Wolverhampton at 10.25am, followed on MSO by a 'South Wales and West of England Express' at 9.30am (Chester dep 10.05am: Shrewsbury arr 11.09am). The Birkenhead to Southampton through service left at 9.35am (Chester dep 10.15am) and arrived at Wolverhampton at 12.15pm, the Manchester to Portsmouth TC having been attached at Wellington. Following this on SO was the 10.30am Birkenhead to Cardiff, arriving at Shrewsbury at 12.22pm. Two Birkenhead to Shrewsbury trains connected with the 'north to west' services: the 12.00 noon (Chester dep 12.37pm: Shrewsbury arr 1.55pm) connected with the Liverpool to Taunton train, continued to Wolverhampton (arr 3.08pm) and terminated at Birmingham; while the 11.20pm (Chester dep 12.20am) connected with the overnight service to Cardiff and the West of England.

The SO 'Cambrian Coast Express' (Aberystwyth dep 10.00am), which ran direct through Shrewsbury, arrived at Wolverhampton at 1.28pm; while the FSO 'Aberystwyth to Birmingham Express' (Aberystwyth dep 2.30pm) was due at Wolverhampton at 6.35pm. The SO 'Isle of Man Boat Express' from Birkenhead to Birmingham left at 2.30pm (Chester dep 3.05pm) called at three stations before reaching Shrewsbury, and also at Wellington (unlike the down train), and arrived at Wolverhampton at 5.07pm (Birmingham arr 5.30pm).

On Sundays the overnight train from Paddington (dep 12.10am) arrived at Birkenhead at 7.35am, though the 1.30am portion via Bicester did not run. There was now no day time departure for Birkenhead until 1.10pm, though the 10.10am via Oxford ran as far as Shrewsbury (arr 3.03pm). The 1.10pm from Paddington left Wolverhampton at 3.55pm, calling at Wellington, Shrewsbury and the usual three stations before arriving at Chester at 5.05pm (Birkenhead arr 6.48pm): there was a considerable improvement on the infamous 9.00am in 1902 which did not reach Birkenhead until 7.35pm! The 6.10pm Paddington to Shrewsbury (arr 9.36pm) left Wolverhampton at 8.40pm and called at most stations. There was also a fast train leaving Shrewsbury at 5.55pm and arriving at Chester at 7.03pm in connection with the Plymouth, Paignton and Cardiff to Manchester train (Shrewsbury arr 5.40pm).

As in 1902, there was only one Birkenhead to Paddington train on Sundays, and this was not until 2.55pm (Chester dep 3.40pm), arriving at Paddington at 9.00pm. There was also the 8.55am from Shrewsbury, via Oxford, which arrived at

Above:
'Saint' class No 2904 *Lady Godiva* is seen at Halton heading the Birkenhead to Deal through train composed of Southern Railway stock.
H. G. Tidey: Real Photos (T6219)

Below:
'Star' class No 4031 *Queen Mary*, shedded at Stafford Road for many years, stands at the north end of Shrewsbury station on an express train bound for Chester — again, the train is of Southern Railway stock.
W. H. Whitworth: Real Photos

Paddington at 2.40pm. The 10.30am from Birkenhead (Chester dep 11.30am) was a fast train to Shrewsbury (arr 12.37pm) to connect with the 'north to west' Manchester to Plymouth service leaving at 12.50pm.

Less changes took place in locomotive workings during the 1930s and early 1940s than on most other GWR main lines. Although the number of 'Castles' at Shrewsbury had gradually increased,

from two in 1935 to eight in 1947, the allocation of 'Stars' had been reduced from 10 in 1938 to four in 1947. In 1938 they were — Nos 4013 *Knight of St Patrick*, 4014 *Knight of the Bath*, 4030 *Swedish Monarch*, 4031 *Queen Mary*, 4044 *Prince George*, 4046 *Princess Mary*, 4053 *Princess Alexandra*, 4061 *Glastonbury Abbey*, 4067 *Tintern Abbey* and 4068 *Llanthony Abbey*. In 1947 they were Nos 4040 *Queen Boadicea* and three of the 1938 engines, Nos 4044, 4046 and 4061.

Further north, Chester remained dependent upon the 'Saints', though its seven engines in 1932 had been reduced to five by 1938 — Nos 2903 *Lady of Lyons*, 2920 *Saint David*, 2928 *Saint Sebastian*, 2931 *Arlington Court* and 2932 *Ashton Court* — while there were also seven 'Halls'. In 1947 there were still five 'Saints', though not the same engines — Nos 2915 *Saint Bartholomew*, 2926 *Saint Nicholas*, 2930 *Saint Vincent*, 2953 *Titley Court* and 2989 *Talisman* — and also one 'Star', No 4013 *Knight of St Patrick*, and a 'Castle', No 5033 *Broughton Castle*, as well as six 'Halls'.

Chester shared the workings with Stafford Road, which retained its 'Saints' until 1945 when they were replaced by some of the new 'Counties'. In 1938, Wolverhampton's 'Saints' were Nos 2926 *Saint Nicholas*, 2941 *Easton Court*, 2981 *Ivanhoe* and 2989 *Talisman*. The 'Counties' were destined to have a very close association with the line, some of their finest work being done north of Wolverhampton. Five of the class were at Stafford Road in 1947, Nos 1016 *County of Hants*, 1017 *County of Hereford*, 1024 *County of Pembroke*, 1025 *County of Radnor* and 1029 *County of Worcester*; and Nos 1016, 1017 and 1025 were to spend their entire lives working from either Stafford Road, Shrewsbury or Chester.

In addition to a dozen or so 'Castles' and four 'Kings', Stafford Road also retained a few 'Stars'. In 1938 they were Nos 4018 *Knight of the Grand Cross*, 4025 *Italian Monarch*, 4058 *Princess Augusta* and 4065 *Evesham Abbey*: Nos 4018 and 4015 were still there in 1947, having been joined by Nos 4031 *Queen Mary* and 4053 *Princess Alexandra* from Shrewsbury and No 4060 *Princess Eugenie* from Landore. 'Halls' and 'Granges' were often to be found on main line passenger work, though the latter were more commonly seen at weekends during the summer months when there were many SO extra trains.

The final timetables issued by the GWR, for the winter of 1947, at last recognised Birkenhead's existence when describing the main line service, which was now 'London, Oxford, Birmingham, Wolverhampton, Shrewsbury, Chester, Birkenhead and Liverpool', With dogged persistence, the company still maintained that Paddington was the obvious London station for any passenger wishing to travel to or from Liverpool!

Although there were still six trains from Paddington to Birkenhead, the up service had been further reduced, to only four trains. The ravages of the war years and the shortage of locomotive coal were reflected in the extended timings. It was now not possible to leave Birkenhead for any station south of Birmingham until 8.30am. Shrewsbury fared better, with two early morning trains to London, leaving at 7.25am and 9.30am, the former arrived at Paddington at 11.20am, but the latter ran via Oxford and was not due until 2.15pm — only 20min prior to the arrival of the 8.30am from Birkenhead (Shrewsbury dep 10.40am).

The only Shrewsbury to Birkenhead fast train, at 4.15pm, provided a connecting service from the 8.45am Plymouth to Liverpool and Manchester train, reaching Chester at 5.22pm (Birkenhead arr 6.11pm). The overnight service and the 9.10am and 11.10am trains from Paddington also provided connections from 'west to north' services. There was still the traditional early morning train from Leamington, now at 7.25am (Wolverhampton dep 9.00am), reaching Chester at 10.56am.

In contrast, there were three fast trains from Birkenhead to Shrewsbury providing connections for the 'north to west' services at 9.20am (Chester dep 10.00am), arriving at Shrewsbury at 11.06am.

The 11.40am and 2.35pm Birkenhead to Paddington trains also connected at Shrewsbury with trains for South Wales and the West of England.

On Sundays there was the usual overnight service, leaving Paddington at 12.05am, but that was all: there was no other train from Paddington to Birkenhead! The 11.10am (with RC) and 6.10pm trains terminated at Shrewsbury (arr 3.12pm and 10.50pm). A fast train from Shrewsbury to Chester, leaving at 4.30pm, provided a connection for the Cardiff to Manchester and Liverpool service (Chester arr 5.40pm — though Birkenhead was not reached until 6.54pm). The 10.35am from Wolverhampton (8.50am from Leamington), which made five stops before arriving at Chester at 12.24pm (Birkenhead arr 1.00pm) was the only other down service.

From Birkenhead there was still the 2.25pm to Paddington (Chester dep 3.40pm), arriving at Wolverhampton at 5.59pm after the RC had been attached at Shrewsbury (Paddington arr 9.20pm). The only other service to Paddington was the 8.00pm from Shrewsbury, via Oxford, due at Paddington at 2.35pm. The morning fast train from Leamington to Birkenhead was balanced by the 7.22pm from Birkenhead (Chester dep 8.00pm) to Leamington, arriving at Wolverhampton at 9.54pm.

1947

DOWN		RC	RC			RC
Paddington, dep	12.05am via Oxford	9.10am	11.10am	2.10pm	4.10pm	6.10pm
Wolverhampton, dep	4.40am	12.22pm	2.09pm	5.11pm	7.19pm	9.25pm‡
Wellington, dep	set down only	12.47pm	2.36pm	5.36pm	7.44pm	9.53pm
Shrewsbury, arr	5.31am	1.04pm	2.52pm	5.52pm	7.59pm	10.08pm
dep	5.46am	1.10pm‡	2.58pm	6.00pm	8.04pm	10.15pm
No of stops	3 (MO5)	3	3	4	3	3
Chester, arr	7.15am	2.24pm	4.11pm	7.14pm	9.15pm	11.31pm
Birkenhead, arr	8.06am	3.05pm	4.50pm	7.54pm	9.57pm	12.16am

‡   Restaurant Car detached
RC Restaurant Car

UP				
Birkenhead, dep	8.30am	11.40am RC	2.35pm	4.30pm
Chester, dep	9.15am	12.22pm	3.17pm	5.00pm
No of stops	3	4	3	3
Shrewsbury, arr	10.34am	1.37pm	4.26pm	6.12pm
dep	10.40am	1.45pm	4.35pm RC	6.28pm
Wellington, dep	11.00am	2.02pm	4.57pm	6.50pm
Wolverhampton, dep	11.27am RC	2.33pm	5.23pm	7.19pm
Paddington, arr	2.35pm	5.40pm	8.40pm	11.45pm via Oxford

RC Restaurant Car to Paddington

Above left:
The ultimate development of Churchward's two-cylinder 4-6-0s, the 'Counties' spent many years working north of Wolverhampton. No 1016 *County of Hants* is seen leaving Wrexham on a Birkenhead to Paddington express in the arctic conditions of the 1947 winter. There are still 201 miles to go — if travelling via Oxford!
Ian Allan Library

Left :
In very different conditions, No 1024 *County of Pembroke* heads a down Chester express north of Shrewsbury on a summer's day in June 1954.
Dr L. N. Owen

Right:
A Paddington to Barmouth Express leaving Ruabon, after reversal, in the charge of Mogul No 7310 and '2251' class 0-6-0 No 2209, on 9 August 1956. Both engines appear to have more than enough coal for the journey ahead!
B. E. Morrison

Above:
Super power for the job, '4700' class 2-8-0 No 4707 at the head of an up train standing in Wellington station in August 1935.   *H. Wheeller*

6 Coals to Birkenhead

'Carrying coals to Newcastle' may have been symbolic of a waste of time, but carrying coals to Birkenhead was an important function of the main line north of Shrewsbury. Freight traffic was the financial backbone of many railways, a number of the earliest lines owing their existence to the need to transport coal. Like the Stockton & Darlington, the NWMR was such a line; and between Ruabon and Chester it was coal rather than passengers which provided the greater part of the company's revenue.

However, ironically, in the long run it was not coal mined in the North Wales coalfield around Wrexham which provided the bulk of the mineral traffic, but that which originated far to the south in the valleys of Monmouthshire and South Wales. That coal was largely responsible for the promotion of the Newport, Abergavenny & Hereford Railway, which transported it northwards from Pontypool on its way to Birkenhead. Commencing in 1856, and using NA&HR engines throughout — by arrangement with the companies concerned — an ever-increasing procession of coal trains travelled northwards. Although the LNWR shared in this coal traffic, tapping the heads of the Monmouthshire valleys by means of its line from Abergavenny to Tredegar and Merthyr, the GWR gained the greater advantage.

At the same time, equally heavy trains of iron ore were hauled southwards to the foundries and iron works in South Wales, especially around Merthyr and Ebbw Vale; and, again, the LNWR shared in the business. Birkenhead was at that time one of the leading ports for the export of coal and for the import of iron ore. Mineral traffic was not the only concern of the port of Birkenhead, as during the 1840s and 1850s it was a major port for the importing of cattle, which required the regular running of special trains formed exclusively of cattle wagons. It was no wonder that both Paddington and Euston cast covetous eyes on the Birkenhead Railway with its profitable traffic!

In the 1860s such mineral traffic was worked from Birkenhead by the small-wheeled 0-6-0s of the '79' class and from Pontypool Road by the Beyer, Peacock 0-6-0s of the '322' class. A few years later, that work was being undertaken from Birkenhead by Armstrong's '927' class or 'Coal Engines', some of which were shedded there for many years. During the early years of this century, the double-framed 2-6-0s of the 'Aberdare' class began to appear on these duties, working from Pontypool Road shed, and these were followed a few years later by the '2800' class 2-8-0s. By 1921, it was Chester rather than Birkenhead which was responsible for such work, there being no less than eight of the '2800' class shedded there — as well as four 'Aberdares'.

General goods traffic over the main line was of considerable volume and importance, as it linked the south of England with Merseyside by way of Basingstoke and Westbury; this being something in which, for once, the LNWR was not in a position to compete! There was also the traffic originating in the great industrial centres of the

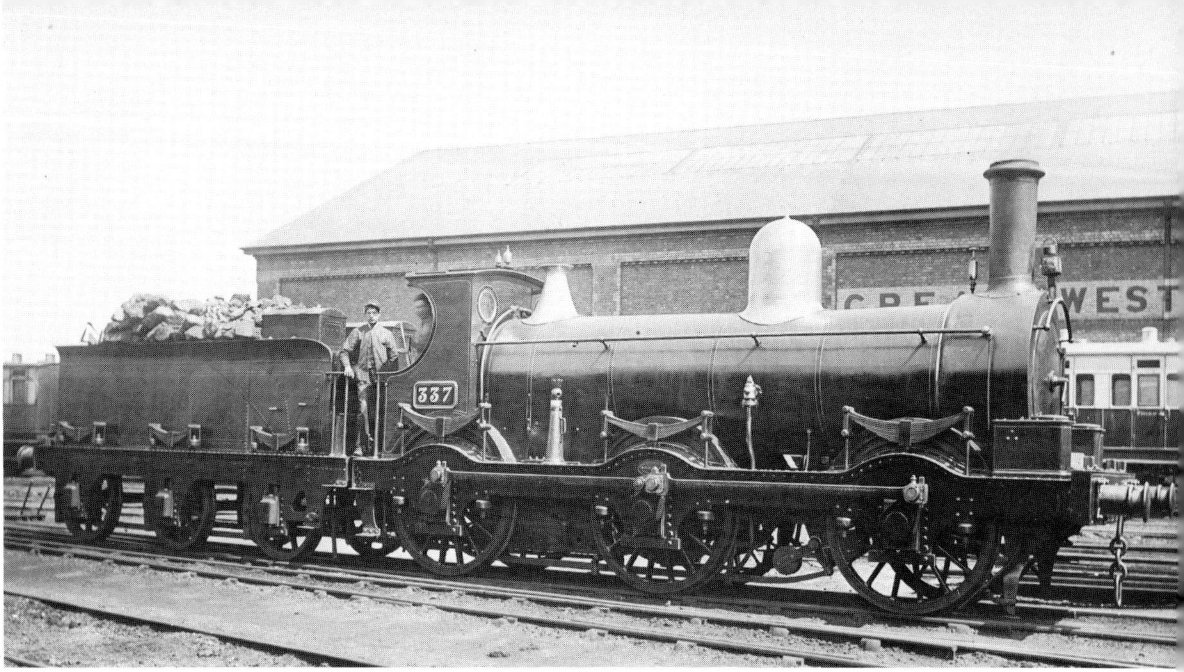

West Midlands, though here the GWR faced keen competition from the other company.

At Birkenhead itself, the GWR had no less than four stations or depots for goods traffic: Canning Street town goods station, Cathcart Street goods station and private wharf, and Morpeth Dock goods station were all on the extension line from the original terminus at Grange Lane; while on the later line leading to Woodside, the company owned Hinderton Road depot. In addition there were extensive coal tips serving the docks and situated on a line to the west of Canning Street goods station.

Ever concerned with Liverpool, the GWR had its own depots in that city, these being the South End depot (Chalenor Street), Manchester Dock depot (renamed after 1930 'Pierhead depot'), Stanley Dock depot and the Langton & North Dock depot. The company also had its own offices in James Street, near the Pierhead. Throughout the week, lorries came across the Mersey by ferry to Morpeth Docks goods station, bringing an average of 160 loads daily — 80 of which arrived after 5.00pm! The record for such traffic was 300 loads in one day! Morpeth Dock was reached over lines of the Mersey Docks & Harbour Board, from a junction near Canning Town goods station, and this must have been one of the most profitable leases ever made by the company. Some 400 wagons, carrying 1,700 tons of goods, were

Above:
The '322' class, 30 engines built by Beyer, Peacock & Co in 1864 and 1866, were among the most handsome and successful of their type. No 337, seen here at Chester after rebuilding at Wolverhampton in 1882, was originally No 325. It was not withdrawn until April 1919.
Ian Allan Library

Below left:
The first engines built specially for mineral traffic on the GWR were the 0-6-0s of the '79' class. No 84 is seen as fitted with a cab and Armstrong chimney after being 'renewed' at Wolverhampton in 1877. It was withdrawn in 1912.
Ian Allan Library

Right:
Armstrong's small-wheeled 'Coal Engines' of the '927' class were built in 1874. Most of them spent their entire lives working from either Birkenhead or Chester — where No 937 is seen after being rebuilt at Wolverhampton in 1891. It was withdrawn in February 1923, from Birkenhead.
Ian Allan Library

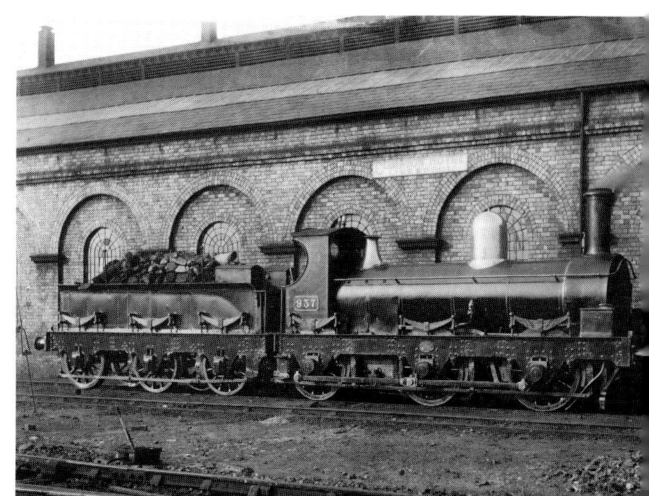

dispatched each day over the GWR's lines. Morpeth Dock also had a barge dock for goods which were 'barged' across the Mersey to and from ships anchored on the Liverpool side of the river.

The Special Instructions No 2 'Liverpool Goods Traffic' dated 1927 and issued from the Chief Goods Manager's Office, Paddington, stated: 'Traffic for shipment in lots of 32 tons and upwards can also be barged direct from Birkenhead to alongside ships in any of the Liverpool Docks, thus avoiding congestion that may exist on the quays'. One is surprised that the publicity experts at Paddington didn't use the slogan 'It's quicker by barge'! The importance attached to the Liverpool traffic may be estimated by the following instructions in the same publication: 'Every effort should be made by Agents and Canvassers to get traders to consign traffic by the Great Western Route via Chester and Birkenhead except as herewith mentioned, and the Liverpool Goods Manager should be notified of any consignments, to or from Liverpool, which have been carried part way only by this company, so that the consignees or senders may be canvassed for future traffic to be sent by the Great Western route throughout'.

These Special Instructions were accompanied by a large-scale map showing all the GWR goods

Above:
Nearly one third of the 'Standard Goods' engines, such as No 704, were to be found in the Northern Division. No 704 is seen in original condition, apart from the fitting of side sheets to the weather board, and prior to receiving number plates. Built in 1872, this engine was withdrawn from Taunton in March 1923. *Ian Allan Library*

Below:
Churchward's Moguls were equally at home on passenger or goods workings. No 4348 heads a class 'F' fast goods at Chester in the 1920s. *LGRP courtesy of David & Charles (17646)*

Above right:
2-8-0 No 3802 of the '2884' class, climbs from Saltney Yard to Saltney Junction, heading for Chester, 14 August 1954. *S. D. Wainwright*

Right:
Carrying class 'E' headlamps, 'ROD' class 2-8-0 No 3029 at the head of a Crewe to Oxley sidings express freight passing Ruckley sidings between Wellington and Wolverhampton, 4 August 1954. *G. Bannister*

depots and stations in Liverpool and Birkenhead. In addition, the company's staff were reminded of Special Form No 1372 which was to be used to report 'consignments which have passed by indirect or disadvantageous routes or by our competitors' routes throughout'. Nothing was left to chance: however, it was not made clear as to whether 'disadvantageous routes' were to be judged from the point of view of the customers or of the GWR!

A similar Special Instructions No 1 dealt with 'Manchester Goods Traffic' and revealed that the GWR had a goods station at Liverpool Road (though not mentioning that this was by courtesy of the LMS — late LNWR) and depots at Duncan Street Yard — 'for mineral and station to station

traffic' — and at Cross Lane, for cattle. In this instance, the Special Instructions concluded with the statement, 'Express train services are maintained in both directions'.

Until the early 1890s, the 9.50pm Paddington to Manchester was the fastest standard gauge goods train on the GWR running with a limited load of 27 wagons as far as Reading and 31 wagons beyond that point. However, it was a long way behind the fast goods trains run between London and Manchester by both the Great Northern and Midland Railways (whose routes were considerably longer) — though the LNWR does not appear to have offered a great deal of competition to the GWR in respect of speed.

As with the passenger engines, there was a slow

descent for the various classes of goods engines from working the principal trains to being relegated to local 'pick-up' work or shunting. Gooch's '57' class and 14 of the '131' class were very thoroughly 'renewed' at Wolverhampton and continued to work for many years afterwards. Apart from No 60 (at Reading), all the '57' class ended their days in the Wolverhampton Division (as the old Northern Division had become), and were to be found over the entire line from Leamington to Birkenhead. No 316, the last sandwich-framed 0-6-0 on the GWR, was withdrawn in November 1927 from Tyseley.

In 1911, Birkenhead's goods engines were '57' class Nos 57, 63 and 318; 'Standard Goods' Nos 428, 691 and 785; '360' class No 365; and 'Coal Engines' Nos 932, 934 and 937. It would probably be difficult to find another GWR shed at which, at that date, the entire allocation of goods engines consisted of double-framed 0-6-0s. No 937 probably spent its entire life working from Birkenhead, as it was still there in 1921 — when six of the seven 0-6-0s at that shed were still 'double-framers'!

From the mid-1880s, Dean's '2301' class supplemented and then supplanted the older double-framed engines of the 'Standard Goods' class; while by about 1920 the 'Aberdares' were to be found working between Oxley and Chester. In 1921 four of the class were shedded at Chester and two were at Croes Newydd. The GWR's other — and more normal — 2-6-0s of the '4300' class handled a considerable amount of main line goods traffic, as well as working a number of the express trains. The growth of vacuum-braked trains brought about an increase in the number of Moguls allocated to sheds such as Birkenhead, which had only two members of the class in 1921 but no less than 10 by 1938.

A shortage of locomotives during World War 1 led to the GWR being loaned engines by several other companies (though they, in turn, lent some 0-6-0s to the LNWR!). Among the engines received on loan were six of the Lancashire & Yorkshire's 0-8-0s, which worked for several months in 1918 between Pontypool Road and Chester (the allocation being shared between the

Below:
Unusual motive power, even for a fast goods train is provided by 'Armstrong' class 4-4-0 No 4171 *Armstrong* seen here on a down train near Chester in the mid-1920s — and making heavy weather of the task! *LGRP courtesy David & Charles (17647)*

Right:
Steam and smoke are also evident as 'Modified Hall' No 6986 *Rydal Hall*, in charge of a southbound express freight, tackles the climb up the bank near Gresford on 1 June 1964. *Derek Cross*

two sheds). According to the late Eric Mason, 'they even managed to win approval from the GWR men both for their comfortable footplates and ability to pull loads without being thrashed'. Praise indeed: one can imagine that the verdict would have been quite different had it been LNWR 0-8-0s, with their notoriously inadequate brake power, which had been borrowed! From 1922 onwards, the 'ROD' 2-8-0s of Great Central design and sold to the GWR by the Government, were also to be found on mineral or 'unfitted' goods workings from Pontypool Road and Wolverhampton.

The '2800' class 2-8-0s were well represented by 1921, with eight at Chester (though only one at Wolverhampton); however, by 1938 the only one shedded north of Oxley was working from Croes Newydd shed. In 1947 Oxley and Chester had three each, two were at Birkenhead and one at Shrewsbury. Although eight of the 'ROD' engines on loan from the Government were at Wolverhampton in 1921 — including Nos 6001, 6002 and 6003 — a presage of 'Kings to come'? — none were at any of the northern sheds. There were nine at Wolverhampton in 1938, three being at the 'passenger' shed at Stafford Road — despite these engines not being fitted with vacuum brakes! They were still at Stafford Road and Oxley in 1947, when there were also two at Croes Newydd. By that time, there were also World War 2 'Austerity' engines; two apiece at Chester and Croes Newydd, and a dozen at Oxley.

A regular traffic from the Banbury area was provided by ironstone trains bound for Stewarts & Lloyds, Wrexham, and the Brymbo steelworks. These trains were usually worked by 'Aberdares'

or by 'ROD' class 2-8-0s, though the '2800' class were also used. Following the demotion of the 'Aberdares' from long-distance workings they were allocated to such sheds as Chester and Croes Newydd, both sheds maintaining their allocation through the 1920s and 1930s. There were still four at Chester and two at Croes Newydd in 1938, as in 1921; though by 1947 only No 2662 remained, at Chester. Following the withdrawal of many of the 'Aberdares' during the 1930s, some of the GWR's largest tank engines, the '7200' class 2-8-2Ts, were shedded at Oxley for working northwards over the main line and to Crewe. There were four of them at Oxley in 1938, while by 1947 there were no less than nine.

During the war years, a number of LMS '8F' class 2-8-0s, built at Swindon and working on the GWR, were to be found north of Wolverhampton, as were some of the US Army 2-8-0s which were on loan to the company for a year or two. Among other wartime visitors were LNER 'O4' class 2-8-0s, identical in design to the 'ROD' class: some of these visitors were returning to former haunts, as they had worked on the GWR while on loan between 1919 and 1922. Also on loan from the LNER were a number of ex-North Eastern 0-6-0s of Class J25 , whose presence was due to the transfer to the War Department of nearly 100 of the 'Dean Goods' engines.

Despite the number of 'Dean Goods' which had been drafted to the former Cambrian Railways' lines, the number shedded north of Wolverhampton increased between 1921 and 1938.

Above:
Majestic in repose outside Chester shed, Churchward's magnificent '4700' class 2-8-0 No 4702. These engines were regularly used on fast vacuum-fitted goods trains such as the well-known Birkenhead Meat Train. September 1937.
Ian Allan Library

In the former year, there were three at Shrewsbury, two at Chester and one at Birkenhead, with about a dozen at Wolverhampton: in 1938, Shrewsbury had 10 (largely on acount of through workings to and from the former Cambrian system via Welshpool); there were still two at Chester, and Croes Newydd had four; while six were at Oxley and one was at Stafford Road. However, by 1947 only No 2513 at Chester remained; thus that shed had both the remaining 'Dean Goods' and the remaining 'Aberdare'.

Some of the work formerly done by the 'Dean Goods' was taken over by the new '2251' class, a number of which went to the northern sheds during the 1930s. By 1947 the collection of 'Dean Goods' formerly to be found at Shrewsbury had been replaced by seven of the newer engines — one of which, No 3217, was very new indeed, having been built during the last week or two of the GWR's existence.

Throughout the war years Birkenhead retained its allocation of about a dozen Moguls, at that time the largest engines shedded there. By 1947 there were also two 'Granges', Nos 6819 *Highnam Grange* and 6878 *Longford Grange* and No 4704, one of Churchward's mighty and truly magnificent mixed traffic 2-8-0s of the '4700' class, second only to the 'Kings' in size and power. When first built in 1922-3, there had been three of these engines at Oxley, for working the night express goods trains between Wolverhampton and London, but in those days the '4700' class — like the 'Kings' — were not allowed to work north of Wolverhampton. At Birkenhead, No 4704's special duty was the working of the well known Birkenhead Meat Train.

At the turn of the century, the Birkenhead Meat Train consisting of 30-40 vans, vacuum-braked throughout and with a fitted brake van, ran non-stop to Oxley Sidings (86 miles) and then to Acton (139 miles), where it passed on to the Metropolitan Railway for Smithfield; the average speed being 40mph. In 1905 this train was being given a clear run from Shrewsbury to Madeley Junction, being advised to the latter box from the Abbey Foregate box: passing the latter point at 6.25pm it took only 23min to cover the intervening 15¾ miles.

Passenger engines were used throughout between Birkenhead and Acton. In 1911, Birkenhead shed had two 'Bulldogs', Nos 3416 *Frank Bibby* and 3453 *Dominion of Canada*, specially for this duty: by 1921 these had been replaced by two Moguls, Nos 4308 and 5327. During the interwar years, Old Oak Common 'Stars' and 'Castles' were often used, with '4700' class 2-8-0s appearing on occasions.

Although the GWR's premier express passenger trains received the most publicity and were endowed with a definite glamour — though the main line north of Wolverhampton never had anything remotely resembling the 'Cheltenham Flyer'! — the company's excellent publicity department ensured that the public, not least those with commercial interests, were also informed about the excellence of the fast goods trains which served most parts of the system. Indeed, the GWR had been among the pioneers of such services way back in an age when most other companies were content to run mammoth trains of loose-coupled wagons at what were often monumentally slow speeds! First introduced in 1905, between Acton and Bristol, the number of such trains increased rapidly. However, meat and fish trains were much older, among them being the 'Birkenhead Meat'.

Inventive as ever in such matters, the company's staff lost little time in naming the more important trains, though there were some historic names dating back to the broad gauge days for a few trains. Thus the ingenuity which in earlier days had christened the 'Flying Dutchman' and the 'Zulu' (not to mention the celebrated broad gauge goods train, the 'Tip') produced a collection of titles — some of which found their way into the company's publications — for what were officially 'Vacuum fitted and Accelerated E Freight'.

Birkenhead vied with Paddington for second place in the 'league table' of named freights, Bristol and Wolverhampton having by far the largest number — about 15 each. The Birkenhead 'namers' were:

3.35pm	Birkenhead to Smithfield	'The Meat'
6.05pm	Birkenhead to Pontypool Road	'The Feeder'
8.20pm	Birkenhead to Paddington	'The General'
9.05pm	Birkenhead to Cardiff	'The Mersey'
10.50pm	Birkenhead to Bordesley Junction	'The Birmingham Market'
11.35pm	Birkenhead to Oswestry	'The Cambrian Pioneer'
9.10pm	Bordesley Junction to Birkenhead	'The Shipper'
6.50pm	Bristol to Birkenhead	'The Farmer's Boy'
9.10pm	Paddington to Birkenhead	'The Northern Flash'
2.45am	Wolverhampton to Birkenhead	'The Northern Docker'
12.45am	Wolverhampton to Birkenhead	'The Flying Skipper'

There were also the following trains which ran over at least part of the main line north of Wolverhampton:

9.45pm	Cardiff to Saltney	'The Spud'
7.45pm	Manchester to Bristol	'The Mon'
8.42pm	Manchester to Wolverhampton	'The Early Riser'
11.40am	Southall to Crewe	'The Grocer'
7.35pm	West Depot to Manchester	'The Lancashire Lad'
4.00am	Wolverhampton to Crewe	'The Northern Exchange'
8.35pm	Worcester to Crewe	'The Sparagras'

While some of these names had an obvious connection with either the places concerned or the traffic conveyed, others appear to defy any attempts to explain their origin or significance!

Many of these trains ran over the Shrewsbury to Chester section of the main line; though some travelled via the Crewe Branch, which always carried a considerable amount of freight traffic. In 1927, up to eight trains ran in each direction on weekdays between Oxley Sidings and Crewe — all under either 'E' or 'F' headlights; while the 4.00am Oxley to Manchester Accelerated 'E' took a GWR engine to Manchester (Liverpool Road), returning at 8.42pm SX. Two trains ran to and from the Stourbridge area: the 8.05pm Cradley to Crewe 'F', via Wombourne, was the return working of the 4.00am Crewe to Stourbridge Junction; while the 1.50am MX (MO 4.25am) Stourbridge Junction to 'Crewe F' returned as the 8.35pm from Crewe.

There were also regular workings between Worcester and Crewe: the 9.45pm Worcester to Crewe Vegetables 'Accelerated E' returning as the 9.35pm from Crewe; 2.10pm SXRR Littleton & Badsey Fruit (Passenger Rated) 'C' and 8.35pm SX Worcester to Manchester, via Wombourne, 'C' (SO 8.35pm to Crewe 'E'). Southbound, there was the 12.50am MX Crewe to Worcester, via Wombourne, 'E' and the 10.50am MXRR Crewe to Worcester 'Returned Veg and Fruit Empties and Coaching Stock' 'C' (which also covered ECS for Shrewsbury and Birmingham).

From the West of England there was the SXRR Broccoli Train to Crewe 'C', and from the London area a daily Southall to Crewe 'Margarine Train' also running under 'C' headlights. Two 'F' trains ran from Oxley to Crewe, and there was also a 5.30pm RR Perishables; while from Crewe there was the 9.50am Crewe to Oxley 'F' Goods and three others shown as RR.

The Cradley and Stourbridge trains were worked by 'Dean Goods' 0-6-0s, though the MO 4.25am from Stourbridge Junction required an engine of Group D (probably an 'Aberdare'): in all other instances where the Engine Group was indicated it was 'D', under which both the 'Aberdares' and '4300' class 2-6-0s were included. The Worcester to Manchester through goods was worked only as far as Crewe; while the 4.30pm Littleton & Badsey to Crewe Fruit changed engines at Oxley.

A through goods service from Bristol to Manchester had been introduced as early as August 1871, long before there was any prospect of the Severn Tunnel being constructed and two years before the first GWR standard gauge track was laid in Bristol. This apparently impossible feat was achieved by using the Midland's line from Bristol to Gloucester, and then the Gloucester to Hereford line which had been 'narrowed' in July 1869, after which the train continued over the joint line to Shrewsbury! At first, reversal as well as change of engine was required at Gloucester, but from April 1873 the train regained GWR metals at Standish Junction (the Swindon to Gloucester line also having been 'narrowed') instead of using the Midland line into Gloucester.

Unlike some other lines, the GWR was a great believer in using tank engines; not least in using 0-6-0 saddle tanks for all manner of duties — including main line passenger trains and long-distance coal trains! A wide variety of engines, the earlier ones having double frames, but mostly built at Wolverhampton, was to be found at every shed north of Wolverhampton. There were also a few of the Swindon-built engines of the '1076' class, just as a number of the '1016' class were to be found in the South -- which appears to have been an insistence on variety for its own sake!

Although a few of the large 2-6-2Ts worked from Croes Newydd for some years — Nos 3163 and 3172 being there in 1921 — most of the coal traffic from the North Wales coalfield was worked

Below left:
No 1802 was one of the last of the '645' class to be built, in 1881. Fitted with pannier tanks in 1922, it was superheated in 1925 — but the elements were later removed. Seen here at Chester in July 1935, it was withdrawn two years later. *W. Potter*

Above:
No 1773 of the later '655' class, seen here at Chester in July 1935, reveals that there were differences in chimneys as well as in cabs and bunkers! Built as a saddle tank in 1893, No 1773 became a pannier tank in 1927 when it was also superheated (again, the superheater was later removed). It was not withdrawn until 1950.
W. Potter

by 0-6-0Ts, many of which had been rebuilt as pannier tanks. In the mid-1920s something much larger and more powerful appeared, when a few of the new '5600' class 0-6-2Ts were sent north, Oxley, Shrewsbury, Croes Newydd and Chester all having engines of that class. A few of the large 2-6-2Ts were also to be found working from Birkenhead: Nos 3145, 3169 and 3185 being there in 1911; while 10 years later Nos 3131, 3133 and 3186 were at that shed.

Despite the advent of the new '5700' class 0-6-0PTs, which were used on a wide variety of duties, a gradual infiltration of the old Northern Division by the older Swindon-built engines continued. A few of the '1854' class had arrived by 1920, as had a few of the '2721' class, at that time the newest and most powerful 0-6-0Ts on the GWR. An 'odd man out' was No 1824, at Croes Newydd, and the only member of the '1813' class to be found anywhere north of Oxford.

However, in 1938 the majority of the older engines were still of Wolverhampton origin; even without taking into account the numerous smaller engines of the '1901' and '2021' classes. Only Croes Newydd was immune from invasion by the newer '5700' class engines, which were too heavy for most of the local branch lines; though there were four of the lighter-weight engines of the '7400' class for the Bala to Blaenau Festiniog line. In 1947 nearly 50 of the '5700' class were in use, including one at Croes Newydd; while No 9408 of the new '9400' class was at Oxley.

The immediate postwar years saw the wholesale withdrawal of many of the old pannier tanks, some of which had been 'reprieved' from the scrap line in 1939. By 1947, none of the older engines remained at Birkenhead or Chester, though nine were still to be found at Croes Newydd and its sub-sheds; while one remained at Shrewsbury and there were two at each of the Wolverhampton sheds. For the first time in 70 years, none of the Wolverhampton-built large 0-6-0Ts was to be found at Wellington.

There remained the smaller engines of the '1901' and '2021' classes; not least at Birkenhead for working over the dock lines and at Croes Newydd for the colliery branches. By 1947, all four engines at the latter shed were of the '2181' class which had been rebuilt from the '2021' class in 1939-40. Having been given increased brake power for working on steep gradients, they had also — in typical GWR fashion — been given new numbers. However, their work remained the same, as they ensured that coal mined in the North Wales collieries reached the main line. A century after the opening of the first section of the NWMR it was still engaged in 'carrying coals to Birkenhead'.

7   The Shropshire Branches

Wellington to Nantwich (The Crewe Branch)
The origins of the Crewe branch were two small companies, the Nantwich & Market Drayton Railway and the Wellington & Drayton Railway, the northern section of nearly 11 miles being the first to be constructed. Opened on 20 October 1863, and worked by the GWR as an isolated line to which access was only possible over the LNWR line from Shrewsbury, it did not become GWR property until 1897. On 16 October 1867, the southern section, 16 miles long, was opened; and the GWR henceforth described the combined line as being the Crewe branch. The Wellington & Drayton Railway was absorbed by the GWR in 1896.

The initial service over the Nantwich & Drayton Railway consisted of four trains each way between Crewe and Market Drayton on Weekdays only, with a fifth train each way on Wednesdays. The line was of double track and there were three stations, at Market Drayton, Adderley and Audlem, though all trains also called at the LNWR station at Nantwich. The service was worked from Market Drayton, where a single-road engine shed and a 35ft diameter turntable were provided.

Below:
When antiquity characterised the Crewe branch! Seen at Wellington on 28 April 1922, 'Stella' class No 3204 was the latest in a long line of 2-4-0s to work on that line. Built in 1885, No 3204 was withdrawn in 1929 — only two years after being superheated. *H. G. W. Household*

Right:
The largest and most important station between Wellington and Nantwich was Market Drayton, the junction for the North Staffordshire's line from the Potteries. A late 19th century view of the station, looking from the south. *Lens of Sutton*

Below right:
From the turn of the century: the station staff at Audlem pose somewhat self-consciously for the camera! *Lens of Sutton*

Audlem had a goods shed, but at Adderley there was only a siding and a loading bank. On the southern section, the station at Crudgington, Peplow, Hodnet, and Tern Hill all had a goods

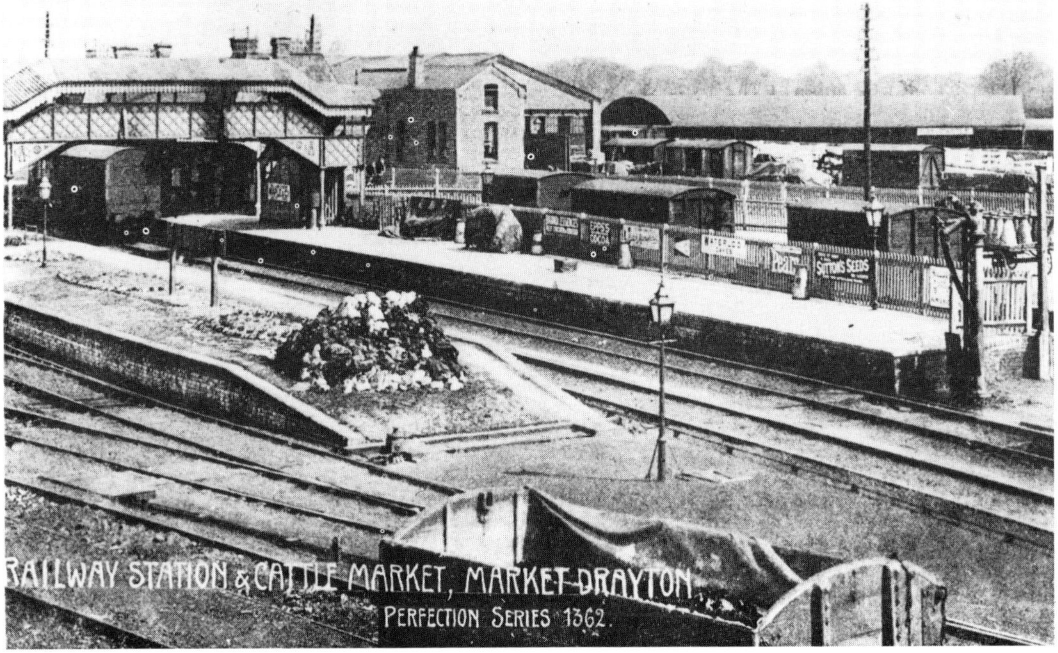

RAILWAY STATION & CATTLE MARKET, MARKET DRAYTON
PERFECTION SERIES 1362.

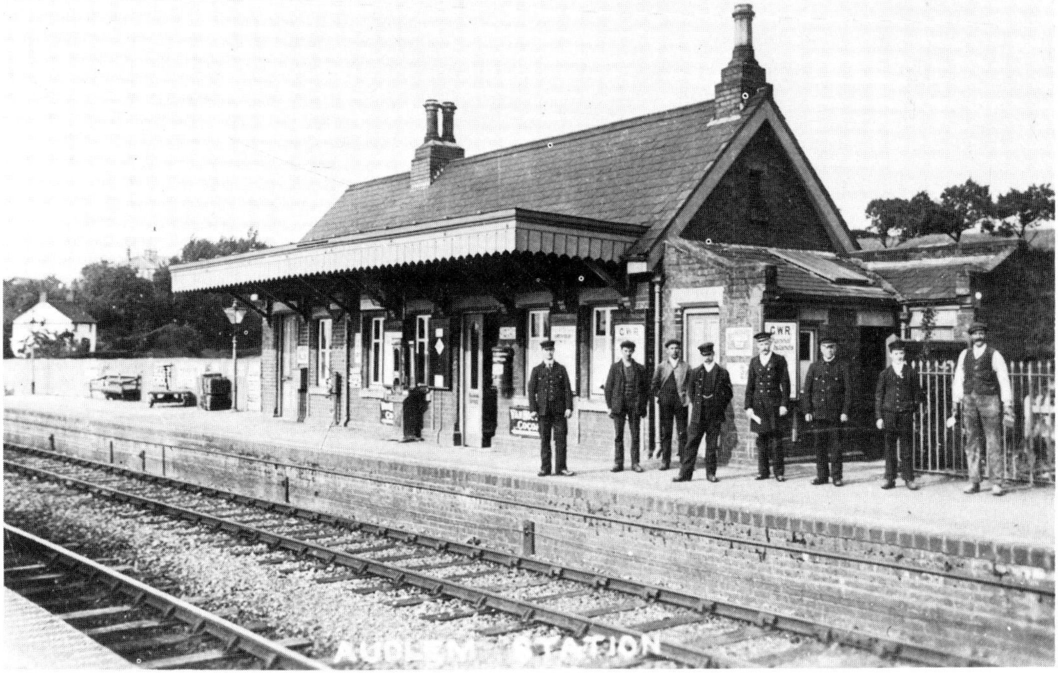

AUDLEM STATION

shed and sidings; while all stations had a signalbox. Again, the line was of double track.

The layout at Market Drayton was much more extensive, especially after 1870 when the North Staffordshire Railway's branch from Silverdale was opened. Run-round facilities were provided behind the down platform, together with a number of additional sidings; the goods shed and yard being situated on the up side, adjacent to the engine shed. The latter was handed over to the NSR in February 1870, though it is probable that the shed at Wellington did not come into use until 1876. However, the GWR continued to use the shed at Market Drayton, and in 1889 they installed a larger, 40ft diameter, turntable. At a later date, the lines behind the down platform were extended to join the main line to the south of the station, thus making that platform into an island.

The GWR also shared with the LNWR the ownership of an engine shed at Gresty Lane, Crewe. Why the LNWR had any interest in the premises is a mystery. Gresty Lane was of the most modest proportions, having only two roads and no turntable — so that GWR engines had to use that at the neighbouring LNWR shed at Crewe South. Opened in about 1870, possibly when the NSR took over the ownership of the shed at Market Drayton, it was extended in 1913 to provide accommodation for about half-a-dozen engines, which was the number allocated in 1921, when there were four 4-4-0s and two 0-6-0s; though in later years it housed only one or two.

The Crewe Branch was the very last section of double track on the GWR to be worked by 'time interval', a practice which continued until August 1891. There was little alteration made to the

Above left:
Unusual motive power for a GWR train leaving the citadel of the former LNWR, Crewe station. The '3571' class 0-4-2Ts were normally to be found working between Chester and Birkenhead. Note the vintage carriage stock c1930. *W. Potter*

Bottom left:
Among the 2-4-0s whose last years were spent working on the Crewe branch were several members of the '3232' class. No 3234, seen at Crewe station on 15 March 1925, had a few more miles to run before being withdrawn in December of the following year. *W. Potter*

Above:
The Crewe branch was an important route for freight traffic. Having joined the main line at Wellington, No 2802 heads a Crewe to Stoke Gifford fast freight — which will travel via Wombourn — as it passes through Codsall station in March 1954. *G. Bannister*

stations during this century, though a number of halts were opened during the 1930s: most unusually, in this instance, they were not connected in any way with the introduction of auto-trains.

The GWR used the line to provide through services to and from Manchester (London Road) from 1867 onwards, which replaced the short-lived service via Bushbury Junction and the LNWR. For many years these included TC between Padding-ton and Manchester, for the benefit of Reading, Oxford and Banbury passengers; and there was also a through service in each direction between Worcester and Crewe. The former service was withdrawn as a consequence of the opening of the new route via Bicester; while the latter was cut back to terminate at Crewe, and latterly ran in the northbound direction only. The line was also used for various special workings as well as for the considerable number of goods trains mentioned in Chapter 6.

Which engines were used on the isolated Market Drayton to Nantwich and Crewe section between 1863 and 1867 is not known, but they are likely to have been tender engines from one or other of the absorbed lines. With the opening of the line from Wellington it is likely that some of the Wol-verhampton-built 2-4-0Ts were used — shedded either at Market Drayton or at Crewe — as several of the class were employed in their early days on local and branch duties from Wellington.

However, during the 1870s the first of what was to be a long succession of 2-4-0 tender engines took over these duties; and for the next 60 years such engines were to become a familiar sight — and eventually a hallowed tradition — on the Crewe branch. The first of these were three of the '481' class; Nos 12, 19 and 20 built in 1869, the only engines of the class to be sent to the Northern Division. At the beginning of this century some of the double-framed engines of the '149' class were working on these duties, which they continued to do until withdrawn: Nos 150, 151, 154, 155 and 156 all ended their lives on the Crewe branch before being withdrawn between 1916 and 1920.

Above:
When this photograph of 2-6-2T No 4409 was taken at Wellington, in August 1935, engines of that class were a recent introduction to the line between Wellington and Craven Arms. A truly incredible mixture of carriages on this train!
H. Wheeller

Below:
Despite being quite a small station, Horsehay & Dawley had at least three members of staff when this view of the station was taken — probably at the turn of the century — to be used as a Christmas card! The white 'T' diamond on the station building is most unusual, as there was also the usual one on the signalbox. *Lens of Sutton*

Above right:
Much Wenlock undoubtedly possessed the most imposing station buildings to be found between Wellington and Craven Arms, though the station never had more than a single platform.
Lens of Sutton

The Wolverhampton-built engines of the '111' class do not appear to have been used on this line, though No 3231 of the similar '3226' class worked to Crewe during its last years when shedded at Wolverhampton. Other engines which ended their lives on the branch included No 810, the last of the '806' class, and some of the '3232' class, Nos 3234 and 3240 being at Wellington in 1921. Several of the small-wheeled, double-framed engines of the

'3201' or 'Stella' class also spent their last years on these duties: Nos 3204 and 3507 were working to Crewe in 1922-23, and No 3505 was also on that line prior to withdrawal in 1929; while Nos 3201, 3205 and 3518 were withdrawn from Wellington between 1931 and 1933. Finally, there were some of the '3206' or 'Barnum' class, which lasted until 1937: among the last survivors were Nos 3221 (withdrawn August 1933), 3223 (withdrawn May 1936) and 3210 and 3222 (withdrawn March 1937), while No 3220 was shedded at Wellington as early as 1921.

By the early 1920s 4-4-0s were also working regularly one the Crewe branch. In 1921 the allocation at Gresty Lane was 'Duke' class No 3267 *Cornishman* and 'Bulldogs' Nos 3314 *Mersey*, 3362 *Albert Brassey* and 3400 *Winnipeg*; though there were none shedded at Wellington, whose only tender engines were three 2-4-0s, Nos 3220, 3234 and 3240. In the 1930s there was a succession of 4-4-0s, comparable with that of the 2-4-0s in earlier years: among these were 'Duke' class No 3266 *Amyas*, 'Bulldogs' Nos 3309 *Maristow* (withdrawn 1934), 3405 *Empire of India* (withdrawn 1937), 3414 *Sir Edward Elgar* (withdrawn 1938) and 3445 *Flamingo* (which was transferred to Stafford Road prior to 1938), and the hybrid 'Dukedog' No 3208 *Earl Bathurst*. The last 4-4-0 to be shedded at Wellington was 'Bulldog' No 3417 *Lord Mildmay of Flete*, which was withdrawn in 1948.

The eventual successors to the long line of four-coupled engines were the large 2-6-2Ts of the '5100' and '5101' classes, a number of which were shedded at Wellington from the mid-1930s onwards. A couple of these engines, together with a '5700' class pannier for the branch 'pick up' goods, were normally at the Gresty Lane shed in the postwar days. Goods engines in former days were in keeping with the succession of 2-4-0s used on the passenger trains. In 1921, No 363 of the '360' class and No 312 of the '131' class — two of the oldest 0-6-0s on the GWR — were the only goods engines shedded at Crewe.

The GWR made brave efforts to persuade the public that this was no mere branch line, despite the local nature of the passenger service for the most part — though it was a valuable route for a number of long-distance goods trains. Thus Manchester always figured in equal prominence with Wellington and Crewe at the head of the timetables; in 1902, the service was 'Wellington, Crewe and Manchester, with connections to the North Staffordshire line, via Market Drayton'. The Wellington to Crewe section was only a small part of the table, with times being shown to and from the more important stations between Paddington and Birmingham, stations on the West Midland Section, and places such as Bournemouth and Portsmouth via Basingstoke. Full details were

also given for connections between Manchester and Huddersfield, Halifax and Leeds, while they were also given from Crewe to the principal stations on the main line to Carlisle, Edinburgh and Glasgow (the latter by both the Caledonian and Glasgow & South Western routes!).

Although reduced to half a page by 1932, details were still given for Paddington and main line stations to Birmingham, Worcester, Stourbridge Junction and Dudley; and for Portsmouth, Bournemouth and Southampton. Although no mention was now made of connections northwards from Manchester or Crewe, full details continued to be given for what was now described as the 'North Staffordshire District'. In 1947 there was simply the service between Wellington and Crewe, with connections to and from Manchester, but no mention was made of any stations south of Wellington.

Through the years the service consisted of about half-a-dozen trains in each direction between Wellington and Crewe on Weekdays, with one or two on Sundays, and one or two additional trains to and from Market Drayton. Apart from some through trains between Manchester and the south coast during the inter-war years, all trains stopped at every station.

In 1902, trains left Wellington at 7.38am, 9.50am, 11.40am, 2.55pm, 5.43pm and 9.02pm for Crewe, and at 1.50pm for Market Drayton. The 11.40am was the 9.55am Worcester to Manchester (London Road) through train; while the 2.55pm had TC from Paddington to Manchester detached from the 9.45am train to Birkenhead at Wellington. The 5.43pm conveyed TC from Birmingham to Manchester which were 'slipped' at Wellington by the 2.10pm Paddington to Birkenhead corridor train. Finally, the 9.20pm was a through train from Wolverhampton to Crewe.

The first departure from Crewe was at 6.55am (there being no connection from Manchester), and this arrived at Wellington at 8.13am to connect with the 6.15am. Birkenhead to Paddington Corridor Train (Wellington dep 8.28am). The 9.40am had TC from Manchester (dep 8.35am) to Paddington (arr 3.30pm) conveyed to Wolverhampton by the 8.15am from Birkenhead and taken forward by the 9.30am Birkenhead corridor train. The next train was not until 1.03pm this being the 11.50am from Manchester with TC both for Worcester (arr 5.05pm at Foregate Street, attached to the 3.45pm Wolverhampton to Hereford) and for Paddington (arr 7.37pm) — the latter being attached to the 12.00 noon train from Birkenhead. The remaining trains, at 3.10pm, 5.10pm and 6.50pm, all terminated at Wellington; while the 8.05pm ran only as far as Market Drayton (arr 8.40pm). The latter station was thus the terminal point for trains from Wellington and Crewe for which there was no return working!

On Sundays there was an early morning train from Crewe at 7.25am, which connected with the

7.50am Shrewsbury to Paddington (arr 3.50pm); and an evening train from Wellington at 7.40pm, with connection from Crewe for Manchester, but none from Wolverhampton.

In 1932, the summer timetables provided a service of seven down trains and six up trains. Departure times from Wellington were at 7.35am, 9.50am, 11.46am, 3.16pm, 3.40pm, 5.50pm and 9.30pm. The 11.46am was the 9.42am from Worcester to Crewe; while the 3.16pm was the 'Bournemouth & Portsmouth to Manchester Express', calling only at Market Drayton, and arriving at Crewe at 4.00pm (Manchester arr 4.50pm), being TC detached at Wellington from the Bournemouth to Birkenhead train. All trains had connections for Manchester.

Departure times from Crewe were at 6.25am, 9.35am, 11.00am, 1.00pm, 5.50pm and 6.40pm, all except the first having a connection from Manchester. The 11.00am consisted of the TC from Manchester (dep 10.10am) to Portsmouth and Bournemouth, the only stop being Market Drayton, which were attached to the Birkenhead train. The 9.35am continued to Wolverhampton, but there was now no through service to Worcester. Except on Saturdays, the 8.10pm ran to Market Drayton, but was extended to Wellington SO.

The service on Sundays now had two trains in each direction. However, neither of the trains from Wellington, at 9.15am and 5.40pm, had good connections from Wolverhampton, though both had excellent connections from Shrewsbury! In contrast, both trains from Crewe — at 6.45am and 11.00am — had connections both for Wolverhampton and for Shrewsbury. The 3.20pm to Market Drayton returned to Wellington at 4.25pm to connect with the 2.55pm Birkenhead to Paddington.

By 1947 there had been a reduction to five trains each way between Wellington and Crewe, with two return workings between Wellington and Market Drayton. Departure times from Wellington were 7.30am, 10.00am, 12.00 noon, 1.00pm (to Market Drayton), 2.50pm (also to Market Drayton), 5.55pm and 9.25pm; the 12.00 noon

being the 9.35am Worcester to Crewe. Departure times from Crewe were 6.05am, 9.30am, 12.54pm, 5.10pm and 8.40pm: however, none of these continued to Wolverhampton. The trains from Market Drayton to Wellington were at 8.00am and 3.50pm; thus there was either an ECS working in each direction between Wellington and Market Drayton or the 1.00pm did not return until 8.00am, the following morning!

There were still two trains in each direction on Sundays; at 8.15am and 10.55pm from Wellington, and at 6.40am and 8.35pm from Crewe. The late evening train from Wellington provided a connection from the 6.10pm Paddington to Shrewsbury; similarly, the 6.40am from Crewe connected with the 8.00am Shewsbury to Paddington. With considerable ingenuity, however, the timetable arranged for the 8.35pm from Crewe to arrive at Wellington 12min *after* the departure of the last train to Wolverhampton and Birmingham, at 9.27pm!

Wellington to Much Wenlock and Craven Arms
Like the Crewe branch, the line from Wellington to Marsh Farm Junction, north of Craven Arms, was not opened throughout for several years. Associated with this line was the much older branch from Madeley Junction to Lightmoor, the S&BR's only branch line, which had been opened on 1 June 1854.

When the Severn Valley Railway (worked by the former West Midland Railway) was opened from Hartlebury to Shrewsbury on 1 February

Below left:
No 3623 is on the mid-morning train from Craven Arms as it stands in Presthope station on 17 November 1951; however, the headlamp code suggests that it is a light engine! *G. Bannister*

Above right:
On the western extremity of the line from Wellington, No 4401 runs into Rushbury station on its way to Craven Arms on 5 April 1951, not long before the passenger service was withdrawn. The absence of passengers waiting to board the train reveals the reason for closure. The signalman is carrying the staff for the final five-mile section to Marsh Farm Junction. *Dr L. N. Owen*

Right:
Somewhere along the line! A delightful study of No 4401 and the branch train, in spring sunshine, somewhere in Shropshire. Yet again, according to the headlamp No 4401 is running as a light engine: something which appears to have been a regular practice on this line! *Dr L. N. Owen*

Above:
The notice board which said it all! No 1412 with the Oswestry auto-train stands in the bay at Gobowen on 21 July 1951. *R. C. Riley*

1862, a short branch was also opened from Buildwas to Much Wenlock. The latter was the Much Wenlock & Severn Junction Railway — whose title was almost as long as its original line of 3½ miles. Both these lines were on the west side of the Severn, to the east of which were two branches to Lightmoor; the line from Madeley Junction, about 4 miles long, and the Wellington & Severn Junction Railway, 4½ miles long, from Ketley Junction. The latter line was opened on 1 May 1857, but until 1 July 1861 it was worked by the Coalbrookdale Iron Co. The GWR then took it over and opened it to passenger traffic.

Two short sections were opened simultaneously on 1 November 1864 to connect Buildwas and Lightmoor. The Much Wenlock Railway opened just under a mile of line from Buildwas Junction to Coalbrookdale, and the GWR opened a section 1½ miles long from Lightmoor to Coalbrookdale. There was thus a through line from both Wellington and Madeley Junction to Much Wenlock. West of the latter town, the section of nearly three miles to Presthope came into use on 5 December of the same year, and the final 11 miles from Presthope to Marsh Farm Junction were opened on 16 December 1867: both sections of line were the property of the Much Wenlock Railway, which was absorbed by the GWR in 1896. The distance from Wellington to Craven Arms was 28 miles.

The only engineering works of any magnitude were the Royal Albert Bridge across the Severn at Buildwas and the Coalbrookdale Viaduct, which was 264yd long. There was also a short tunnel, 207yd long, at Presthope. The extension from Much Wenlock to Presthope involved by-passing the original terminus, the new station being sited nearer to Buildwas. However, the old premises continued to be used as the goods station and as the site of the small engine shed.

All the stations, at Much Wenlock, Presthope, Longville, Rushbury and Harton Road, had only a single platform and none, except Much Wenlock, served a community of any size, so that the potential passenger traffic can never have been large. Apart from Much Wenlock and Presthope (where there was considerable traffic from the Lilleshall lime works), the facilities for handling goods traffic were also limited. In the 1930s three halts were opened in a forlorn attempt to increase passenger traffic — long after a steam railmotor service, introduced in 1905 between Shifnal and Craven Arms, had been abandoned! Much Wenlock, Presthope and Rushbury stations had signalboxes. Passing loops were provided at Much Wenlock and Presthope; while in later years the loop siding at Harton Road was also used for 'running round'.

The Much Wenlock Railway joined the Severn Valley Railway to the south of Buildwas Station, where it had its own platform at a higher level and on a sharp curve. Between Buildwas Junction and Lightmoor the line was of double track, the remaining sections being single track. Coalbrookdale and Lightmoor stations had two platforms and a signalbox. No passenger trains used the latter station in 1902: in 1932 and 1947 it was shown in the timetables as 'Lightmoor Platform'.

Between Lightmoor and Ketley Junction there were stations at Horsehay & Dawley (where extensive sidings served the Horsehay Iron Works); at Lawley Bank, where there was merely a single platform without any sidings, though a signalbox was provided; and at Ketley, where further sidings were situated. Three halts were opened between 1932 and 1936. The former S&BR branch from Madeley Junction had only one station, Madeley; this was originally Madeley Salop, and in later years Madeley Court, and had one platform, a crossing loop, and a couple of goods sidings with a goods shed. Though there were a number of private sidings to collieries and works, no signalbox was provided. The passenger service was always exigious and was finally withdrawn on 21 September 1925, the line having previously been closed to passengers in 1915 — only to have the service restored in July 1925! It remained open for goods traffic, especially in connection with the Buildwas power station.

For many years the engines employed were the usual 0-4-2Ts and 0-6-0STs; though one or two of the Wolverhampton-built 2-4-0Ts may have worked on the line from Wellington in its earliest days, and 'Metro' class 2-4-0Ts may also have been used during the early 1900s when one or two were shedded at Wellington. The maximum loads for passenger trains in either direction were 96 tons for 0-6-0s and only 72 tons for the 0-4-2Ts, there being a rather nasty climb at 1 in 40 through Farley Dingle.

From a note found inside an old Block Telegraph Register at Madeley Junction signalbox, dated 1905, it is possible to identify one of the 0-6-0STs in use at that time — 'Presthope engine 2706. Tubes leaking badly. Send another tank engine to B'was at once. H. Creed'.

In 1935 the small-wheeled 2-6-2Ts of the '4400' class were introduced, five of the 11 engines of that class being shedded at Wellington for the remaining years of the GWR. As they were allowed to take 125 tons, they represented a considerable advance in power over the 0-6-0Ts; though the traffic, especially beyond Much Wenlock, rarely required the provision of more than three carriages. One or two of the '4400s' were always sub-shedded at Much Wenlock; in 1921 the allocation was 0-4-2T No 557 and 0-6-0ST No 1531, in 1938 it was one '4400' class and an 0-6-0PT, and in 1947 it was two 2-6-2Ts.

In 1902 there was only one train from Wellington to Craven Arms — and this was not until 4.30pm! The only other trains to Craven Arms were the 6.25am 'mixed' from Much Wenlock and the 9.30am from Shifnal (Wellington passengers travelled to Shifnal on the 8.55am Wellington to Paddington train). Presthope had an additional train from Wellington at 3.05pm, and there were three trains to Much Wenlock — at 11.08am, 7.05pm and 9.10pm (the latter being 'mixed'). There were also two trains from Shifnal to Much Wenlock, at 4.05pm and 5.47pm. The latter was a through train from Wolverhampton (dep 5.18pm) and returned from Much Wenlock at 7.20pm as far as Buildwas, where it again reversed and then continued over the SVR to Shrewsbury (arr 8.23pm). The only other train was the 8.32am from Wellington to Buildwas; though on Saturdays the 12.45pm Wolverhampton to Shifnal was extended to Coalbrookdale, returning at 1.45pm to Solihull.

There were two trains from Craven Arms to Wellington, at 8.15am and 6.38pm, and a mixed train 11.40am to Much Wenlock (arr 1.05pm) replaced on Mondays by a passenger train at 11.35am (Much Wenlock arr 12.23pm). Between Much Wenlock and Wellington there was also two trains, at 7.30am and 1.45pm, while the 3.05pm Wellington to Presthope returned at 4.15pm. The only trains to Shifnal were the 8.45am from Madeley (for which were was no outward working) and the 2.50pm from Much Wenlock, which connected at Shifnal with the 1.20pm Leamington to Oswestry, and returned at 4.05pm; though on Saturdays there was also the 1.45pm Coalbrookdale to Solihull. Finally, there was the 3.05pm from Horsehay (Dawley) to Wellington, another train with no outward working.

The service on Sundays consisted of one train in each direction between Wellington and Much Wenlock, leaving Wellington at 9.35am and returning from Much Wenlock at 6.55pm.

In 1905 a railmotor service, using steam railcars, was introduced between Shifnal and Craven Arms. This commenced from Much Wenlock, where a railcar was shedded, with the 8.10am to Shifnal, followed by the 9.25am Shifnal to Craven Arms and the 1.55pm Craven Arms to Shifnal (arr 3.32pm). However, as there was also a 2.10pm railmotor departure from Shifnal to Much Wenlock, a second railcar was required: this was probably provided from Wolverhampton, with the two railcars working on alternate days and spending alternate nights at Much Wenlock.

Below:
Headquarters of the Cambrian Railways, Oswestry formerly also had a much more modest station belonging to the GWR. The latter premises may be seen on the right, after becoming Oswestry Goods station. 'Dean Goods' No 2408 is on an up goods, while some choice vintage carriage stock is on the left. 6 August 1935.   *H. Wheeller*

Above:
An unusual engine to find on an auto-train, domeless-boilered 0-6-0ST No 2124 at Oswestry in 1931. The former GWR station is behind the train. Note the revenue-earning water tank!
J. A. G. H. Coltas

Below:
Two of a class which became synonymous with Oswestry and the former Cambrian line, 'Dukes' Nos 3268 *Chough* and 3263 (formerly *St Michael*) at Oswestry in 1936. Note the numerous differences between the two engines.
C. R. L. Coles

There were considerable differences in the service in 1932, as the Madeley branch no longer had any passenger trains. There were now two trains from Wellington to Craven Arms, at 8.17am and 3.00pm, as well as the early morning train from Much Wenlock (at 6.30am). The 8.17am replaced the 8.32am to Buildwas, while the 3.00pm had formerly been the 3.05pm to Presthope: the 4.30pm formerly the only through train from Wellington to Craven Arms, ran only as far as Buildwas, and there was now a 5.25pm train to Harton Road. There were four trains to Much Wenlock, with a fifth on Saturdays (at 10.25pm).

There were three trains from Craven Arms to Wellington, at 7.50am, 11.05am and 4.30pm; while the 5.25pm Wellington to Harton Road returned at 7.05pm. There were four Much Wenlock to Wellington trains, with a fifth on Saturdays (the 8.00pm being the outward working of the 10.25pm from Wellington), and two from Coalbrookdale, at 6.25am and 5.05pm (the latter being the return working of the 4.30pm Wellington to Buildwas). There were now no trains on Sundays.

In 1947 the two Wellington to Craven Arms trains ran at the same times as in 1932, as did the 6.30am from Much Wenlock. Five trains ran from Wellington to Much Wenlock, which had another SO (at 10.00pm) and one from Ketley (where there was a large industrial firm) SO at 12.45pm. The early morning train to Wellington now commenced from Buildwas at 6.00am, instead of from Coalbrookdale, as did the later afternoon train (dep 4.55pm) — for which there was no outward working. The three Craven Arms to Wellington trains were at similar times to those in 1932; but there were now only three trains from Much Wenlock, the evening train running nearly an hour later on Saturdays (SX 7.05pm: SO 8.00pm). As in 1932, there were no trains on Sundays.

Goods workings over the branch in 1927 were as follows: 6.45am Wellington to Presthope (arr 10.00am), returning at 10.15am to Hollinswood (arr 12.57pm), Hollinswood (dep 1.50pm) to Lightmoor and Wellington (arr 5.33pm); 11.25am Wellington to Much Wenlock (arr 2.03pm) — RR Presthope and return: Much Wenlock (dep

3.50pm) to Wellington (arr 6.49pm); 8.35am Much Wenlock to Craven Arms (arr 10.50am): Craven Arms (dep 11.30am) to Much Wenlock (arr 2.20pm) RR Buildwas and return; 8.05am Hollinswood to Buildwas (arr 11.00am) return to Shifnal (arr 1.07pm): Shifnal (dep 2.45pm) to Buildwas (4.45pm/6.40pm) return to Shifnal (arr 7.47pm).

Gobowen to Oswestry

The short branch, not quite 2½ miles long, from Gobowen to the market town of Oswestry was opened on 23 December 1848. Originally intended to be only the initial section of a much longer branch to Llanymynech, it was left to the Oswestry & Newtown Railway (later part of the Cambrian Railways) to proceed beyond Oswestry. For the first 13 years the branch provided the only rail communication between Oswestry and the rest of the country, Oswestry station serving as the railhead for Mid Wales. However, in the summer of 1861 the Oswestry & Newtown Railway was opened for traffic, with its own premises adjacent to those of the GWR, and this was to affect the branch very considerably.

Initially, the volume of traffic — especially sheep and cattle-passing over the branch increased; but the construction of further lines in Mid Wales and to Whitchurch, in 1864, created a through route between the LNWR and Aberystwith which resulted in the diversion of a considerable amount of passenger and goods traffic which had formerly passed over the branch to Gobowen and the GWR main line. The LNWR were assiduous in their attentions to the interests of the Cambrian Railways. The formation of the Cambrian Railways resulted in Oswestry becoming the headquarters of the company, where its main offices and locomotive works were situated. In consequence, the GWR found itself in an inferior position, despite having been established there since 1848.

The amalgamation of the Cambrian Railways with the GWR on 1 January 1922 had considerable consequences, and partly reversed the decline which had set in nearly 60 years previously. The GWR station at Oswestry was closed to passenger traffic, though retained as the goods station, and the branch trains henceforth used the former Cambrian station which was improved and enlarged. The engine shed at Gobowen was also closed. There was a great increase in the volume of goods traffic passing over the branch, as the GWR had no intention of routing such traffic via Whitchurch and the newly-formed LMS! The only other development was the opening of Park Hall Halt ('For Hospital') during the 1920s.

As the S&CR possessed only tender engines, apart from two 0-4-0Ts used on the colliery

Above:
Welsh cattle must have been small! An unusual short cattle wagon (of GWR origin) at Oswestry in 1935. *H. Wheeller*

branches around Wrexham, and no turntable was provided either at Gobowen or Oswestry, the first engines to work the branch must have always worked tender-first in one direction. From the late 1860s the '517' class 0-4-2Ts were employed for over 60 years until the advent of the '4800' class in 1934. In 1901, No 547 was at Gobowen for the branch passenger trains, and '850' class No 2010 and '655' class No 2711 were the shunting and goods engines; however, one of the 0-6-0STs must have also been used for passenger duties, as the timetable required the use of a second engine at times. In 1921, the allocation was auto-fitted 0-4-2T No 829 and 0-6-0ST No 1773.

Although the use of auto-trains became well-established during the 1920s, these were integrated into the service which covered the main line as far north as Chester. Many of the branch trains continued to be formed of ordinary stock, as were those trains which ran between Oswestry and Chester or Shrewsbury.

In 1902 the service was as follows:

Gobowen to Oswestry: 23 trains + 1 WO 7.10am to 10.40pm.
Oswestry to Gobowen: 22 trains + 1 WO, 1 ThuSO 7.00am to 10.20pm
(10.40am, 1.48pm and 6.30pm ex-Oswestry; 11.43am ex-Gobowen were mixed)

The first train being from Oswestry, and the last being from Gobowen, meant the running of a light engine or empty train twice daily. At 6.11pm trains were shown as simultaneously arriving at and departing from Gobowen — despite the branch being single track! There was no Sunday service; however, the timetables stated that an omnibus ran from Gobowen to Oswestry (New Swan Inn) at 10.55am and 6.20pm, the times from Oswestry being 9.40am and 5.00pm — 'meets up and down trains at Gobowen'.

Service in 1932:
Gobowen to Oswestry: 25 trains + 1 WO 7.20am to 10.55pm (11 auto-trains)
Oswestry to Gobowen: 26 trains + 1 WO 7.40am to 9.50pm (11 auto-trains)

The engine(s) now being shedded at Oswestry, this still entailed a light engine or empty stock working twice daily. Several auto-train workings were through trains to or from Ruabon, Wrexham or Chester. The WO trains were the same return working from Wrexham as in 1902. There was still no Sunday service.

Service in 1947:
Gobowen to Oswestry: 25 trains 7.10am to 11.15pm (7 auto-trains)
Oswestry to Gobowen: 25 trains 7.35am (to Ruabon) to 10.28pm (7 auto-trains)

There was now a service on Sundays, with seven trains from Oswestry and eight from Gobowen. The 6.45am from Gobowen was an auto-train — the only one in either direction — providing a connection from the 12.15am overnight train from Paddington which called at Gobowen at 6.05am 'to set down passengers only'. Why passengers for Oswestry were required to 'cool their heels' on Gobowen station for 40min on winter mornings was known only to the timetable compilers! The first ordinary train was the 9.45am from Oswestry and the last was at 8.52pm from Gobowen. There was a long interval between the 11.47am from Gobowen and the 4.15pm from Oswestry, as the service was provided solely to connect with the up and down main line trains.

As well as the transfer trips between Oswestry and the main line, there were also through goods trains between Oswestry and Birkenhead and Saltney. In 1927, the Saltney to Oswestry train arrived at 11.35pm (SO 12.00 midnight) and returned MX at 1.00am; while the Birkenhead Goods arrived at 1.58am and returned at 3.50am MX (Sundays dep 3.30am). The latter ran to Oswestry under 'Accelerated E' lights, but returned as an 'F' train — as was the Saltney Goods. On Wednesdays — Market Day at Oswestry — there was a cattle train to Oxley (dep 7.15pm) and another RR to Chester (dep 6.50pm) under 'E' headlights. There was also a 5.15am working from Oswestry on Sundays, 'Engine, Van and Guard' worked by '2.40am Whitchurch Engine and Guard', which returned an hour later — 'Conveys Van Third with Passengers and Newspaper traffic off 12.10am Paddington and any wagons for Central Wales Division arriving at Gobowen by late Goods ex-Birkenhead Saturday'. Perhaps the travellers on Sundays mornings in 1947 with their auto-train were not so badly off after all!

Below:
While the wagons may not be short, the train certainly is! 0-6-0PT No 5745 passes over Dark Lane crossing on the Stirchley branch on its way to Randlay's Brickworks. *G. Bannister*

8   Moor and Mountain

Westwards from Ruabon, through Llangollen, Corwen and Bala, to Dolgelley and Barmouth, and north-westwards from Bala to Blaenau Festiniog, ran two of the GWR's most scenic routes. Moor and mountain were the dominating features, though the Ruabon to Barmouth line followed the course of two river valleys — the Dee and Wnion — for much of its length. Rhobell Fawr, Aran Benllyn and Aran Fawddwy towered over the line between Bala and Dolgelley, while Cader Idris dominated the horizon ahead when running from Drws-y-Nant towards the coast. At the beginning of this century, a travellers' guide declared, 'The Rail Route from Bala to Festiniog is probably the wildest and most impressive hour of rail travelling in England and Wales'.

Ruabon to Dolgelley and Barmouth
Although the main line from Chester reached Ruabon as early as November 1846, it was not until December 1861 that the Vale of Llangollen Railway was opened from Llangollen Line

Right:
Llangollen station, looking towards Ruabon. The unusual staggered platform awnings, with two separate sections on the up platform should be noted. 1949.
LGRP courtesy David & Charles (19235)

Below:
0-4-2T No 4828 and auto-trailer No 178 at Ruabon in 1938. Most of the working life of this trailer was spent on the line between Ruabon and Barmouth. *H. Wheeller*

Junction, half-a-mile south of Ruabon Station, to Llangollen, a distance of 5½ miles. The opening brought the railway to Acrefair and Trevor, situated in an area of brickworks and chemical firms, as well as to Llangollen which was just becoming a favoured holiday centre for exploring the beauties of the upper reaches of the River Dee. The station at Llangollen was built so close to the river, that the down platform was almost on its bank. The opening of the Vale of Llangollen Railway, which was always worked by the GWR, though not absorbed until 1896, resulted in the closure of Llangollen Road Station situated on the main line between Cefn and Chirk.

Following the absorption, the line was doubled as far as Llangollen Goods Junction — nearly half-a-mile beyond the passenger station — in 1898. The extensive goods yard adjoined a canal wharf, and three very long sidings were provided specially for stabling carriages from Bank Holiday Special trains.

Having been the terminus of the original SBBR line, Ruabon had both an engine shed and a turntable; though the shed had been closed when the line was absorbed into the GWR in 1854. However, the building appears to have continued in use as a stabling point for several years — probably until 1865 when a shed was opened at Corwen — while the turntable remained in use and was later replaced by one of larger diameter on a different site.

Above:
0-4-2T No 1416 with a rather mixed train leaving Berwyn with its impressive black and white timbered station building.
J. L. Smith collection per R. C. Riley

Left:
Llangollen station signalbox. *S. C. Dent*

Right:
Corwen station, with 0-6-0ST No 772 (one of the few engines of the '645' class never rebuilt as a pannier tank) on a down train. The awning on the up platform was of a most unusual 'cantilever' pattern. *J. L. Smith collection per R. C. Riley*

Below:
Bala Junction station, with 0-6-0s Nos 3200 and 3201 double-heading a train from Ruabon to Barmouth. 1951. *R. C. Riley*

The 10 miles of the Llangollen & Corwen Railway (also absorbed by the GWR in 1896) were opened to a temporary terminus at Corwen on 8 May 1865. The LNWR had already reached the town, their line from Denbigh having been opened to a temporary terminus in September 1864. On 1 September 1865 a permanent station, used by both companies, was opened. A large two-road engine shed, owned jointly and used by both the GWR and the LNWR, was opened to the west of the station, a 45ft diameter turntable being provided. There were two signalboxes, East and West, situated half-a-mile apart.

The single track line between Llangollen and Corwen had stations at Berwyn, Glyndyfrdwy and Carrog, and there was a short tunnel to the west of Berwyn. Berwyn's station building was a noble edifice, the upper storey being in the traditional black and white style; while Carrog's massive building might well have been converted from a centuries-old manor house — despite the absence of any local community of any size. For much of the way, the railway followed the course of the River Dee.

Corwen remained the terminus for only 14 months, as on 16 July 1866, the Corwen & Bala Railway (also absorbed in 1896) was opened as far as Llandrillo, a distance of 4¾ miles, with an intermediate station at Cynwyd. The final section was opened to Bala (near the later Bala Junction), a distance of just over six miles, on 1 April 1868, there again being only one intermediate station, Llanderfel, to the west of which there was a fairly long tunnel. As before, the railway followed the course of the River Dee.

Four months later, on 4 August, the entire

18¼ miles of the Bala & Dolgelley Railway were opened, the line passing from the valley of the Dee and over the mountain watershed to join the valley of the River Wnion at Garneddwyn, the maximum gradient being 1 in 58. Stations were opened at Llanuwchllyn, Drws-y-Nant and Bontnewydd. Thus the line was completed, the 44½ miles having been constructed by no less than four companies! Although the three eastern companies were not absorbed until 1896, the Bala & Dolgelley was taken over by the GWR as early as 1877.

In 1862 the Aberystwyth & Welsh Coast Railway had been authorised to construct a line from Barmouth Junction to Dolgelley, intended as a defensive action against the GWR's proposed advance westwards from Ruabon. By the time the first section as far as Penmaenpool — aptly described as being 'in the middle of nowhere' — had been opened in July 1865, the A&WCR had become part of the Cambrian Railways and it was the latter company who extended the line to meet the Bala & Dolgelley's line just to the west of Dolgelley station on 21 June 1869.

No engine shed was provided either at Bala or Dolgelley, despite the latter station being nearly 30 miles from Corwen and an engine always being required to remain there overnight! Corwen's shed remained responsible for almost the entire working of the services until the opening of Croes Newydd in 1902, though a few duties were worked from Chester and from the shed opened at Bala in 1882.

In 1882 the Bala & Festiniog Railway was opened from Bala Junction. A new Bala station, much nearer to the town, was opened on the new line. Although shown on maps of the GWR system, Bala Junction did not appear in the timetables. In 1902, Bala station times were shown for trains arriving from *Corwen* in the down direction with departure times for Festiniog and Dolgelley; however, although there were arrival times from the latter stations in the up direction, the departure times were stated to be for *Ruabon*! The omission of any reference to Bala Junction, except in a footnote stating 'passengers to and from Corwen and Dolgelly have to change at Bala Junction by most of the trains' meant that a casual reading of the timetables gave the impression that trains always left Bala before they arrived there!

In 1922 the Cambrian Railways, with its Barmouth Junction to Dolgelley branch, became part of the GWR. The stations at Penmaenpool, Arthog and Barmouth Junction now appeared in the GWR's timetables for the first time — though the service had always been described as being to Dolgelley and Barmouth. Also acquired was the two-road engine shed at Penmaenpool, annexed by the Wolverhampton Division to become a sub-shed to Croes Newydd and used for the over-night stabling of engines working to Barmouth from Ruabon, as well as being the home of the tank engine used on local trains between Barmouth and Dolgelley. There was no turntable, the triangle at Barmouth Junction being used to turn engines. The ex-Cambrian line was improved by the strengthening of the track and bridges, though Penmaenpool remained the only crossing place, the work being completed by 1927.

Corwen shed's importance declined after Croes Newydd was opened, and in April 1927 it ceased to be used by the GWR. A number of improvements had been made in the latter years of the 19th century, including the provision of a larger, 55ft diameter, turntable. Among the earlier occupants

Below left:
'Bulldog' class 4-4-0 No 3358 *Tremayne* at Bala Junction in August 1935, this being one of the regular engines on the Chester to Barmouth trains at that time. *H. F. Wheeller*

Below:
Making sure that all can understand. A bilingual warning notice at the up end of the island platform at Bala Junction, 1953. *Real Photos (K1865)*

Below right:
Mogul No 6316 heads a down passenger train at Garneddwyn in 1959. This halt was unusual in having a passing loop with two platforms and a signalbox. *E. Frangleton*

of the shed would probably have been one or two of the 2-4-0Ts built at Wolverhampton in 1864-66. Their successors were 0-6-0STs and '517' class 0-4-2Ts, the latter eventually being replaced by some of the '3571' class. Six of these engines, Nos 3572, 3574, 3575, 3578, 3579 and 3580, were shedded at Corwen in 1901, when there were also seven 0-6-0STs, Nos 654, 758, 768, 773, 775, 1501 and 1560, all belonging to the '645' or '1501' classes. In 1921 the allocation consisted of 'Stella' class 2-4-0 No 3505, 'Dean Goods' 0-6-0 No 2431, and '1501' class 0-6-0STs Nos 1514, 1515, 1533 and 1557.

The GWR never made up its mind about the correct description of the line. Although in later years the majority of trains ran to and from either Wrexham or Chester, no indication of this was given in the table headings! In 1902 it was 'Corwen, Bala, Blaenau Festiniog, Dolgelley and Barmouth', Ruabon not being mentioned! In 1932 it had become 'Llangollen, Dolgelley, Barmouth and Pwllheli' (the Bala to Blaenau Festiniog line now being shown in a separate table), still without any mention of Ruabon. By 1947 it had, at last, become 'Ruabon, Dolgelley and Barmouth'; however, Ruabon's inclusion was at the expense of any mention of connections or through trains from Wrexham and Chester.

In 1902 the down service commenced with the 6.55am Corwen to Bala (arr 7.22am) which returned at 7.50am as a through train to

Above:
A little further down the line, Wnion Halt was much more typical of such stopping places on this and many other lines. The waiting passengers would appear to have a Mogul apiece!
LGRP courtesy David & Charles (19215)

Birkenhead (arr 10.07am) which did not stop at Chester. The remainder of the service consisted of the following trains: To *Dolgelley* — Ruabon dep 7.50am (no connection for Barmouth); 9.42am; 3.15pm TC from Paddington (dep 9.50am) to Barmouth (arr 5.50pm) making only four stops between Ruabon and Bala Junction; 4.10pm TC from Birkenhead (dep 2.55pm) to Barmouth (arr 6.55pm) — except on Saturdays this was the last train to Dolgelley; SO 7.10pm: *To Llangollen*

12.05pm: *To Corwen* — 1.35pm and 6.10pm TC from Birkenhead (dep 4.45pm): *To Bala* — 7.10pm SX and 10.25pm TC from Oswestry (dep 9.00pm) to Bala (arr 11.15pm).

The up service commenced with the 6.55am from Llangollen (Ruabon arr 7.13am) and the 7.50am Bala to Birkenhead (Ruabon arr 9.05am). The first train from Dolgelley was at 8.35am (Ruabon arr 10.46am), followed by the 10.35am TC Barmouth to Paddington (arr 5.20pm) taken forward by the 11.47am from Birkenhead (Ruabon arr 12.35am); 3.05pm TC Barmouth to Birken-head (arr 7.01pm) and TC Llangollen to Wolverhampton (arr 6.50pm) taken forward by the 4.15pm from Birkenhead (Ruabon arr 5.05pm); and 7.00pm to Chester (arr 10.30pm) (Ruabon arr 9.42pm). Other trains were — *Corwen* dep 1.50pm (Ruabon arr 2.40pm) and *Bala* dep 5.00pm (Ruabon arr 6.25pm, SO extended to Wrexham arr 6.36pm).

The service on Sundays was confined to the late afternoon and evening. It commenced with the 4.55pm Corwen to Ruabon (arr 5.42pm), connecting with the 9.00am Paddington to Birkenhead

100

and the 4.20pm Birkenhead to Knowle & Dorridge, and returning at 6.05pm to Corwen (arr 6.50pm); and it concluded with the 6.55pm Dolgelley to Chester (arr 9.55pm).

Apart from the 3.15pm from Ruabon, with TC from Paddington to Barmouth, which took 1hr 45min, the typical journey time between Ruabon and Dolgelley in either direction was 2hr 10min. Six engines were needed daily for passenger work, the workings being shared between Chester and Corwen sheds, with engines being exchanged between the sheds on alternate days in some instances.

The use of tank engines on the Dolgelley line ended when 2-4-0 tender engines of the '3201' ('Stella') class were sent north to Chester and Croes Newydd sheds. In 1921 there were five at Chester, while Croes Newydd and Corwen had one each. A few of the 'Barnums' were also employed on these duties in the 1920s and 1930s and these remained until Nos 3211 and 3216 were withdrawn from Croes Newydd in December 1934 and May 1935 respectively. The 'Stellas' had disappeared from the line by the late 1920s.

Until the completion of the track improvements in 1927, 'Blue route' engines were not allowed to work over the line: they were then allowed to work as far as Barmouth Junction, but it was not until 1929 that they were permitted to work into Barmouth itself. This introduced further double-framed engines to the line, in the form of 'Bulldogs' and 'Aberdares'. No 3314 *Mersey* was the first 'Bulldog' to reach Barmouth Junction (on 17 August 1928); while the first 'Aberdare' to work a goods train over the line was No 2617. 'Bulldogs'

Above left:
The fireman on Mogul No 6339 prepares to collect the train staff for the ensuing single line section, a recurring task on the line from Llangollen to Barmouth.
LGRP courtesy David & Charles (6630)

Left:
Yet another Mogul. No 6303 heads an up ballast train passing through Dolgelley station — with a lovely assortment of station barrows on the platform. *P. L. Wells*

Above:
Reflections! 0-4-2T No 4812 propels the Dolgelley to Barmouth auto-train near Arthog on an idyllic day. 13 August 1935. *H. Wheeller*

Right:
A bilingual warning notice near Arthog. It was ironic that the locally promoted Cambrian Railways used only English for their warning notices: it was left to the GWR to provide warnings in Welsh from 1922 onwards!
H. Wheeller

used in the 1930s included Nos 3342 *Bonaventura*, 3358 *Tremayne*, 3359 *Tregeagle*, 3369 *David MacIver*, 3423 (not named) and 3450 *Peacock*.

However, the use of the tank engines did not cease entirely, as '3600' class 2-4-2Ts and '5100' 2-6-2Ts were used on occasions during the early 1930s. It was the '4300' class Moguls which gradually took over the greater part of the work, being used both on passenger and on goods trains. There were three Moguls at Croes Newydd in 1938 (when the only 'Bulldog' was No 3450 *Peacock*), but by 1947 the number had increased to 10, and there was also one of the light-weight 4-6-0s of the 'Manor' class, No 7817 *Garsington Manor*.

Early in this century, steam railmotors had been used on a local service between Wrexham and Llangollen, and the last was not withdrawn from this work until April 1934: a similar local service between Corwen and Ruabon ceased in July 1915.

Above:
Prior to the advent of the '4800' class, the '517' class 0-4-2Ts such as No 1160 — seen here at Barmouth (with trailer No 178) — worked all the auto-train services between Ruabon and Barmouth, with some trips along the coastal line as far north as Harlech. *Lens of Sutton*

Below:
Cut down to size by the mist-covered peaks of Cader Idris and the wide stretches of the Mawddach estuary, a Barmouth to Ruabon train headed by a 'Manor' crosses Barmouth Bridge. *R. E. Vincent*

Above right:
The GWR ran to Barmouth long before 1922. Tender-first, a 'Dean Goods' heads a very mixed train out of Barmouth c1900. *Ian Allan Library*

A few months after assuming control of the former Cambrian Railways, the GWR introduced a steam railmotor service between Dolgelley and Barmouth in August 1922 (with some workings to and from Dyffryn-on-Sea), Steam Railcar No 39 being used. In July 1927 this was replaced by an auto-train, and by the summer of 1932 the service included three return trips along the coast line to Harlech or Portmadoc. Later in the 1930s, auto-trains with '4800' class 0-4-2Ts were used between Ruabon and Llangollen or Bala, and were integrated into the auto-service between Chester or Wrexham and Oswestry.

The service in the 1932 summer timetables was a great improvement on that provided in 1902. Most trains now ran to and from Chester or Wrexham, while some ran beyond Barmouth to give through services to and from Pwllheli. Most trains still called at all stations and halts — a number of the latter having been opened during the 1920s.

Down service 1932

To Barmouth — 7.43am (7.20am Chester); 9.41am (9.00am Chester); 1.30pm (12.00 noon Birkenhead to Barmouth and Pwllheli) (TC Paddington dep 9.10am) calling only at Llangollen, Corwen, Bala Junction and Dolgelley; 3.05pm (1.08pm Birkenhead to Barmouth and Pwllheli) (TC Paddington dep 11.10am); 5.20pm FSO (4.20pm Chester); 6.35pm (5.55pm Chester): also SO 11.00am (TC Birkenhead [dep 9.35am] and Manchester [Exchange] [dep 8.55am] to Pwllheli).

To Bala — 12.30pm (12.25pm Wrexham) and 4.00pm: *to Llangollen* — 5.20pm FSX (4.20pm Chester); also auto-train workings between Ruabon and Llangollen or Corwen. A road motor car leaving Corwen at 3.45pm ran to Dolgelley (arr 6.00pm) via Bala (arr 4.45pm).

Up service, 1932

This still commenced with an early morning train from Llangollen (dep 7.26am) which ran to Chester (arr 8.54am), followed by the 7.30am Bala to Birkenhead (arr 9.57am).

From Barmouth — 7.40am to Ruabon (arr 10.00am); 10.25am SX (9.00am Pwllheli to Birkenhead TC (arr 1.57pm) and Paddington TC (arr 5.05pm); 10.20am SO (TC Pwllheli and Barmouth to Birkenhead, arr 1.37pm); 10.32am SO (TC Pwllheli and Barmouth to Paddington, arr 8.05pm); 12.10pm FSO (10.30am Pwllheli TC to Birkenhead (arr 3.22pm) and Manchester (Exchange) (arr 4.07pm); 1.18pm to Wrexham (arr 3.38pm); 2.40pm to Chester (arr 6.00pm) 7.15pm to Chester (arr 10.19pm).

From Bala — 3.00pm to Wrexham (arr 4.54pm) and 5.45pm to Wrexham (arr 7.27pm). *From Llangollen* — 6.05pm FSX to Ruabon (arr 6.23pm).

There were now three trains in each direction between Ruabon and Llangollen on Sundays; leaving Ruabon at 3.10pm, 4.20pm and 6.35pm, and arriving back from Llangollen at 4.07pm, 6.07pm and 8.16pm. The first of these was the 2.35pm from Chester, while the last terminated at Chester at 8.55pm. The 4.07pm arrival at Ruabon connected with the 2.55pm Birkenhead to Paddington (arr 9.00pm); while the 6.55pm from Ruabon provided a connection from the 5.55pm fast train from Shrewsbury. Corwen was served by

Above:
Foretelling the end of steam? A permanent way department internal combustion-engined trolley at Barmouth in 1938. *H. Wheeller*

Below:
Bala station in the 19th century, with '517' class 0-4-2T No 539 on a train of period carriages. The road vehicles are also worthy of note, especially the horse bus. *Lens of Sutton*

a road motor, which connected at Llangollen with the first and last trains. There were two journeys each way, leaving Corwen at 2.50pm and 6.50pm and arriving back at 4.24pm and 8.45pm. Only the 2.50pm from Corwen served any of the intermediate stations, the other journeys running 'non-stop'.

The Dolgelley and Barmouth 'local' auto-train service, with its three trips along the coast line, commenced at 8.50am and concluded at 10.30pm, between which times the engine and train covered just under 250 miles, which must have been one of the highest daily totals for any auto-engine, especially for one of the old '517' class 0-4-2Ts.

Down service 1947
To Barmouth — 7.15am (7.03am Wrexham); 9.31am (8.40am Chester) TC Pwllheli; 2.10pm (1.15pm Chester) TC to Pwllheli; 3.45 fast train to Barmouth and Pwllheli, connection from 11.10am Paddington to Birkenhead; 7.00pm (5.50pm Chester), connection from 2.10pm Paddington to Birkenhead.

To Llangollen — 7.00am; 8.25am auto-train (the only train in either direction to call at Sun Bank Halt!) and 5.07pm (4.20pm Chester); *to Bala* — 1.20pm auto-train (1.05pm Wrexham); 4.00pm (3.45pm Wrexham) and 9.34pm (9.20pm Wrexham).

Up service 1947
Still commencing with an early morning train from Llangollen (dep 7.35am) to Chester (arr 8.52am), followed by 7.18am Bala to Chester (arr 9.19am) and 9.10am auto-train Llangollen to Chester (arr 10.41am).

From Barmouth — 7.18am to Ruabon (arr 9.43am), connection from Pwllheli (dep 5.50am), connection with 9.30am Birkenhead to Paddington (arr 2.35pm); 10.10am to Chester (arr 1.21pm), connection from Pwllheli (dep 7.45am), connection with 11.40am Birkenhead to Paddington (arr 5.40pm); 1.12pm to Wrexham (arr 3.35pm), fast train connecting with 2.35pm Birkenhead to Paddington (arr 8.40pm) TC Pwllheli (dep 11.30am) to Wrexham; 2.35pm to Chester (arr 6.05pm), connection from Pwllheli (dep 12.45pm),

connection with 4.20pm Birkenhead to Paddington (arr 11.45pm); 7.15pm to Chester (arr 10.40pm). *From Bala* — 3.25pm auto-train to Wrexham (arr 4.55pm) and 5.50pm to Wrexham (arr 7.16pm): *from Llangollen* — 5.40pm to Ruabon (arr 5.57pm).

There was now no service on Sundays. In 1947 the local auto-train service at the far end of the line was confined to the Dolgelley and Barmouth section, apart from school trains between Dolgelley and Drws-y-Nant. Compared with the old '517' class engines, such as No 1160, which had formerly worked the service, No 1434 — the regular engine at Penmaenpool in 1947 — led an easy life!

A fairly heavy goods traffic passed over the line, especially between Ruabon and Bala Junction. In 1927, there were three goods trains in each direction. The 4.05am Mail and Goods, 'F' headlamps, detached mail vans at Bala Junction and reached Dolgelley at 6.12am, being followed by the 4.45am Barmouth Goods (arr 8.45am) and the 8.05am Dolgelley Goods (arr 3.28pm) which stopped at Corwen from 9.05am to 10.40am and terminated at Barmouth Junction at 5.25pm. The first up goods left Barmouth Junction at 5.50am, reaching Ruabon at 11.32am. The 12.35pm from Dolgelley ran via Bala (2.50pm to 4.20pm) and, with extended stops at Corwen and Llangollen Goods, did not reach Ruabon until 7.52pm. Finally, there was the 6.40pm from Barmouth Junction reaching Ruabon at 11.58pm. The up Mail was combined with the 7.15pm Barmouth to Chester — a train still running in 1947.

A through goods working to Blaenau Festiniog left Ruabon at 5.45am; while the 9.20am Bala to Ruabon Goods spent over two hours at Corwen before arriving at Ruabon at 3.04pm. There were also morning and evening RR return workings between Ruabon and Bala. Further goods traffic reached Ruabon attached to the 3.00pm and 5.45pm passenger trains, both of which were mixed. Also shown in the WTT as mixed was the 5.55pm auto-train from Corwen! Corwen was also served by an evening return working from Ruabon, which spent nearly two hours there; while Llangollen had a morning RR working from Ruabon.

On 7 September 1945 a major accident occurred when the 3.35am Mail and Newspaper train from Chester, 16 wagons and covered vans, hauled by Mogul No 6315, plunged into a gap in the embankment about two miles beyond Trevor. In the early hours of the morning the Llangollen Canal, which ran alongside and above the railway, had broken its banks and washed away the line for nearly 200ft to a depth of some 40ft. Approaching the disaster area at about 35mph, with the crew unaware of any danger, the train plunged into the breach. The engine struck the far wall of the breach before coming to rest on its side; while the train plunged over and around it. Fire broke out almost immediately and destroyed all the vehicles with the exception of the Guard's van.

Fireman Geoffrey Job was thrown out of the cab of No 6315, landing more than 100ft away and almost buried in mud. Although suffering from shock and burns, a broken wrist and a fractured ankle, he attempted to make his way to Llangollen to report the accident. Guard Fred Evans was rendered unconscious and awoke to find himself trapped in his van, surrounded by flames. Managing to escape through the window, he climbed along a broken rail to safety; and after setting warning detonators on the line, made his way along the line towards Trevor signalbox.

The non-arrival of the train at Llangollen resulted in the shunter being sent along the line, by road in a Post Office van(!), to find out the cause of the delay. He returned with the horrific news of the disaster. The first that signalman Williams at Trevor knew about the incident was when guard Fred Evans staggered into his box and blurted out the terrible news. Driver Jones had died in the cab of his engine, and such was the appalling condition of the site that it was not until two days later that the rescuers reached his body — to find his hand still gripping the brake handle in a futile attempt to stop his train from running into the breach.

The boiler of No 6315 was recovered in one piece, but the rest of the engine was cut up on the site. Restoration of the embankment was not completed until 17 September, the train service commencing again on 20 September.

Bala to Blaenau Festiniog
The 22 miles of the Bala & Festiniog Railway were opened for traffic on 1 November 1882, with stations at Bala, Frongoch, Arenig, Trawsfynydd, Maentwrog Road and Festiniog. The line was single track, with crossing places at Bala, Arenig and Trawsfynydd. Bala, Trawsfynydd and Festiniog were the most important stations, each having two platforms; while a small single-road engine shed and turntable were provided at the new Bala station. Though worked by the GWR, the company was not absorbed until 1910. This long independence was despite the fact that the GWR owned a short extension of the line from Festiniog to Blaenau Festiniog which had been opened in 1883.

The Bala & Festiniog was not the first railway to reach Festiniog, this distinction belonging to the little Festiniog & Blaenau Railway, opened as early as 1868 on the same 1ft 11½in gauge as the neighbouring Festiniog Railway from Portmadoc. The GWR purchased the little line, only 3½ miles long, and obtaining possession on 1 April 1883,

lost no time in converting it to standard gauge: it was opened on 10 September! There was one intermediate station, at Manod, near which the GWR built a small engine shed adjacent to Tan-y-Manod siding and installed a 45ft diameter turntable. Only one platform was provided at Blaenau Festiniog, the other face of which was used by the narrow gauge Festiniog Railway while there was a large goods shed, cattle pens and sidings, as well as interchange sidings with the narrow gauge company's lines.

Blaenau Festiniog was at that time, and for many years afterwards, the capital of the then-extensive North Wales slate industry; while Arenig possessed large quarries which were to produce mineral receipts for that station of over £10,000 per annum! In later years, Arenig station was quite over-shadowed by the vast bulk of the adjacent stone-crushing plant.

Above:
Cwm Prysor, with its crossing loop, out on the lonely moors — not the snow fences on the right. 1950. *LGRP courtesy David & Charles (24863)*

Below:
Trawsfynydd station c1900, with a 0-6-0ST on a short goods train from Blaenau Festiniog. *Lens of Sutton*

The line traversed much wilder and more desolate countryside than did the line to Dolgelley (or any other GWR line except the 'mountain railway' to Princetown). It was the nearest approach on the GWR to the Highland Railway's original main line across the desolate wastes of Dava Moor: like the latter, it was often subjected to snow drifts in winter — in 1947 only the finials of the signalposts were visible above the snow near Arenig! The breaking down of the telegraph on the section between Arenig and Trawsfynydd was accepted as being a likely occurrence, and the Appendix to the Chester Division WTT contained special provisions for the anticipated event:

'Should the weather indicate a heavy fall of snow during the night such as is likely to break down the telegraph communication on the section between Arenig and Trawsfynydd, the Station Masters at Arenig and Trawsfynydd, after the last train of the day has passed, and before leaving duty, will communicate with each other, and if they consider it necessary, are hereby authorised to withdraw an electric token from the instrument at Arenig to enable the snow plough to pass over the section the following morning.'

The line climbed from 600ft above sea level at Bala to over 1,200ft at Cwm Prysor, a distance of 11 miles. Northbound, the worst gradients were 1 in 60 at Frongoch. 1 in 50 at Arenig and 1 in 55 at Cwm Prysor — though there were similar, though shorter, climbs between Maentwrog Road and Manod. Southbound, the steepest section was from Trawsfynydd to Cwm Prysor at between 1 in 60 and 1 in 55. There were numerous speed restrictions, with the maximum permitted speed being only 15mph at several places, one being the passing loop two miles north of Cwm Prysor station (opened during the early years of this century). Several halts were opened on the southern section of the branch, and at Teigl between Festiniog and Manod, prior to 1932; while others were opened later at Bryncelynog and Trawsfynydd Lake.

The provision of two engine sheds for the Blaenau Festiniog branch was in contrast to the lack of any at Dolgelley. However, very shortly afterwards, a third shed was provided! This was at that very bleak spot, Trawsfynydd, where a brick-walled lean-to building was added to the goods shed to provide stabling for one engine. The reason for this profligacy appears to have been the running of an early morning workmen's train to Blaenau Festiniog. No turntable was provided. Tan-y-Manod did not have a long life, being closed in 1906; however, it remained in use as a servicing point, and was still in excellent condition, with turntable and water column still in use, at least 30 years after officially closing! The normal allocation appears to have been one 0-6-0ST — in 1901 this was No 760 of the '645' class.

Extensive army firing ranges were opened near Trawsfynydd in 1903 and these required the running of special troop trains during their periods of use. A troop yard was built just beyond the station, in 1910, and this had its own platforms — both being over 450ft long — one of which was narrowed for about half its length to provide a gun platform and end-on dock. Troop trains were usually double-headed, and in later years Moguls were sometimes employed — in pairs!

Below:
The special military sidings and platform were situated just to the north of Trawsfynydd station. The Royal Field Artillery entraining after manoeuvres, c1910. *Lens of Sutton*

The line was mostly worked by 0-6-0STs of Wolverhampton origin, their use extending for over half a century. Some of the old '1501' class engines, rebuilt as pannier tanks, were still to be seen on passenger trains — often of vintage, clerestory stock — during the 1930s. However, some of the '517' class 0-4-2Ts were also used in earlier days, a modest load of four or five 4-wheelers being the limit of their capabilities.

In 1902 the Bala to Blaenau Festiniog service was included in the same table as that between Ruabon and Dolgelley. There were four down trains, leaving Bala at 7.00am, 9.30am, 11.34am and 5.44pm. The 7.00am was a mixed train as far as Trawsfynydd, but while lingering there from 7.52am to 8.27pm it shed its goods portion and completed the journey as a passenger train: in 1927, the 1.25pm goods from Bala to Blaenau Festiniog changed into a mixed train — again while lingering at Trawsfynydd! There was also a mixed train from Trawsfynydd to Blaenau Festiniog, at 4.15pm, but it was not clear if this had also commenced its life in a humbler guise.

There were only three up trains, leaving Blaenau Festiniog at 7.55am, 2.30pm and 7.05pm for Bala; but there were also two to Trawsfynydd, at 9.35am and SX 12.05pm mixed — on Saturdays the latter ran as a passenger train, leaving at 12.50pm. There were also several local workings in each direction between Bala and Bala Junction, providing connections for the Ruabon and Dolgelley trains, as well as one or two through trains to or from Ruabon or Chester. The only train on Sundays was the 7.48pm Bala to Chester (the 6.55pm from Dolgelley, which arrived at Bala at 7.43pm).

Two or three engines were required from Bala shed each day, as well as one from Tan-y-Manod and another from Trawsfynydd. Although the 7.50am Bala to Birkenhead was worked by a Corwen engine, the 5.00pm to Ruabon (SO to Wrexham) and back was worked from Bala shed. In 1921 there were only three engines shedded on the branch; 0-4-2Ts Nos 555 and 1477 at Bala, and 0-6-0ST No 1808 at Trawsfynydd, so that some turns must have been worked from Corwen.

In 1932 the Bala to Blaenau Festiniog branch was shown in a separate table, with five down trains and an additional train on Saturdays. The early morning train from Bala still spent over half-an-hour at Trawsfynydd; departure times were 6.45am, 9.20am, 11.50am, 1.15pm and 5.35pm, with a late evening train SO at 8.50pm. There was also the SX 3.45pm mixed train to Arenig (arr 4.22pm), returning at 5.00pm.

As in 1902, there was one train less from Blaenau Festiniog than from Bala, departure times being 7.35am, 9.00am, 2.20pm and 7.10pm, with a 4.25pm SX train to Trawsfynydd. The SO 12.20pm mixed train to Trawsfynydd continued to Bala as a goods; while the 4.25pm SO ran through to Bala (being shown in the 1927 WTT as 3rd class only), taking the place of the SX 5.00pm Arenig to Bala. There were no trains on Sundays.

Three engines were still required, with a fourth engine working between Bala and Bala Junction. Tan-y-Manod shed having been closed, the first train from Blaenau Festiniog each morning was worked by the Trawsfynydd engine which had worked up on an unadvertised Workmen's Train. This engine and that of the 5.35pm from Bala (returning from Blaenau Festiniog at 7.10pm) ran to Tan-y-Manod to take water — Blaenau Festiniog possessing no water column!

The older 0-6-0PTs were still being used on both passenger and goods workings; their eventual replacements being some of the new '7400' class engines, the first of which was built in 1936. By 1938, there were four of the class at Croes Newydd and its sub-sheds — when Bala had two 0-6-0PTs and two 0-4-2Ts of the 5800 series. Only one engine was shedded at Trawsfynydd, and in 1947 this was No 1706 of the Swindon-built '1854' class; by which time, Bala had four 0-6-0PTs and two 0-4-2Ts.

In 1947 the service had reverted to the 1902 level, with only three trains in each direction;

Top left:
Manod in 1951, with a mixed train — of a sort! — headed by No 7440. *R. C. Riley*

Top right:
Blaenau Festiniog. A general view of the station in the 1920s, with the narrow gauge lines of the Festiniog Railway on the left. *Lens of Sutton*

Right:
Blaenau Festiniog in 1937, with 0-6-0PT No 2702 at the head of an unusually long train for the line: the third carriage appears to be of Cambrian Railways origin. *Dr I. C. Allen*

though there was an additional train on Tuesdays and Thursdays and another (at a different time) on Saturdays. An afternoon return working between Bala and Trawsfynydd ran two hours earlier on Saturdays and returned from Blaenau Festiniog (having run empty from Trawsfynydd). There were two Blaenau Festiniog to Trawsfynydd trains, at 11.15am and 4.25pm, both being SX, the former being replaced SO by the 11.50am. Also on Saturdays there was a morning train from Arenig to Bala and a later evening one from Blaenau Festiniog to Trawsfynydd. Departure times were — from Bala: 6.45am, 9.00am (Tuesdays and Thursdays), 11.55am, 5.35pm and 8.55pm (SO); from Blaenau Festiniog: 7.10am, 9.15am (Tuesdays and Thursdays), 2.20pm, 4.15pm (SO) and 7.15pm. Several trains were now 3rd Class Only, though none was auto-worked.

Despite the complicated timetable it was possible for the service to be worked by three engines — two from Bala and one from Trawsfynydd — with a fourth engine being required on Saturdays. Bala shed also worked two trains to Chester and back each day.

In 1927, in addition to the daily through goods from Ruabon to Blaenau Festiniog, there was the 1.25pm from Bala (mixed from Trawsfynydd); while from Blaenau Festiniog there was the 11.25am SX to Bala (SO 1.20pm from Trawsfynydd) and the 3.10pm from Manod (Blaenau Festiniog RR 2.55pm). The SX evening return working between Trawsfynydd and Arenig could,

if necessary, begin from Maentwrog Road, Pengwerne siding or even from Blaenau Festiniog! Another RR goods was an early morning return working between Bala and Trawsfynydd Reservoir Siding. The SO 11.50am Bala to Arenig Goods returned as the 12.35pm passenger train, hence the WTT note 'To convey empty coaches only if running late'. Finally, there were several local trip workings between Blaenau Festiniog and Manod or Tan-y-Manod.

With the vagaries of both weather and timetables, the local staff needed to be men of dedication and of more than average ability. The enginemen also needed to be a tough breed: only with the advent of the '7400' class 0-6-0PTs and the '5800' 0-4-2Ts did they receive the benefit of enclosed cabs on their engines, despite having to face the fury of the winter weather as they battled across moor and mountain.

9 North Wales Mineral

Wrexham had been an important agricultural centre during the Middle Ages, but it was the discovery of coal and iron deposits which brought about the town's development. The extensive coal measures stretched from Cefn Mawr in the south through Coed Poeth and Brymbo towards Caergwrle. However, the industry had only local significance as the area was devoid of adequate means of transport until the NWMR was opened. Even when the Ellesmere Canal had been opened, the roundabout journey via Whitchurch and Nantwich meant that traffic covered a distance of 60 miles to reach Chester; the distance by rail was just over 12 miles!

The first developments took place in the latter years of the 18th century, Ffrwd Ironworks and Ffrwd Colliery at the upper end of the Moss Valley being opened sometime before 1796; while Westminster Colliery, further down the same valley, was working in the early 1800s. Other early collieries were Brynmally and Ffosygo. All these were the targets of the NWMR when the original, but abortive, mineral branch was proposed.

The first mineral branch to be constructed came into use in July 1847. It ran from Wheatsheaf Junction (Rhos Robin) to Minera, the site of a large limestone quarry and limeworks, a distance of six miles, with branches to a number of collieries; the total distance being about 11 miles. The line included two tunnels and two rope-worked inclines, known locally as 'brakes'. Initially, two mineral trains were run daily —

Below:
Coed Poeth station was the original terminus of the passenger service which commenced in November 1897: following the introduction of Steam Railmotors in June 1905, the service was extended to Berwig Halt. The station saw its last passenger train on 31 December 1930, but was still in good condition in 1948.
LGRP courtesy David & Charles (18005)

Right:
Although the Moss Valley branch was opened in 1882, there was no passenger service until 1905 when steam railmotors began running to Moss Crossing Halt. The service was withdrawn at the end of 1930. Note the check rail.
LGRP courtesy David & Charles (6232)

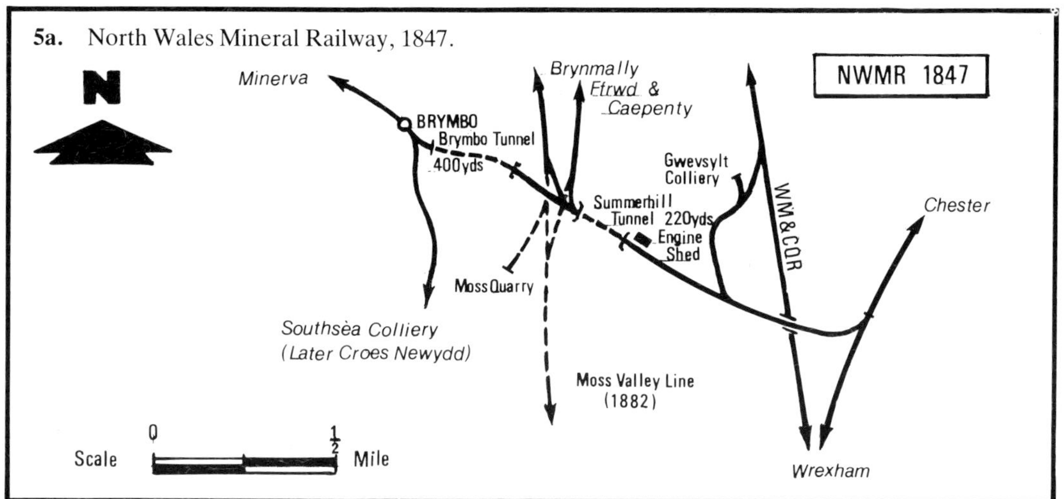

Nos 15 and 16, no doubt, being the engines employed.

Two small engine sheds were provided, at Brymbo and Summerhill. The former was replaced by another building in 1872 (when the Wrexham & Minera Extension Railway was opened); rather strangely, the new building appears to have been smaller than the original shed. Brymbo and Summerhill remained in use until 1902, being closed when the Croes Newydd shed was opened. In 1901 there were three 0-6-0STs at Brymbo, No 779 of the '645' class and Nos 2061 and 2064 of the '2021' class — one of the latter being sub-shedded at Summerhill. The majority of the passenger, goods and mineral turns were worked from Chester prior to Croes Newydd being opened.

Further south, a short single-track mineral branch was opened from Gardden Lodge Junction (Ruabon) to Aberderfyn, a distance of 1¾ miles, on 1 August 1861. The line was constructed under agreement with local landowners — as was a later extension of 1¼ miles to Legacy — opened on 27 August 1876, so no Act of Parliament was required. Known as the Ponkey Branch, it was originally built to serve two large brickworks, though in later years it also carried coal for the Rhos Gas Works, raw materials and the products of a local furniture factory, and petrol traffic.

A few months later, the Wrexham & Minera Railway was opened on 22 May 1862, between Croes Newydd Junction and the Southsea Branch of the old NWMR line from Wheatsheaf Junction at Broughton, to the south of Brymbo. This was a double-track line, about 3½ miles long; the other mineral branches being single track. The original line between Moss and Brymbo, including the 400yd long Brymbo Tunnel and one of the rope-worked 'brakes' was then abandoned. The existence of the incline is commemorated by the

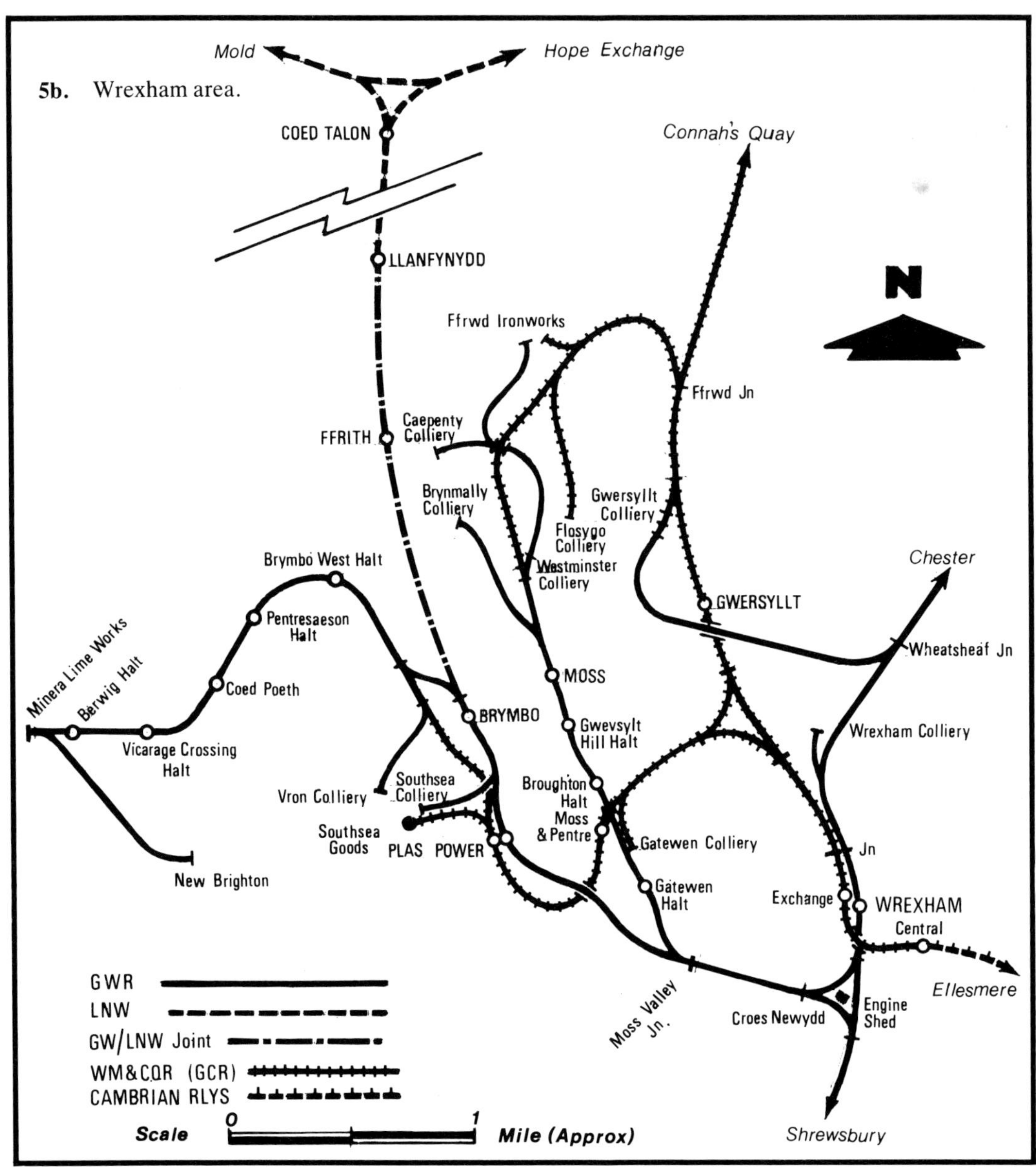

name of the Brake Methodist Church, Moss, opened in 1885. The original line which remained in the Brymbo area still had considerable gradients. The section between Brymbo and Coed Poeth was subject to a general speed limit of 20mph, while there were several local restrictions.

Impetus for the opening of the new line, and the partial abandonment of the original branch, was probably given by the prospect of rival lines, the Wrexham, Mold & Connah's Quay Railway Act having been passed in August 1862. This brought another railway to Wrexham, though it was not until 1887 that the WM&CQR reached Brymbo (a passenger service to that town commencing in 1889) and the Vron Branch was not opened until 8 October 1888.

On 2 January 1872 the Wrexham & Minera Extension Railway (a joint venture of the GWR and LNWR) was completed and opened. Its title was somewhat of a misnomer, as it ran from Brymbo Junction to Coed Talon on the LNWR's line from Mold, a distance of not quite three miles, and passed nowhere near Minera! Opened as a mineral line, it remained as such until 1897 when a passenger service was commenced on 13 November between Brymbo and Mold.

112

Further south, the Moss Valley line was opened from Moss Valley Junction, on the Wrexham & Minera line, to a junction with the original NWMR line from Wheatsheaf Junction on 11 May 1882, a distance of almost two miles. Again, this was shortly before the WM&CQR obtained an Act of Parliament, in this case for its line to Brymbo (18 August 1882). The line from Wheatsheaf Junction, including the remaining incline and tunnel, was gradually closed and abandoned; the section from Gwersylt to Moss was closed in October 1908, and eventually it was reduced to a short line to Wheatsheaf Yard.

The Moss Valley line served the Ffrwyd Ironworks and the Caepenty, Brynmally and Westminster Collieries, all originally reached over the old line. The line serving Westminster and Caepenty Collieries (and the ironworks) was closed in 1917 (Westminster Colliery to Ffos-y-go) and 1925 (Moss to Westminster Colliery); while the Brynmally Colliery line was closed in 1935.

In 1896 the GWR acquired the Pontcysyllte branch, 3½ miles long, which ran from the canal basin at Pontcysyllte, near Trevor, to Llwyenion

Above:
Legacy, on the Rhos branch, was only a halt, despite having a signalbox and being the junction 'station' for the passenger service over the Ponkey branch. The latter service was withdrawn in March 1915, but the trains between Wrexham and Rhos continued to run until the end of 1930.
LGRP courtesy David & Charles (18349)

Below:
Rails reached Rhos from the south, from Pontcysyllte in 1867, but it was not until 1901 that the line was opened from Wrexham. Although the passenger service was withdrawn at the end of 1930, the line remained open for goods and was in regular use for the running of football specials. The Llwyenion brickworks are on the left. 1949.
LGRP courtesy David & Charles (18351)

on the outskirts of Rhos. This was nominally the property of the Shropshire Union Railway & Canal Co, which had been in LNWR hands since 1847 — and the latter Company retained the

Above:
Among the select band of small tank engines kept at Croes Newydd specially for the local colliery branches was ex-Birkenhead Railway 0-4-0ST No 96, seen here in Croes Newydd shed c1930. No 96 was withdrawn in 1935. *Lens of Sutton*

ownership of a short length of line (10 chains) at the canal basin. Many years previously, the GWR had built a short line from a westward-facing junction just beyond Trevor Station (on the Dolgelley line), which connected with 20 chains of privately owned track running to Edward's Siding (over which the GWR was allowed to work [by agreement] to reach the Pontcysyllte Branch).

The origins of the line, which was much older than the NWMR (or the GWR) were to be found in the Ruabon Brook Tramway opened as early as 1805 from the canal at Pontcysyllte to Acrefair, past the Kynaston Ironworks and Colliery. It was owned by the Ellesmere Canal Co, who had obtained an Act for its construction in 1794, and who extended it to Plasmadoc Colliery in 1808. At a later date a second line from Acrefair to Wynn Hall Colliery was opened; while another line from Ruabon (Wynnstay Colliery) through Plas Madoc to the Delph Brickworks was opened as a tramway in 1829, crossing the Wynn Hall line on the level near Plas-y-Wern.

From 1860 onwards these lines were converted to railways, the Wynn Hall line being extended to the Llwyenion Brickworks at Rhos in 1867. This work was carried out by the Shropshire Union Railways & Canal Co who had taken over the Ellesmere Canal in 1846 — only to find themselves leased by the LNWR in the following year. The line from Wynnstay to Delph was worked by the New British Iron Co until 1886, then by the Wynnstay Colliery Co; however, the Pontcysyllte Branch had been worked by the LNWR, an engine being stabled in a most unusual combined engine shed and warehouse, part of which was built *over* the canal basin!

Although retaining ownership of the line on which the shed was situated, the LNWR handed over the building to the GWR who then proceeded to allocate an engine there. In 1901 this was 0-6-0ST No 1979 of the '1901' class, which were the heaviest engines allowed to work over the newly-acquired line. The shed was closed in the following year when Croes Newydd was opened; however, the branch goods engines still took water there — a man being sent from Wrexham about twice a week to ensure that water was pumped up into the water tank. The line must have taxed the powers of the '1901' class engines, was there were considerable gradients for much of the way. From Rhos to Pant was 1 in 54, and further south there was over half-a-mile at 1 in 37. Maximum speeds in either direction were strictly limited; 10mph between Trevor and Wynn Hall, and 15mph between Wynn Hall and Brook Street (Rhos).

The Plas Madoc branch, which was linked to the GWR by a junction from down sidings half a mile south of Ruabon station (the junction being under a bridge carrying a private line to Wynnstay Colliery across the main line), was regarded as being an extended siding and worked accordingly, never meriting any mention in the WTT.

The last line to be opened, in 1901, was from Rhos Junction, just south of Croes Newydd, to join the recently-acquired Pontcysyllte branch at Rhos. It passed through the terminus of the Ponkey branch at Legacy, where a station was opened — other stations being at Rhostyllen and Rhos. The latter station had a small goods yard and sidings serving brickworks, but horse and cattle traffic was dealt with at Legacy (though also occasionally handled at Rhos passenger station).

The mineral lines were the haunt in earlier years of a select band of small tank engines, most of which were 0-4-0STs. These included No 15, built 1847, which spent over 50 years working around Wrexham before being withdrawn in 1904, and No 16 — also built in 1847, but withdrawn in 1879. Both engines which successively carried the number 45 worked for many years in the area; the second No 45, built at Wolverhampton in 1880, was mostly employed there until withdrawn in 1938. Although originating on the Birkenhead Railway, Nos 95 and 96 had close associations with the Wrexham Coalfield. No 96 appears to have spent most of its long life in the area — built in 1853, it was not withdrawn until 1935. No 95 was less faithful, as it spent several years in South Wales from about 1899 and went south again in 1922.

Nos 91 and 92, which were among the first standard gauge engines to be purchased by the GWR also worked in the area. Although No 91 lasted only until 1877, when it was 'cannibalised' and parts used for the rebuilding of No 92, the latter engine went on working around Wrexham for nearly 60 years longer — until 1936. A similar engine, No 342, acquired from Chester General Station Commissioners, also spent its GWR service at Wrexham until withdrawn in 1931. It is significant that the withdrawal of these veterans coincided with the closure of some of the oldest collieries.

Although these branches were all opened for mineral traffic, some passengers were also carried on occasions. As early as 1847 there was an excursion from Brymbo to Birkenhead: how the passengers descended and ascended the two 'brakes' is not known! In about 1866 a passenger service was begun on the Wrexham & Minera Railway, which was jointly leased by the GWR and the LNWR between 11 June 1866 and 1 July 1871, but this was soon discontinued — possibly when the joint lease expired and the GWR took over the line. However, a permanent service commenced on 24 May 1882 between Wrexham and Coed Poeth. A service over the Wrexham & Minera Extension Railway, between Brymbo and Mold, worked by the LNWR, commenced on 15 November 1897. This was followed by the introduction of passenger trains on the newly-opened Rhos branch in October 1901 — an event not unconnected with the proposed electrification of the street tramway between Wrexham and Rhos!

The service on the Wrexham & Minera line was described as the Coed Poeth Branch, the stations being Plaspower, Brymbo and Coed Poeth. In 1902 there were four trains in each direction, with an additional train to Brymbo and back on Thursdays and Saturdays; while there was also a SO late evening train in each direction. The first train was from Coed Poeth, at 8.45am, the first departure from Wrexham not being until 9.40am: the last train from Coed Poeth was at 6.00pm (SO 8.00pm), that from Wrexham being at 7.20pm (SO 8.50pm). There was no service on Sundays.

The Brymbo and Coed Talon branch also had four trains in each direction between Brymbo and Mold, worked by the LNWR from Mold. These connected at Brymbo with trains to and from Wrexham, and there was an additional train in each direction on Wednesday and Saturday evenings. Again, there was no service on Sundays.

The Rhos branch enjoyed a more frequent service, having five trains in each direction, while there were six on Thursdays and no less than nine on Saturdays. Legacy was a request stop for all trains. The first departure was from Rhos, at 8.15am, the first train from Wrexham not being until 9.15am, with the last trains leaving at 6.50pm and 8.20pm respectively, except on Saturdays when they were at 8.45pm and 9.15pm. As on the other branches, there was no service on Sundays — the majority of the local population held strongly Sabbatarian views!

How these services were worked prior to the opening of Croes Newydd shed in 1902 is something of a mystery, as there were only three 0-6-0STs shedded at Brymbo and Summerhill: there must have been a considerable amount of light engine working to and from Chester. Maximum loads allowed between Wrexham and Coed Poeth were 98 tons for 0-6-0Ts and 70 tons for '517' class 0-4-2Ts — though the respective allowances in the reverse direction were 252 tons and 224 tons! A similar contrast, though not such a great one, was to be found on the Rhos Branch: Wrexham to Rhos 0-6-0Ts 196 tons and 0-4-2Ts 140 tons; Rhos to Wrexham — 280 tons and 252 tons respectively.

The Wrexham District Tramways operated a line between Wrexham and Johnstown, which ran roughly parallel and to the west of the GWR main line (which it crossed near Rhos Junction); although proposed and authorised, an extension to Ruabon was never built. Originally, horse-drawn trams were used, but in 1903 the line was electrified and the service greatly improved. It was in direct competition with the GWR services for Rhos and Johnstown, and the GWR's response to this competition was the introduction of steam railmotors and the opening to passenger services of what had been mineral or goods lines.

The service on the Rhos branch was extended over the northern section of the Pontcysyllte Branch to Wynn Hall, with halts at Brook Street, Pant and Wynn Hall — all in just over a mile! This service commenced on 1 May 1905, there being about eight or nine return workings each day. A few weeks later, on 15 June, the northern end of the Ponkey Branch between Legacy and Ponkey Crossing, just to the south of Aberderfyn, was also given a railmotor service — the stopping places being halts at Fennant Road, Aberderfyn and Ponkey Crossing. In this instance, there were three halts in the course of less than ½ mile!

To the north of Wrexham, the Moss Valley line was also opened to passengers on 1 May 1905, halts being provided at Gatewen, Broughton, Gwersylt and Moss. It was claimed that the latter halt was a railhead for 14,000 people living locally: as the course of most of these branch lines, originally intended for mineral traffic only, tended to avoid villages, the word 'railhead' was probably quite correct! A month later, passenger services on the Coed Poeth branch were extended to serve Vicarage Crossing and Berwig halts (other halts being opened between Brymbo and Coed Poeth).

The service on the Ponkey branch did not have a long life, being withdrawn from 22 March 1915, when the service between Rhos and Wynn Hall also ceased, while the northern section of the Ponkey branch — and that most recently opened — was closed completely from 18 January 1917, as a wartime economy, and the track was lifted. A few years later, after the grouping, the GWR stated that 'there is no case for restoring' the closed section. The original mineral line from Gardden Junction to Aberderfyn remained in use for goods traffic and outlived the GWR. In 1927 there were eight 'Motor' trains in each direction on the Rhos branch, the first leaving Wrexham at 7.25am and the last from Rhos being at 8.45pm; and there was also an evening return working by an ordinary passenger train. The Moss Valley line

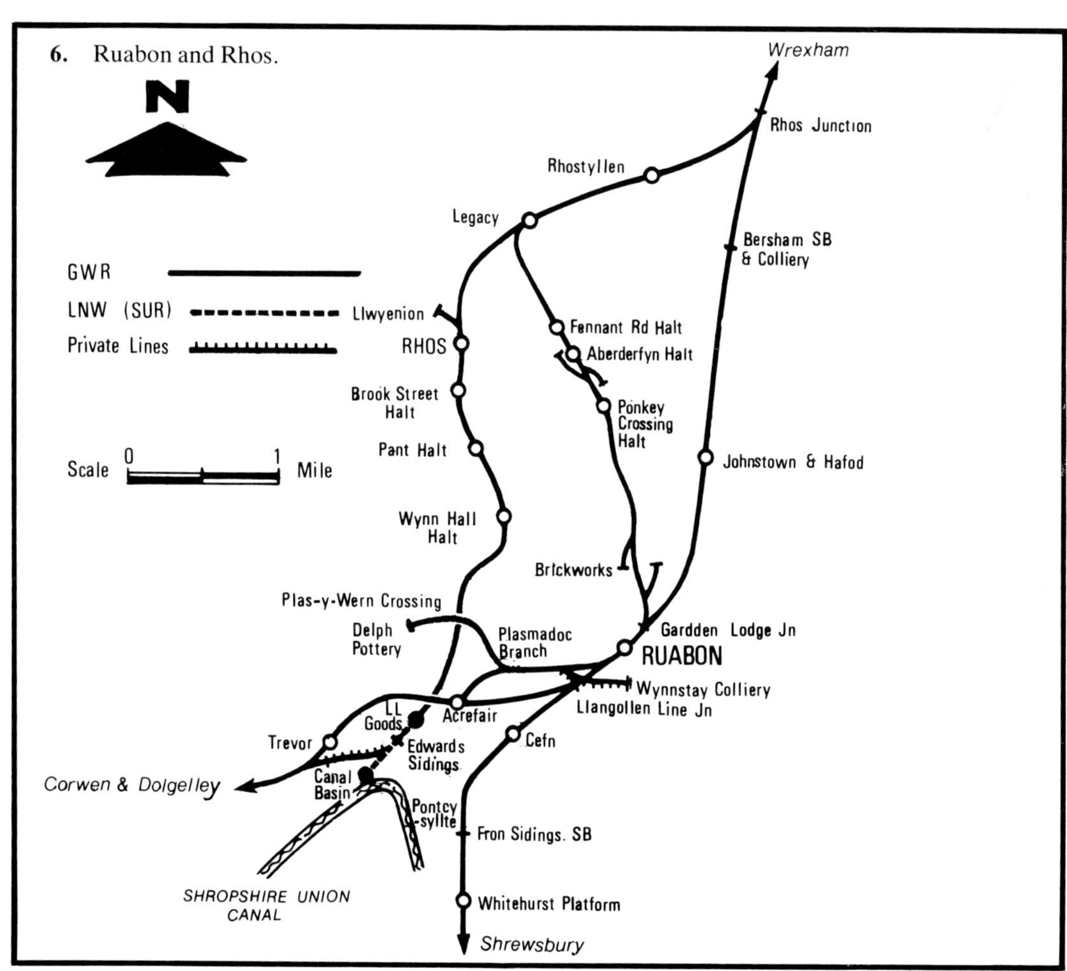

had a similar service by eight 'Motor' trains, which was increased to 12 each way on Saturdays.

On 1 January 1931 all these railmotor services were withdrawn, as were passenger services between Wrexham and Brymbo; though football specials for home matches at Wrexham continued to be run on the Rhos branch for many years. The GCR had abandoned their Wrexham to Brymbo service in 1917. At the height of the railmotor boom, in 1908, there were no less than 10 cars allocated to Croes Newydd for the various branches and for some workings to Llangollen: the latter duty lasted until April 1934 when the last steam railcars were replaced by auto-trains. By 1921, only three railcars, Nos 41, 78 and 91, remained at that shed, but there were at least four auto-fitted engines; Nos 826 and 1156 of the '517' class, and Nos 2120 and 2135 of the '2021' class. The latter were among the four engines which had been converted c1906 for auto-train working in the Plymouth area; while No 2120 was also one of the pair which had been disguised by being clothed in dummy coachwork.

The GWR also introduced motor-buses into the Wrexham area, both as 'feeders' to rail services and for excursion purposes. A double-decker service was run to Farndon in Cheshire, which at times was extended to the village of Aldford from whence passengers could board a river steamer to Chester and then travel back to Wrexham by rail: railway-type tickets were used for these excursions. An oddity of these railway-owned buses was the carrying of oil lamps — side and tail — of a railway pattern, even when the buses were fitted with electrical equipment!

After World War 1, numerous independent operators commenced running buses in the area in competition with the GWR and with the Wrexham District Tramways. However, competition between the railway and the tramway was still most intense. A curious incident that helped to enliven the rivalry occurred when the strongly trade union miners discovered that the tram-waymen were not union members, whereas the GWR busmen were members of the NUR. The

On the Pontcysyllte branch, the site of Wynn Hall Halt (closed March 1915) in 1949. As on a number of branch lines, the old inside-keyed track remained long after it had disappeared from the main line.
LGRP courtesy David & Charles (18353)

trams were at once declared 'black' and the miners either transferred to the GWR buses or cycled and walked to work. It was most unfortunate that at the same time someone at Paddington decided that the buses must collect extra revenue by displaying advertisements — and sets were sent down to Wrexham to be affixed to the vehicles garaged there. Alas, due either to ignorance or 'malice afore-thought', every one of them was for intoxicants — Scotch Whisky, Hollands Gin, Old Port etc. Their appearance was the signal for the elders, deacons and leaders of the numerous Nonconformist chapels in the area to urge the faithful, both in English and Welsh, to 'black' the buses! Non-union, but temperance, trams were preferable to unionised 'intoxicating' buses. 'Chapel' and its authority had greater influence in those days than the union: to the surprise of the busmen and no doubt of some union officials — back went the colliers to travelling on the trams!

After 1931 only the Brymbo and Mold service remained, and this was worked by the LMS. In 1947 the timetables simply informed would-be passengers 'See LMS Company's Time Table'. As in so many other parts of the country, it was the all-conquering motor-bus which brought about the demise of the branch rail services. The GWR at least had the satisfaction of seeing its services outlive those of the rival tramway, the last tram having run on 31 March 1927. It also had the consolation that at least some of the bus services were its own, as by the late 1920s it was operating services from Wrexham to Llay, Brymbo, Pentre Broughton and Rhos — the latter place enjoying a half-hourly service.

The Rhos and Ponkey branches continued to

11.15am — returning on a local goods from Trevor
at 6.45pm. Although the Ponkey branch had a
general restriction of 15mph over the whole line,
the only restriction on the Rhos branch was one of
15mph in either direction at Rhos Junction.
However, on the Pontcysyllte branch although
15mph was allowed north of Wynn Hall, between
the latter point and Trevor the maximum speed
allowed was only 10mph. The maximum speed of
20mph allowed between Brymbo and Coed Poeth
was reduced to 10mph in several places between
Coed Poeth and Berwig; while the Vron and
Wheatsheaf branches were subject to maximum
speeds of 8mph.

have a daily goods working, the former extended
over the Pontcysyllte branch to Trevor — with
Llwyenion being served by a trip working on the
return journey from Trevor (which was allowed
10 minutes extra time owing to the gradients).
Pontcysyllte was also served from Ruabon by an
engine which arrived at Trevor at 6.31am and
spent the day shunting — including an hour's stint
at Llangollen Goods between 10.15am and

Following the closure of the collieries in the
Moss Valley, the Moss Valley branch was closed
completely in 1935 (the northern- and original
section having been closed in 1925). At Brymbo,
the Vron branch was shortened by about ¼-mile
when the Vron Colliery closed in 1930; although
the LNER had continued to work daily trains over
their branch, opened in 1888, the GWR had long
since ceased to provide such a service. In 1924 it
was stated 'the output does not warrant a service'.
The remainder of the branch remained open to
serve the steel works which provided most of the
traffic on the Wrexham & Minera line during the
latter days of the GWR.

One by one, the collieries had come to the end
of their working life: Broughton closed as early as
1878, to be followed by New Broughton in 1910
and Southsea in 1938. The lower section of the old
NWMR's branch survived the GWR by only three
years, Wheatsheaf Junction to Gwersylt being
closed in 1951. However, beyond Brymbo the
original line to the quarries at Minera, opened in
1847, remained in use — and as an active reminder
of the once great days of the North Wales Mineral
Railway.

10 The Birkenhead Joint Lines

Birkenhead was the physical terminus of the GWR's northern main line, though the ultimate destination was, of course, Liverpool! However, the reversal of all but a handful of trains at Chester meant that the lines north of that city formed what was almost a detached section, accentuated by the fact that they were not the exclusive property of the GWR, but were jointly owned, initially with the LNWR and latterly with the LMS.

The Birkenhead Joint Lines originated in a line from Chester to Birkenhead, about 14½ miles long, opened in September 1840 as the Chester & Birkenhead Railway. Added to this, in December 1850, was the line from Chester to Walton Junction, near Warrington, a distance of 16¾ miles. The latter line, the Lancashire & Cheshire Junction Railway, had running powers into Manchester (Exchange), a distance of no less than 40 miles from Chester. Prior to its opening, the new line was amalgamated with the C&BR, the whole concern adopting the title of the newer line. The shorter title of the Birkenhead Railway was adopted in 1859, only a few months prior to the Company ceasing to have an independent existence.

Beyond Chester, the tall signal posts of unmistakable LNWR origin were evidence that this was no longer GWR territory; while in later years upper quadrant signals of LMS pattern confirmed the joint ownership. The WTT No 14 'Chester, Birkenhead, Manchester and Wolverhampton' contained no details of the times during which signalboxes were open for anywhere beyond Saltney Junction — 'For times of signalboxes on these sections see LMS Company's Notice'. Furthermore, trains on the Chester to Manchester line departed from the south end of Chester General station — from whence trains also left for such 'foreign' places as Crewe and Euston. Finally, the LNWR was much in evidence at Birkenhead, where the GWR and LNWR engine sheds stood side by side.

In earlier years, the joint ownership of the lines was apparent in the appearance of the trains. In the immortal words of the late E. L. Ahrons: 'In some respects they were the "jointest" (if I may coin that term) service run by two separate companies. Great Western trains were frequently worked by London & North Western engines, and vice versa. One London and North Western Manchester to Llandudno express was at one time worked from Manchester (Exchange) to Chester by a Great Western engine during 1899-1900.' Although GWR passenger engines do not appear to have enjoyed the hospitality of the LNWR at Manchester, two or three goods engines were regularly stabled at the old Ordsall Lane sheds and, in later years, at Patricroft.

The local train service between Chester and Birkenhead was probably more profitable to the GWR than were the handful of Paddington expresses. The Wirral peninsula found increasing favour among the wealthy business men of Merseyside as the ideal place in which to live. This was aided by the opening of the Mersey Railway — despite the sulphureous fumes of its earlier years — which ended the dependence of passengers on

Below:
0-4-2T No 3579, one of the 10 engines of the '3571' class which worked between Chester and Birkenhead for many years, at Chester General station in August 1938. No 3579 was withdrawn from Birkenhead in 1942. *W. Potter*

The unique 2-4-0T No 1 at Chester shed in 1921 (shortly after overhaul at Swindon), three years before being withdrawn from service.
W. H. Whitworth

Below:
Another unique 2-4-0T, No 3596 of the 'Metro' class as rebuilt with a Churchward enclosed cab and bunker. In Birkenhead shed, July 1937.
W. Potter

the ferry service across the Mersey; though, no doubt, there were those who preferred the ferry boats and the hazard of fog, to the constant smoke of the railway tunnel. Either way, the Birkenhead Joint lines' trains carried them to and from Parkgate, Heswall and — later — West Kirby. Not that the GWR and LNWR enjoyed a monopoly in the Wirral, for there was fierce competition from the thrusting little Wirral Railway, a local line which also served West Kirby — and by a route which was only about one third of the distance by the Joint line!

The West Kirby Branch which served the west coast of the Wirral was one of two lines which joined the main line at Hooton. It was not the first to be opened, that distinction belonging to the double track line along the Mersey side of the Wirral to Helsby on the Chester and Warrington line, a distance of nearly nine miles, which came into use on 1 July 1863. Ellesmere Port was the only place of any size served, and for many years

the service was much less frequent than that on the West Kirby line.

The first section of the latter branch, which was single track, was opened from Hooton to Parkgate, a distance of 4¾ miles, on 1 October 1866. However, the remaining section to West Kirby, just over seven miles long, was not constructed until 20 years later, being opened on 19 April 1886 — just as the Wirral Railway was enjoying the first fruits of the growing commuter traffic! Although the volume of passenger traffic was far greater than on the Helsby line, the branch remained single track — possibly because little goods traffic passed over it, unlike the line to Helsby which had a considerable volume of goods traffic of all kinds as it provided a direct link between Birkenhead and the Manchester area. In later years, a short 'goods only' connecting line was built by the Cheshire Lines Committee from their main line at Mouldsworth to Helsby Junction, just to the west of Helsby Station.

Following the disappearance of the majority of the engines acquired by the GWR as its share of the Birkenhead Railway's assets, the engines used on the joint lines from Chester were principally the double-framed 2-4-0s built at Wolverhampton, of which Nos 111-113 and the majority of Nos 372-377 and 1004-1011 were shedded at Chester. There were some through workings between Birkenhead and Manchester via Chester, one train in each direction being worked daily by one of the three 7ft Singles of the 'Sir Daniel' class which were shedded at Birkenhead. Occasional visits to Manchester were also paid by the '149' or 'Chancellor' class 2-4-0s, of which No 152 was at one time shedded at Birkenhead. In the 1880s the LNWR was using some of the famous 2-2-2s of the 'Problem' or 'Lady of the Lake' class on the Manchester to Chester joint line.

Among the impressive collection of locomotive antiquities, at one time such a distinctive feature of the GWR's Chester engine shed, were a few of the ex-Birkenhead Railway engines. Most of these, including 0-4-2s Nos 104 and 105 and the small 2-4-0s Nos 106-109, worked mainly to Birkenhead as did ex-S&CR 0-4-2 No 33. However, another specimen from the Chester engine museum was a frequent visitor to Manchester, this being 2-4-0 No 894. Built by Kitson & Co in 1868, for the Llanelly Railway & Dock Co, it passed into the ownership of the GWR in 1873. The Llanelly company did not number their engines, but gave them names — in this instance *Napoleon III*; however, the GWR in an uncharacteristically republican action removed the title and reduced the engine to the ranks as No 894. Sent to Wolverhampton two years later, it spent the rest of its life working from Chester until withdrawn in 1906.

The majority of the older 2-4-0s were withdrawn during the early years of this century; though the ex-WMR No 214 was at Birkenhead in 1911, as were the more modern '3232' class engines Nos 3238, 3240 and 3244, and 'Stella' class No 3518. By about 1920 the Chester and Birkenhead line was being worked mainly by tank engines. Most of the '3571' class 0-4-2Ts were to be found on this line after being replaced on the Ruabon to Dolgelley line by the 'Stella' class 2-4-0s. No 3573 was probably the first of the class to work in the Wirral, being the only engine at the small sub-shed at Hooton in 1901. By 1911 Nos 3574 and 3579 were at Birkenhead, and six of the class were shedded there by 1921. The first of the '3600' class 2-4-2Ts to work in the area had arrived by then, when No 3609 was shedded at Chester, and by 1923 there were about half-a-dozen of them: all were withdrawn by 1934.

A unique engine to be found at Chester for some years was No 1, a double-framed 2-4-0T which had begun life in 1880 as a 4-4-0T, but which soon became notorious for its tendency to fracture the light framing to which its bogie was attached. Rebuilt as a 2-4-0T, it worked in the Bristol and Plymouth areas for many years before being sent to Chester. Although it worked mainly to Birkenhead, it is also reported to have reached Wolverhampton on occasions — despite its tanks only having a capacity of 890gal. With 17in × 26in cylinders and 5ft 8in wheels, it latterly carried a standard Belpaire boiler with extended smokebox and top feed, as fitted to the 'Dukes'. Being both powerful and free-running, it was very popular with the engine men. It was withdrawn in July 1924.

Although the Swindon-built 'Metro' class 2-4-0Ts were by no means common engines in the old Northern Division (where they were unknown until the early years of this century when one or two were shedded at Wellington), by the late 1920s they had penetrated as far north as Birkenhead. Nos 1495 and 3569 were shedded there during that period; while No 3596, the unique rebuild with a Churchward cab, was there in 1938. The '3571' class remained at Chester and Birkenhead until the late 1920s, Nos 3572 and 3576 being withdrawn from Birkenhead in 1929. Several were then transferred elsewhere, but Nos 3575 and 3579 were still at Chester and Nos 3577 and 3578 at Birkenhead in 1938. However, all except No 3579 — withdrawn from Birkenhead following an accident in 1942 — had been moved away prior to withdrawal.

The engines which eventually took over the majority of workings in the Wirral were the large 2-6-2Ts of the '5101' class, though there were also a few of the older '5100' class engines. The latter had worked on the line as early as 1911, as had

Above:
A normal 'Metro' class 2-4-0T, No 1495 at Hooton on an auto-train for Helsby c1930. No 1495 was withdrawn in 1938 — from Merthyr, in the Cardiff Valleys Division.
H. G. Tidey: Real Photos (T6305)

Below:
Also at Hooton and bound for Helsby, 2-4-2T No 3629 which would be withdrawn by the end of 1931. The ecclesiastical gothic architecture of the station building was somewhat unusual.
H. G. Tidey: Real Photos (T6304)

some of the '3150' class, Nos 3145, 3169 and 3185 being at that time shedded at Birkenhead; while in 1921 Nos 3131, 3133 and 3186 were Birkenhead engines. It is probable that in earlier days they were more often employed on working goods and mineral traffic (as were those of the class at Croes Newydd) than on passenger work. During and after World War 2, Nos 4120-29 were all shedded at Birkenhead, a most unusual 'block' allocation as far as the GWR was concerned.

A service of steam railmotors between Rock Ferry and Ledsham (the first station beyond Hooton towards Chester) was introduced in July 1923, and within a few years auto-train services were running between Birkenhead or Rock Ferry and Hooton or Ellesmere Port (on the Helsby line). 'Metro' class No 1495 was one of the earliest

Above:
Hooton yet again, with 0-4-2T No 3578 on a train of vintage ex-LNWR stock, bound from Birkenhead to Helsby.
H. G. Tidey: Real Photos (T6300)

Below:
The joint ownership of the former Birkenhead Railway's lines was proclaimed by all the warning notice boards, such as this warning concerning trespass on the line which still survived at Helsby in 1953. The use of black lettering on a white background was most unusual.
Real Photos (K2060)

auto-fitted engines to be shedded at Birkenhead (it was auto-fitted in October 1929), but in 1938 0-6-0PT No 6404 was the Birkenhead auto-engine — with '2021' class No 2095 as spare. By 1947 No 6405 (formerly at Stourbridge) was also at Birkenhead, though No 2095 had migrated south to Stafford Road. The last steam railcar left Birkenhead in April 1933.

The importance attached to individual stations in the Wirral could be estimated from the 1902 timetables, with 'Chester, West Kirby and Liverpool (Landing Stage)' being in heavy type and capitals, while Birkenhead was printed in ordinary type and 'lower case'!

The first departure from Chester was at 2.50am, this being an LNWR train which ran non-stop, arriving at Birkenhead at 3.15am: it was not typical of the service in general! Despite the impressive performance of the 2.50am 'express', the LNWR (and later the LMS) appeared content to let the GWR have the lion's share of the London and Birkenhead traffic; the greatest effort made being the attaching of an occasional through carriage off a North Wales express at Chester, which was sent forward to Woodside at the rear of a semi-fast train. Except on Mondays, the first GWR train left at 6.17am, this being the overnight service from Paddington which arrived at Birkenhead at 6.43am. Apart from the Paddington trains, the service was as follows in Table 1.

The first train on weekdays from Birkenhead was the 6.15am to Paddington. The 11.47am to Paddington, the 'Zulu', had no Chester arrival time shown; while in the table for the main line service to Paddington, only the Chester departure time was shown: it was not intended for those who only wished to travel such a short distance and who could wait for the 12.00 noon train. Similarly, the 4.45pm from Paddington, the down 'Zulu' showed only the times of arrival at Rock Ferry and Birkenhead. All through trains, whether to and from London, the West of England, Cardiff and Corwen or Barmouth, stopped only at Rock Ferry and/or Hooton. Footnotes advised that 'Passengers with Local Picnic Tickets' were not allowed to travel on the 2.25pm Birkenhead to Paddington train or on the non-stop 9.45pm Chester to Birkenhead (the 'Zulu'): there was, apparently, no prohibition to travelling on the 2.50am 'express'! How many picnic tickets were sold in January is not known!

The service on the West Kirby branch was shown in the same table as that between Chester and Birkenhead, and was as in Table 2.

Also SO 1.15pm Birkenhead to Heswall, and SO 10.30pm and 11.50pm Hooton to Heswall; SO 2.20pm Heswall and Birkenhead. The majority of trains in each direction were 'through' between Birkenhead and West Kirby. On Sundays there were four trains each way between Hooton and West Kirby (Hooton 9.05am to 7.30pm: West Kirby depart 9.38am to 8.15pm), all being connections from Birkenhead or Chester trains. Though the last Birkenhead to West Kirby train was at 5.45pm, the last train from West Kirby at 8.15pm had a connection for Birkenhead.

The Hooton to Helsby line had a less frequent service as shown in Table 3.

GREAT WESTERN
AND
LONDON AND NORTH WESTERN
RAILWAYS
JOINT LINES.
NOTICE
ALL PERSONS ARE WARNED NOT TO TRESPASS UPON THE RAILWAYS BELONGING TO THE GREAT WESTERN RAILWAY COMPANY AND THE LONDON & NORTH WESTERN RAILWAY COMPANY JOINTLY, OR UPON THE STATIONS CONNECTED WITH SUCH RAILWAYS, AND NOTICE IS HEREBY GIVEN THAT, PURSUANT TO THE PROVISIONS OF THE GREAT WESTERN RAILWAY ACT, 1883, AND LONDON AND NORTH WESTERN RAILWAY ADDITIONAL POWERS ACT, 1883, EVERY PERSON WHO TRESPASSES UPON ANY SUCH RAILWAYS OR STATIONS IN SUCH MANNER AS TO EXPOSE HIMSELF TO DANGER OR RISK OF DANGER RENDERS HIMSELF LIABLE TO A PENALTY OF FORTY SHILLINGS, AND IN DEFAULT OF PAYMENT TO ONE MONTH'S IMPRISONMENT, FOR EVERY SUCH OFFENCE.
BY ORDER.
FEBRUARY, 1885.

TABLE 1

	No of trains	*First and last departures*	
Chester to Birkenhead	24+1 SO	7.30am (SO 7.10am)	11.05pm
Birkenhead to Chester	26+1 SO	7.05am	11.25pm

Sundays — six trains in each direction, including London trains: leaving Chester 9.45am to 10.05pm and Birkenhead 8.33am to 9.45pm.

TABLE 2

	No of trains	*First and last departures*	
Birkenhead to West Kirby	12	6.20am	9.00pm
West Kirby to Birkenhead	12	7.53am	10.00pm

In 1932 the timetables described the service as being 'Chester, Birkenhead and Liverpool', the West Kirby service being shown in a separate table. A new station had been opened at Port Sunlight, between Spital & Bebington and New Ferry. The first departure from Chester was still in the early hours of the morning, though now at 3.45am. The overnight service from Paddington,

Below:
The outbreak of war in 1939 saw the running of numerous 'Evacuation Specials' from Birmingham, Merseyside and Manchester. Children from Merseyside and Manchester were scattered over a wide area of North and Central Wales, as well as along the Severn Valley line in Shropshire. *G. Osborne collection*

GREAT WESTERN RAILWAY.

(For the use of the Company's Servants only)

Chester Division

Notice of Arrangements

IN CONNECTION WITH

BIRKENHEAD & LIVERPOOL, BIRMINGHAM

AND

MANCHESTER

Evacuation Schemes

ALSO

ALTERED WORKING

OF

Through and Local Passenger Trains

DURING PERIOD OF EVACUATION.

The Train Arrangements shewn in this Notice must not be circulated to the General Public.

F. R. POTTER,
PADDINGTON.   *Superintendent of the Line.*
August, 1939.

6

BIRKENHEAD AND LIVERPOOL EVACUATION SCHEME.

1st and 2nd Days. —EVACUATION SPECIALS.—UP LINE.

STATIONS	W 13	C807L	W 15	W 25	W 16	C818L	W 18	W 19	W 19	W 21	W 22	W 23
Approx. No. of 1st day passrs. per train	750	800	700	...	718	730	820	533	...	795	800	708
2nd day	728	800	...	700	760	800	800	...	526	800	800	...
Approx. Load, 8-wh. Bog.	12	12	11	11	12	12	12	9	8	12	12	22
(destination)	To Barm'uth and Tow'n	11-30 a.m. Liver-pool (Ex) to Sh'ws-bury	12-7 p.m. Tue-brook to W'lsh-hamp-ton 1st Day Only	12-7 p.m. Tue-brook to Bas-ch'rch 2nd Day Only	To New-town and Llan-idloes	12-45 p.m. Sand-hills to Bridg-north	1-45 p.m. Edge Hill to Wrex-ham	To Bl. Fes-tiniog and Bar-m'uth 1st Day Only	To Llan-uwch-llyn and Wrex-ham	1-52 p.m. Breck Road to Aber-yst'th 2nd Day Only	2-45 p.m. Edge Hill to Aber-Wrex-ham	To W'lsh pool 1st Day Only
	d	c	c	c	d	c	c	d	d	c	c	d
BIRKENHEAD dep.	12e20	...	...	...	...	...	...	2f20	...	...	...	...
Grange Lane dep.	12 23	...	...	...	1+10	...	...	2 23	2+10	...	...	3+10
ROCK FERRY arr.	...	...	...	...	1+12	...	...	...	2+12	...	...	3+12
,, dep.	...	...	...	...	1 24	...	...	...	2 24	...	...	3 24
Hooton pass	12 33	...	...	...	1 33	...	...	2 33	2 33	...	...	3 33
Ledsham Junc. pass	12 36	...	...	...	1 36	...	...	2 36	2 36	...	...	3 36
CHESTER STA. arr.	...	1C15	1C30	1C30	...	2C15	2C30	...	...	3C15	3C30	...
,, dep.	...	1E20	1E35	1E35	...	2E20	2E35	...	...	3E20	3E35	...
Chester Cutting pass	12 45	...	...	...	1 45	...	...	2 45	2 45	...	...	3 45
WREXHAM arr.	...	...	...	...	...	...	2 58	...	...	...	3 58	...
,, dep.	1 8	1 43	1 58	1 58	2 8	2 43	...	3 10	3 10	2 44	...	4 10
RUABON arr.	1017	...	...	...	...	...	...	3019	3019	...	...	...
,, dep.	1W22	1 52	2 7	2 7	2 17	2 52	...	3W24	3W24	3 57	...	4 19
L'gollen Gds. Jcn. pass	1 41	...	...	...	...	...	...	C3 45S	C3 45S	...	...	...
Glyndyfrdwy pass	CS	...	...	...	...	...	...	CS	CS	...	...	...
CORWEN arr.	2b 2	...	...	...	...	...	...	...	...	...	...	...
,, dep.	2W15	...	...	...	...	...	...	C4 45S	C4 45S	...	...	...
Llandrillo dep.	CS	...	...	...	...	...	...	CXS	CS	...	...	...
Llandderfel arr.	...	...	...	...	...	...	...	...	4 20	...	...	...
,, dep.	CS	...	...	...	...	...	...	CS	4 30	...	...	...
BALA JUNC. arr.	...	...	...	...	...	...	...	4h26	4 37	...	...	...
,, dep.	C2 37S	...	...	...	...	...	...	4 35	4 45	...	...	...
Llanuwchllyn dep.	CS	...	...	...	...	...	...	CS	4 55	...	...	...
Garneddwen dep.	CS	...	...	...	...	...	...	CS	...	...	...	...
Drwsynant dep.	CS	...	...	...	...	...	...	CS	...	...	...	...
Bontnewydd dep.	CS	...	...	...	...	...	...	CS	...	...	...	...
DOLGELLEY arr.	3X12	...	...	...	...	...	...	...	...	...	...	...
,, dep.	3 25	...	...	...	...	...	...	C5 16S	...	...	...	...
BARMOUTH JC. arr.	3 43	...	...	...	...	...	...	5C28	...	...	...	...
,, dep.	3 54	...	...	...	...	...	...	5E33	...	...	...	...
BARMOUTH arr.	4 b0	...	...	...	...	...	...	5 40	...	...	...	...
GOBOWEN pass	...	2 4	2 21	2 21	2 29	3 g5	...	...	...	4 10	...	4 31
Oswestry arr.	...	...	2 27	...	2MR35	...	...	...	...	4 16	...	4 37
,, dep.	...	...	...	...	2 43	...	...	...	...	4 23	...	4 45
Welshpool arr.	...	...	...	...	...	...	...	...	...	...	...	5 15
Newtown arr.	...	...	...	...	3 40	...	...	...	...	...	...	...
Llandinam arr.	...	...	...	...	4 3	...	...	...	...	...	...	...
Llanidloes arr.	...	...	...	...	4 25	...	...	...	...	...	...	...
Aberystwyth arr.	...	...	...	...	...	...	...	...	...	7 20	...	...
Baschurch arr.	...	...	...	2 27	...	...	...	...	...	...	...	...
,, dep.	...	...	...	2 50	...	...	...	...	...	...	...	...
SHREWSBURY arr.	...	2 30	...	3 5	...	3C30	...	...	...	...	...	...
,, dep.	...	...	...	...	...	3E35	...	...	...	...	...	...
Sutton Bridge Jc. pass	...	...	...	...	...	C3 45S	...	...	...	...	...	...
BUILDWAS pass	...	...	...	...	...	C3 45S	...	...	...	...	...	...
Bridgnorth arr.	...	...	...	...	...	4 20	...	...	...	...	...	...

Column / panel notes (printed vertically in the table):
- *(C807L / W15) Frankton dep. 2-32, Ellesmere arr. 2-57, Welshampton arr. 3-27 p.m.; Oswestry dep. 2-32, Ellesmere arr. 3-10, Welshampton arr. 3-27 p.m.*
- *(W25) Light Engine, Baschurch to Shrewsbury—to turn.*
- *(C818L) g—Precede 2-0 p.m. ex Chester from Gobowen.*
- *(W13) 586 detrain Dolgelley 1st day, and 522 on 2nd day.*
- *(W19 / W21) Dep. Bala Jc. with Bala party 4-43 pm. Bala arr. 4-45 pm. 63 detrain Bala, 13 Festiniog, 363 Blaenau Festiniog, 157 Barmouth. detrain Llandderfel, Bala, Llanuwchllyn.*

b—Continuation of 12-20 p.m. ex Birkenhead:-

	arr. p.m.	dep. p.m.
Barmouth	—	4 30
Barmouth Junction	C S	
Llwyngwril	4 51	5 3
Towyn	5 15	

h—Detach Blaenau Festiniog portion, to be worked forward per Special Train as under:-

	arr. p.m.	dep. p.m.
Bala Junction	—	4 40
Bala	4 42	4 50
Trawsfynydd	C5 20S	
Festiniog	5 30	5 40
Blaenau Festiniog	5 50	

c—Worked by G.W. Co. from Chester.
d—Worked by G.W. Co. throughout.
e—Empty Stock ex Grange Lane 11-45 a.m.
f—Empty Stock ex Grange Lane 1-45 p.m.

Above:
For over 80 years the small 0-6-0STs of Wolverhampton origin were a familiar sight and sound in Birkenhead Docks. No 987 is seen here at Birkenhead shed c1890. *Ian Allan Library*

arriving at Birkenhead at 7.35am was not shown: the 'Isle of Man Boat Express' was not intended for the use of Merseyside commuters! There were eight through trains (London, Bournemouth and Deal) in each direction, the local service being shown in Table 4.

Also about two dozen trains between Birkenhead and Hooton (the majority being to or from West Kirby) and the Rock Ferry and Hooton 'Rail-motor' service. The service on Sundays consisted of 12 trains from Chester (7.00am to 10.05pm) and 10 from Birkenhead (8.30am to 9.50pm), and 10 trains in each direction between Birkenhead and Hooton, none of which were auto-trains.

On the West Kirby line, Caldy station had been opened between Thurstaston and Kirby Park. The service was as in Table 5.

All were through trains to and from Birkenhead. ThSX 5.03pm from Birkenhead ran non-stop from Port Sunlight to Hadlow Road, and the 8.10am from West Kirby was non-stop from Hadlow Road to Rock Ferry (Birkenhead arrive 8.57am). On Sundays there were seven trains in each direction (Hooton depart 8.38am to 8.32pm: West Kirby depart 9.22am to 9.20pm).

There had been a dramatic increase in the frequency of the service over the Hooton and Helsby line, the eight trains in 1902 having been more than doubled (Table 6).

Two of the Hooton and Ellesmere Port workings were by auto-trains. There was now a service on Sundays, of four trains in each direction, the first and last departures being — Hooton 6.50am and 7.53pm; Helsby 7.35am and 8.25pm; while Ellesmere Port had two additional trains from Hooton at 2.43pm and 10.02pm (Ellesmere Port depart 3.00pm and 10.25pm).

By 1947 there had been few changes, the most startling being the omission of Liverpool; not only from the Table heading, but also from the list of stations! (Table 7).

Only seven down and four up trains served all stations, and a number called only at Hooton and Rock Ferry. There was also the local service

TABLE 3	*No of trains*	*First and last departures*	
Hooton to Heswall	8+1 to Ellesmere Port	7.00am	8.00pm 9.35pm EP SO 11.50pm EP
Heswall to Hooton	8	7.55am	8.45pm 10.00pm EP
There was no service on Sundays.			

TABLE 4	*No of trains*	*First and last departures*	
Chester to Birkenhead	28	6.40am	11.05pm
Birkenhead to Chester	29	6.00am	11.20pm

TABLE 5	*No of trains*	*First and last departures*	
Hooton to West Kirby	18+4 Heswall	6.34am	10.00pm
West Kirby to Hooton	18+4 Heswall	6.40am	10.50pm

TABLE 6	*No of trains*	*First and last departures*	
Hooton to Helsby	19	5.33am	10.20pm
Hooton to Ellesmere Port	7+2 SO	6.20am	11.12pm (SO 11.45pm)
Helsby to Hooton	20	6.05am	10.50pm (SO 10.58pm)
Ellesmere Port to Hooton	7+1SO	6.30am	11.35pm

between Hooton and Birkenhead, most of which were to and from West Kirby or Helsby and two return workings by auto-trains between Rock Ferry and Hooton. On Sundays there were 10 trains in each direction (Chester: depart 7.15am to 11.05pm; Birkenhead depart 7.10am to 9.53pm) and four each way between Birkenhead and Hooton which were through trains to and from Helsby.

The West Kirby line's service was considerably reduced from that in 1932 and was less than that in 1902! There were now no trains on Sundays (Table 8).

The electrification of the former Wirral Railway line (now part of the LMS) and the increasing volume of road transport had had a significant effect.

In contrast, the Hooton and Helsby line, in earlier years very much a 'second string', had a service comparable with that provided in 1932. Stanlow & Thornton station had been opened between Ellesmere Port and Ince & Elton; and

Below:
'Saint' class No 2943 *Hampton Court* heads a train of LMS carriages on the joint line near Frodsham, probably a through train from Birkenhead via Helsby. July 1939. *Dr Ian C. Allen*

TABLE 7	*No of trains*	*First and last departures*	
Chester to Birkenhead	28	6.28am	11.42pm
Birkenhead to Chester	27	5.50am	11.10pm

TABLE 8	*No of trains*	*First and last departures*	
Hooton to West Kirby	11+1 SX Heswall	6.20am	9.10pm
West Kirby to Hooton	11	6.17am	7.50pm

Above:
Also near Frodsham, A Birkenhead to Manchester through goods is hauled by 'Aberdare' No 2662 (of Chester). July 1939. *Dr. Ian C. Allen*

There were five trains each way on Sundays (Hooton: depart 8.09am to 9.21pm; Helsby: depart 9.30am to 10.05pm).

Birkenhead shed not only worked most of the Wirral passenger turns, as well as a number of goods trains, but was also responsible for providing engines for working over the extensive dock lines. For the latter work it acquired over the years a considerable number of the small 0-6-0Ts of the '850' and '2021' classes, which were fitted with warning bells, and they were a familiar sight and sound in the dock area for over 80 years! Some of the first members of the '850' class went to Birkenhead as new engines in 1874 (though none of these was still there in 1911); while the last survivor of the '2021' class, No 2069, was withdrawn from Birkenhead in April 1959 — though engines of that class were not used until the 1920s.

although the Ellesmere Port local service had ceased, one train commenced from there (at 7.51am) and there was a morning return working between Hooton and Stanlow & Thornton. The only auto-train was the 10.02am Hooton to Helsby, returning at 10.53am. There were several through trains in the early morning and evening between Frodsham (on the Chester to Manchester line) and Birkenhead; while the 6.15am Chester to Birkenhead ran via Helsby and Hooton.

Below:
Probably one of the last occasions when a double-framed 4-4-0 was to be found at Manchester (Exchange). No 3212 *Earl of Eldon* was only a few weeks old when seen there in May 1937, and its name was removed by the end of June — to be transferred to 'Castle' class No 5055 in August. *W. Potter*

TABLE 9	*No of trains*	*First and last departures*	
Hooton to Helsby	12+5 SX: 7 SO	5.24am	10.45pm
Helsby to Hooton	11+4 SX: 6 SO	6.10am	10.00pm SX
			10.07pm SO

At an earlier date, two small saddle tanks of NA&HR origin, Nos 194 and 195, had worked in the docks for several years. Built in 1854 by Dodds & Co as 0-4-2 tender engines (with Dodd's wedge motion), they had been rebuilt as saddle tanks in 1865 (No 195) and 1872 (No 194). The latter engine remained a 0-4-2ST, but No 195 lost its trailing wheels and became an 0-4-0ST. They were taken out of service in 1881 and 1879 respectively. At the same time, the ex-S&CR 0-4-0ST No 16 was also working in the docks. The original dock shunting engines, Birkenhead Railway Nos 6 and 39 (GWR Nos 95 and 96) later deserted Birkenhead for Chester and the colliery lines at Wrexham.

Among other immigrants working at Birkenhead for many years were two small 0-6-0STs with outside cylinders, Nos 1392 and 1394, which had begun life as side tanks on the far-away Cornwall Minerals Railway, for whom they had been built by Sharp, Stewart & Co in 1873-74. After rebuilding as saddle tanks in 1883 they were sent to Birkenhead for dock work and remained there for over 20 years. No 1392 was withdrawn in 1906, and No 1394 left Birkenhead the following year after being involved in an accident.

In addition to the Cathcart Street goods line, there were a couple of other short branches in Birkenhead. The original C&BR system included a branch, ½-mile long, to Monk's Ferry, and another branch was opened to Tranmere Pool in December 1863. The only other development was a junction with the Mersey Railway at Rock Ferry, which came into use on 15 June 1891.

The Chester to Manchester section was in many ways less obviously part of the GWR system, despite the presence in former years of numerous little double-framed 2-4-0s and, at a later date, the double-framed 'Flower' and 'City' class 4-4-0s — none of which could ever have been thought to have belonged to the LNWR or its successor, the LMS. The 'Flowers' were used on the line from about 1912 until they were withdrawn in the late 1920s (though only two of the class, plus a 'City', were shedded at Chester in 1921). However, as late as 1937 it was still possible to leave Manchester (Exchange) in a train headed by a double-framed 4-4-0, as the 'Dukedog' No 3212 *Earl of Eldon* was working between Chester and Manchester.

That the GWR was only a 'grace and favour' visitor to the line between Warrington and Manchester was emphasised by footnotes contained in the 1902 timetables. Passengers were informed that 'GWR tickets are not available' by certain trains; while in other instances they were only available between Chester and Warrington. Even in 1932, GWR tickets could not be used on one train between Chester and Manchester; but as

Above:
More usual visitors to Manchester in the late 1930s were the Moguls. No 6332 (of Chester) heads a train of LMS carriages in May 1937. *W. Potter*

this left Chester at 2.20am it is not likely that many would-be passengers were frustrated!

In 1902 there were 13 trains from Chester to Manchester, with 15 in the opposite direction — and an additional train on Saturdays. Apart from two 'middle of the night' trains, leaving at 2.32am and 4.30am, the first departure from Chester was at 7.25am, which stopped at all stations to Warrington and then at the principal stations to Exchange (arr 9.16am). Most trains stopped only at Warrington and Newton-le-Willows, taking just over an hour. The last train was at 8.50pm. The first train from Manchester was at 6.50am and the last at 10.40pm (the latter being one of the trains on which GWR tickets were available only between Warrington and Chester). The local service from Chester to Warrington consisted of five trains, stopping at all stations, but there were only two in the opposite direction.

On Sundays, apart from the 2.32am and 4.30am, there was only one train from Chester to Manchester — at 6.55pm, this being the only one on which GWR tickets could be used. Passengers from Manchester fared better, there being trains at 8.00am, 6.00pm and 10.40pm; though, as on weekdays, GWR tickets were available only between Warrington and Chester on the latter train.

In 1932 there were about 20 trains each way between Chester and Manchester. Apart from the 2.20am, the first train from Chester was at 7.55am and the last was at 9.15pm; while from Manchester

the first and last departures were at 7.25am and 10.20pm respectively. The local Chester to Warrington service consisted on three trains on Mondays, four on Saturdays — and two on other days! There were three trains from Warrington to Chester, with a fourth on Saturdays; also at 8.50pm from Newton-le-Willows. On Sundays, apart from the 2.20am, six trains left Chester for Manchester between 7.05am and 8.40pm; however, there were only three from Manchester, at 7.50am, 10.10am and 10.40pm, though there were also two from Warrington — at 12.35pm and 1.55pm (the latter being 'non stop' as in 1902).

By 1947, the service had been reduced to about a dozen trains each way; the first from Chester being at 7.32am (other than the traditional 'middle of the night' one, now leaving at 2.40am) and the last at 9.20pm; while the first and last trains from Manchester were at 7.50am and 10.20pm. There was only one Chester to Warrington train (SX 5.43pm: SO 1.25pm) and two in the opposite direction; while the 12.05am was 'non stop', the 7.25am served all stations. There was now a fairly intensive local service between Chester and Frodsham (which also had morning and evening trains to and from Birkenhead), with about a dozen trains in each direction: the first and last trains from Chester were at 5.38am and 7.58pm (SO 11.15pm), while those from Frodsham were at 8.10am and 11.24pm — some of these trains were extended to and from Birkenhead via Helsby.

On Sundays there were four trains from Chester to Manchester between 7.35am and 7.20pm and three to Frodsham while there were five trains from Manchester to Chester between 8.55am and 10.20pm, but only two from Frodsham (10.22am

Above:
Cleanliness par excellence. 'Chancellor' class 2-4-0 No 152 and an '850' class 0-6-0ST (probably No 987) stand in front of the GWR shed at Birkenhead c1890. *Ian Allan Library*

and 8.36pm). Several stations were now closed on Sundays.

By the 1920s, the GWR's WTT contained no details of any Chester and Manchester passenger trains, but gave full details of all goods workings — there being 17 trains in each direction: several ran to or from Patricroft, and they included services between Manchester and Hereford and Bristol via the 'North to West' route.

Following the disappearance of the double-framed 4-4-0s of the 'Flower' class, Moguls, 'Halls' and 'Saints' were to be found on the Chester and Manchester line; though one or two 'double framers' were still to be seen on occasions, such as 'Dukedogs' on passenger trains and 'Aberdares' on goods workings. However, there was little to remind anyone of that time, half-a-century previously, when the Premier Line's Manchester to Llandudno express was regularly hauled to Chester by a GWR double-framed 2-4-0 built at Wolverhampton. Though such workings to and from Manchester were only by the possession of running powers over the LNWR (LMS) line from Warrington, GWR engines and trains ran to the latter place by right of ownership. For it was Warrington and not Birkenhead (or Liverpool!) — albeit by only two miles — that was the furthest point on the Great Western Railway 'North of Wolverhampton'.

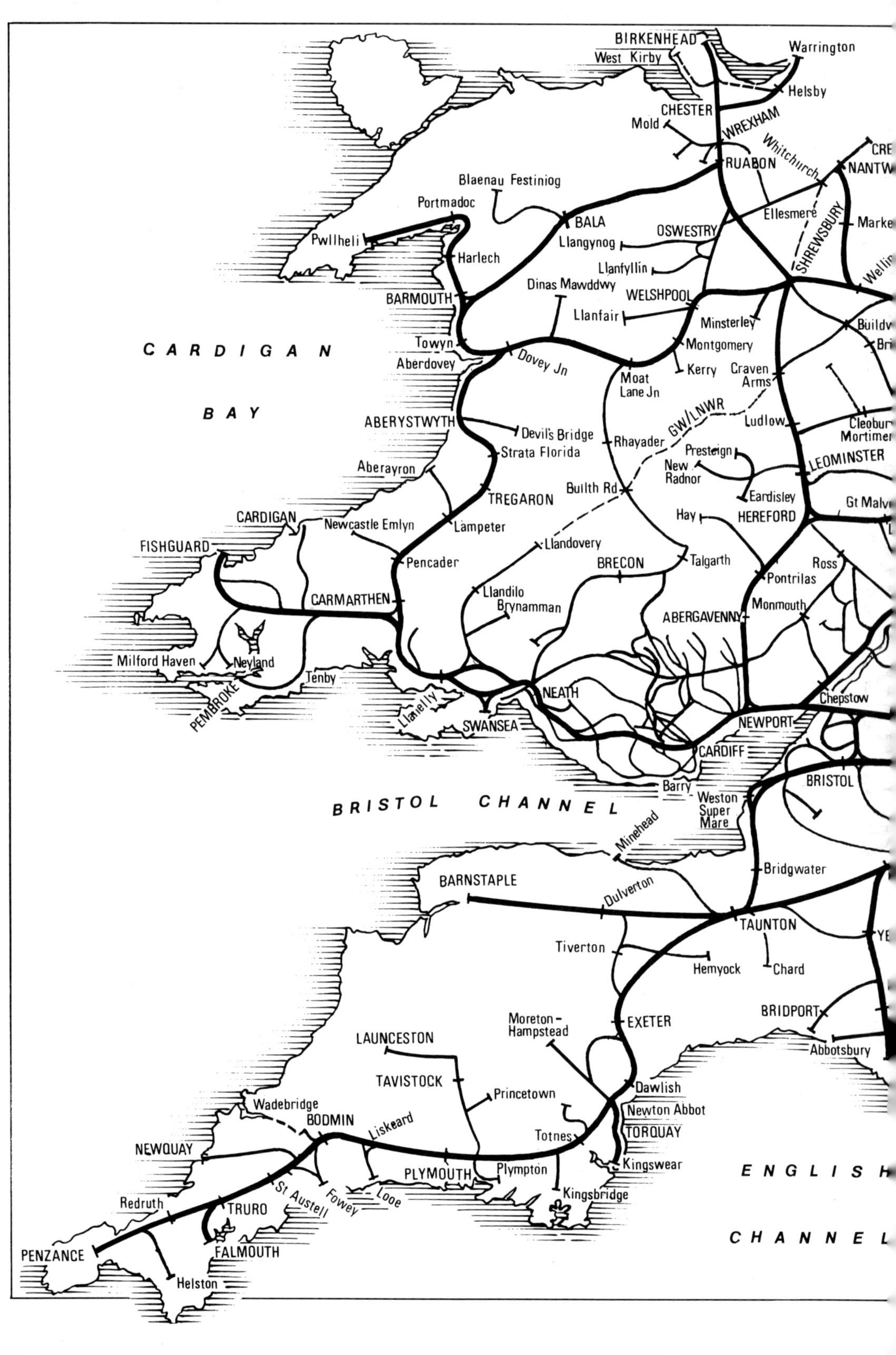

BIRKENHEAD
Warrington
West Kirby
Helsby
CHESTER
Mold
WREXHAM
CRE
Whitchurch
RUABON
NANTW
Blaenau Festiniog
Ellesmere
Marke
Portmadoc
BALA
OSWESTRY
SHREWSBURY
Pwllheli
Llangynog
Harlech
Llanfyllin
Wellin
Dinas Mawddwy
WELSHPOOL
BARMOUTH
Llanfair
Minsterley
Buildv
CARDIGAN
Montgomery
Bri
Towyn
Dovey Jn
Kerry
Craven
Aberdovey
Moat
Arms
BAY
Lane Jn
GW/LNWR
ABERYSTWYTH
Devil's Bridge
Ludlow
Cleobur
Strata Florida
Rhayader
Mortimer
Aberayron
Presteign
LEOMINSTER
New
Builth Rd
Radnor
CARDIGAN
Eardisley
Gt Malve
Newcastle Emlyn
Lampeter
TREGARON
Hay
HEREFORD
FISHGUARD
Llandovery
Pencader
BRECON
Talgarth
Ross
CARMARTHEN
Llandilo
Pontrilas
Monmouth
Brynamman
ABERGAVENNY
Milford Haven
Neyland
Tenby
NEATH
Chepstow
Llanelly
NEWPORT
PEMBROKE
SWANSEA
CARDIFF
BRISTOL
Barry
Weston
Super
BRISTOL CHANNEL
Mare
Minehead
Bridgwater
BARNSTAPLE
Dulverton
TAUNTON
YE
Tiverton
Hemyock
Chard
BRIDPORT
Moreton-
EXETER
Hampstead
LAUNCESTON
Abbotsbury
Dawlish
TAVISTOCK
Princetown
Newton Abbot
Wadebridge
TORQUAY
NEWQUAY
BODMIN
Liskeard
Totnes
Plympton
ENGLISH
PLYMOUTH
Kingswear
Redruth
St Austell
Fowey
Looe
Kingsbridge
PENZANCE
TRURO
CHANNEL
FALMOUTH
Helston